Literature in the Dawn of Sociological Theory

Literature in the Dawn of Sociological Theory

Stories That Are Telling

Sarah Louise MacMillen

LEXINGTON BOOKS
Lanham • Boulder • New York • London

Published by Lexington Books
An imprint of The Rowman & Littlefield Publishing Group, Inc.
4501 Forbes Boulevard, Suite 200, Lanham, Maryland 20706
www.rowman.com

86-90 Paul Street, London EC2A 4NE

Copyright © 2022 by The Rowman & Littlefield Publishing Group, Inc.

Chapter Five: Parts of this chapter were previously published in *Soundings* and used with permission. MacMillen, Sarah L. 2020. "From Herland to #MeToo: Utopia or Dystopia?" *Soundings* 103 (2): 243–263.

All rights reserved. No part of this book may be reproduced in any form or by any electronic or mechanical means, including information storage and retrieval systems, without written permission from the publisher, except by a reviewer who may quote passages in a review.

British Library Cataloguing in Publication Information Available

Library of Congress Cataloging-in-Publication Data Available

ISBN: 978-1-7936-2805-3 (cloth)
ISBN: 978-1-7936-2807-7 (pbk.)
ISBN: 978-1-7936-2806-0 (electronic)

*This book is dedicated to all of the humanists in my life—
family, friends, mentors, colleagues, and students.*

Contents

Acknowledgments	ix
Chapter One: Literature in the Dawn of Sociological Theory	1
Chapter Two: New England Shadows: Hawthorne, *Faust*, and the American Spiritual Character	23
Chapter Three: *Moby Dick* as Modern Epic: "Symphony" in a Broken Ontology	41
Chapter Four: Literary *Metanoia* and the Sociological Imagination in Joseph Conrad: Colonialism and Western Idealism	61
Chapter Five: Women and Men: The Tragicomic	83
Chapter Six: Suspending Modernity: Gender and History in Virginia Woolf's *Orlando*	101
Chapter Seven: The Absurd Christian: The Sociological Imagination of Dostoevsky	123
Chapter Eight: Conclusion: Stories in the Dawn of Capitalism—Crisis and Narrative in Boccaccio's *Decameron*	141
References	155
Index	167
About the Author	169

Acknowledgments

Why is a sociologist writing about literature? This is a question often repeated by countless persons—from family to friends to critics—during the last few years of this project. This was an important challenge and a constant reminder of why literature is increasingly devalued in the social sciences and wider academic spheres. But it was also a nudge for me to make a case that the literary imagination is important not only within sociology's theoretical traditions, but literature also illuminates the realities of social life beyond the limits and scope of sociological inquiry and methodology.

First, credits to earlier versions of these papers and their helpful audiences and reception. Portions of these papers appeared at several conferences. A few (preliminary remarks on) chapters were presented at the Midwest Sociological Society: Chapter Two on Hawthorne in 2016 and Chapter Five on Charlotte Perkins Gilman's *Herland* in 2019. Harry Dahms edited an issue of *Soundings* (Pennsylvania State University Press) where an earlier edition of Chapter Five appeared. A version of the Virginia Woolf chapter was presented at the American Sociological Association (ASA) in 2017. The Boccaccio chapter was presented at Self & Society conference, an affiliate of ASA, in 2020. And sections of the *Moby Dick* paper were delivered at Self & Society in 2015, and the International Social Theory Consortium in 2021. The thumbnail sketches of the Dostoevsky chapter were published in my University of Pittsburgh colleague Ryan McDermott's venture, the *Genealogies of Modernity*'s blog in 2020.

I first studied literature within higher education, under the direction of my major in Classical Studies and Religion at Boston University. A seminar with the former president of the American Academy of Religion, Ray Hart, was a deep inspiration to the chapter on *Moby Dick*. Other influences in reading literature as a wider force shaping culture, psychology, and sociology included Loren "Jay" Samons II, Stephanie Nelson, Stephen Esposito, Robert Richardson, Roye E. Wates, Michael Zank, Herbert Mason (and graduate student assistants), Geoffrey Hill, Fr. Lucien Richard, and Adam Seligman. My undergraduate mentoring was uniquely formative for this type of project in that it encouraged not only analytical rigor, but also interdisciplinary imagination in approaching literature.

I would also like to recognize my mentors from my Ph.D. program in Sociology at University of Notre Dame. Especially the theory and culture scholars, they challenged me to utilize and apply my training in the humanities in connecting with the broader questions of sociological inquiry. I would especially like to thank Eugene Halton, Lyn Spillman, Andrew Weigert, Kevin Christiano, Robert Fishman, and Samuel Valenzuela.

Colleagues inside and outside of Duquesne University were key players in commenting on ideas, chapter sketches, and reviewing portions of the manuscript. Many thanks to: Mike Irwin, Matt Schneirov, Dan Burston, Charlie Rubin, John Mitcham, Christina DiGangi, Lauren Langman, George Lundskow, Gene Halton, Harry Dahms; and especially Fr. George Piggford, Charles Robert Thorpe, and the Rev. Kevin Kalish.

Gratitude also for Duquesne's McAnulty College for Liberal Arts, for their funding of an undergraduate research project with a very bright and talented Honors College student, Bridget Fitzpatrick. This research project launched a portion of the chapter on Virginia Woolf. My Survey (SOCI 101) sections from 2011–2018 also deserve a tip of the hat for reading and discussing Virginia Woolf's *Orlando* and Joseph Conrad's *Heart of Darkness*. My Duquesne students are a constant encouragement for me in "keeping it real and relevant."

My family has been there from the very beginning of my intellectual pursuits. Encouraging my interest in "boy" literature: when my high school teacher said to me, "Girls don't like Conrad and Melville" my uncle, (the late) James Tappenden, gave me his copy of *Heart of Darkness*. I also thank my nuclear family—Martha, Kenneth, Andrew, and Elizabeth—and my extended family, and friends for their continual support.

I'm indebted to Courtney Lachapelle Morales and others at Lexington Books for valuing the project, words of encouragement, and their careful editorial comments along the way. Finally, a great deal of appreciation for my dear friend, and colleague from Notre Dame times: Miriam Rainbird, a historian and literary scholar, whose careful editing brought forth clarity to the core ideas of this book. She, like Socrates says of teaching, is an intellectual midwife.

All errors and lacunae remain my own.

July 2021
Pittsburgh, Pennsylvania

Chapter One

Literature in the Dawn of Sociological Theory

The discipline of sociology and its accompanying methods are relatively new in the human sciences, when compared to the fields of literature, philosophy, theology and history. In fact, sociology is rather "young"—but the qualitative division(s) may find a theoretical inheritance through reading literature. There is an "inseparability of great literature and social life" (James 2001, 125). The mid-nineteenth to early twentieth century is of particular historical significance for both literary and sociological history—reflecting the results of industrialization and the transition from rural to urban modes of life, the emergence of proto-feminist theory, and early reflections on colonialism/globalization. Additionally, as evidenced by the sociologically driven fiction of famed author Charles Dickens, this historical period was one where the novel was more far-reaching to a wider audience than an inchoate-stage "scientific" armchair sociology. Dickens is well known in that his fiction fostered social change, or at least sociological awareness, more effectively and widely than an elite social scientific discourse.

The major contribution of this book of essays is to highlight the sociological observations contained within a selection of works of fiction that were published around the period of the emergence of the "classical" canon of sociological theory—namely the era of Tocqueville, Marx, Weber, Durkheim, Simmel, Tönnies, and DuBois. What these sociological theorists offer in their "greatest works" is a series of "landscapes" as "distinctive and compelling as any to be found among the greater novels or paintings of their age" (Nisbet 2017, 7). The bulk of these sociological theorists concerned themselves with the contrast between "country/city"—in Tönnies's famous definitions of *Gemeinschaft/Gesellschaft*—also to be observed in Impressionist paintings and novels (Nisbet 2017, 7).

This historical period also anticipates a transitional moment in aesthetics, suggested by Lukács' (1971) discussion of the "historical to personal" method of the novel in the late nineteenth century. The question of *society* as an abstraction produces the next stage of abstraction in the psychological subjective. The classical theorist Georg Simmel described this emergence of "subjectivity" as both problematic and freeing in *The Metropolis and Mental Life* (1903). The philosophical and artistic portrayal of the rupture between "essence and appearance" was a result of the emotional degradation resulting from a shift in emphasis on the qualitative to the quantitative, as discussed by Simmel, utility and exchange values in Marx's *Capital* (Goldmann 1975, 8). Marx's project moved in a way different from history. His goal for the proletariat was for it to overcome the "once coherent" structures of worldviews, ethics, and a shared consciousness. "The old" must be overcome by the new. However, as we see with the sweeping "false nostalgia" throughout modern history's fascist and white supremacist narratives that resurge time and time again—especially amidst the "castle ruins" of the rustbelt, that the "new consciousness" is perceived with skepticism. Today, what David Brooks (2000) has called the "bourgeois-bohemian" avant-garde is no longer the call of transformation for the proletarian voices—today's Becketts, Brechts, and Riveras are the products of elite schools and institutions. Privilege now usurps the stances of the marginalized. The voice of the unifying, organic intellectual (Gramsci 1971) is lost. Lukács anticipated this: "Modernism in general was objectively elitist and thus estranged from the 'people' in every practical sense" (Adorno et al. 2007, 14). With new economic and cultural production schemes, the ghosts haunting the new "precariat" classes are such "castle ruins" of a past flourishing of industry instead of a revolutionary hope of solidarity. Contemporary postmodern cultural discussion has dissolved into the conflicts of identity politics, and fueled by vapid mechanics of pop culture in everything. Mass culture (Adorno et al. 2007) pervades everything; it is a part of moral consciousness in discourse on romantic love, politics, to psychology and self-help manuals for "success," to liturgical music in religious settings.

LITERATURE AND A CRITICAL SOCIOLOGY

Franssen and Kuipers introduced a special issue of *Cultural Sociology* with the statement: "Literature is the artform of the nation state . . . and helped to convey and form national identities" (2015, 292). This volume argues that, by selecting several texts for analysis, literature also creates the possibility for an early stage of *critical sociology*, and a nascent analysis of social problems as they carry into the twenty-first century, unresolved, including: totalitarianism, secularization, capitalism, sexism, homophobia, racism, imperialism. The reflective/critical moment in these nineteenth- to twentieth-century novels is radical in its own way; perhaps more radical than today's artistic creations, which suffer heavily from the fracturing of identity politics.

The general attestation in critical aesthetic theory leading up to Lukács's *Theory of the Novel* harkens back to figures like Boccaccio in his *Decameron*: with hell outside, humans internalize, reflect, playfully storytelling while making sense of the world. However, the emergence of the postmodern "psychological" novels are the byproduct of human flourishing. How so? One could say that lo and behold, the problems of pestilence and mass war have been solved, certain utopias have been realized, ushering forth a new era of narcissistic self-exploration and the breaking down of aesthetic order: "Thus art becomes problematic precisely because reality has become non-problematic" (Lukács 1971, 17). As a turning point, reflecting on the dream gone haywire, in the disaster of World War I, Lukács contends, however, that the

> problems of the novel form are here the mirror image of a world gone out of joint. This is why the "prose" of life is here only a symptom, among many others, of the fact that reality no longer constitutes a favorable soil for art; that is why the central problem of the novel is the fact that art has to write off the closed and total forms which stem from a rounded totality of being—that art has nothing more to do with any world of forms that is immanently complete in itself. (Lukács 1971, 17)

Lukács observes that this is for historical-philosophical reasons, and not mere epiphenomena of an aloof aesthetic. The abstract, absurdist literary commentary within the likes of Kafka, Camus, and others, leading into the "postmodern," are an historical byproduct of greater sociological shifts. But the first presentation of dis-order in the modern lingers in the moral questions invoked by the very notion of society's breakage and contradictions as they are present in the mid 1800s to early 1900s examples of Hawthorne, Melville, Conrad, Gilman, Woolf, and Dostoevsky. The idea of "problematic" existence—as it is rooted within the mechanisms of production and the trajectories of capitalism—is the concern of the literary imagination even before the dawn of sociological theory. As it is inherited by sociology, these literary figures anticipate the "deep contradictions in the relationships of production and in the consequent social relationships" and the base of this society creates a "dynamic and internally contradictory process" (Williams 1977, 82). Contradiction and paradox are ripe for literary exposition and poetic exploration, in a way that the pursuit of academic and scientific critical analysis undermines in its quest for univocal statements of reality. The tensions of capitalism create opportunities for dramatic stories and narrations. The broken promises of civilization—ripe for the tragic-realist imagination—presents an opportunity for the radical critique of the very ground of society. The emergence of capitalism produced wealth and grandeur, but also poverty, violence, disorder, and alienation (Williams 1977, 18). This key aspect of "appearance and reality"—a testing of the claims of what would come to be called the social construction of reality by Peter Berger and others—is an important literary trope in the emergence of the sociological imagination within fiction.

REPRESENTATION AND AUTHORSHIP: SOCIOLOGICAL PERSPECTIVES IN LITERATURE

The question of authorship, authenticity, and intentionality emerges here as well. As student of Lukács, Lucien Goldmann extended the discussion of the novel form and its sociological significance into the 1960s. Reflecting Hegel's "The True is the All," Goldmann suggests, "the true subject of cultural creations are . . . social groups and not isolated individuals . . . but the individual creator belongs to the group" (Goldmann 1975, ix). Reflexivity and worldview are just as important factors as the individual psychology, personality, or situation of the author. For example, this tension might play out in anachronistic recent reception scholarship on Joseph Conrad's *Heart of Darkness* and Herman Melville's *Moby Dick*. Before claims of their sexism or racism—a reader should remember the importance of an *emic* function of these texts as they function as an ethnography not only of the "exotic" characters and places in the plot, but also of Euro-American culture itself. Given that positioning of an interpretation of the text, the author develops a critique of *his own world* even while displaying some of the brutalities of the stories' main characters.

Marxian perspectives are rooted in the idea of the social conditioning of authorship—"a legal-political social structure corresponds to social consciousness" and wherein the "mode of production conditions the social, political, and intellectual life" (Marx, in Williams 1977, 75). Within early twentieth-century critical analysis, Plekhanov's distinction between "base and superstructure" reflects the way in which the creations of artists, novelists, composers, and so on, are in turn products of the "base"—cultural forms and social consciousness are representations of the larger foundational class and power/state framework. Ideologies then reflect the collective psyche, with its basis to be drawn from material reality, the social existence of real humanity. Thus, there is a connection between intellectual and material development that potentially can reflect the social problems that humanity faces (Williams 1977, 80–81). This emergence of the "critical writer" who sees the illusions and realities of society in early stages of capitalism shows the problematic nature of the capitalist system. In Marx's *Economic and Philosophic Manuscripts* (1844) the estrangement, or fracture, between "what is and what ought to be," a self as an acting agent in the world, is driven by the condition of life in capitalism (Fromm 2004, 37). Life then "only appears as a *means of life*" and therefore, "the objectification of man's species life" (Marx, "Alienated Labor" in Fromm 2004, 84). Alienation is a key concept in grasping the place of the sociological author at the dawn of the discipline. The experience of some form of reflective alienation gives way to sociologically driven "authorship." Authors' techniques of characterization, plot, language, symbol, both utilize and transform the conventions of literature to navigate through the problematic experiences of modernity (Williams 1977, 173–179). Thus writing, in sociological fiction, is both a) the sociological product of material culture, wherein the products of consciousness and language are determined by social beings and social bases and b) the reflective commentary and critique of the superstructure of consciousness. The second part relating to the creative-reflective capacity is derived from the author as both located within, and critical of, the sociological setting. The moments of creative reflexivity in sociological authors are rare and as Williams notes, it is a response to changes in social formations (Williams 1977, 209).

Lukács and Goldmann see that the novel gives us the "problematic hero" and a "degraded" search for authentic values in a world that has fallen—it tries to capture something that has been lost. The hero searches amidst a breakage with the world (Goldmann 1975, 1–2). *Moby Dick* presents an important example of this rupture—literally a ruptured person (Ahab struck by lightning), a ruptured narrator in Ishmael (a neurotic/intellectual type attempting to do manual labor in a condescension to the worker), and finally a ruptured ship in the climax of the plot. Goldmann argues, following Rene Girard, that the rupture is a symptom of an "ontological sickness"—and an increase of metaphysical desire. For the late modern, the absence of inner joy creates ontological insecurity, despair, and anxiety in the emergent consumer society (Fromm [1968] 2021, 116). A society which focuses on efficiency and the production of "useful things" therefore gives way to "useless people" (Fromm [1968] 2021, 114). The theme of ontological longing presents itself here. Marlow longs for wisdom and is disgruntled by the "façade" of European life that lives in the shadows of brutalities in *Heart of Darkness*. Ishmael longs for wholeness (and maybe some sanity) in the *Pequod*. Virginia Woolf's Orlando longs for love, and comfort in his/her own skin. In *Brothers Karamazov,* the ethical vacuum of their father Fyodor suggests a breakage from all senses of moral congruity with the past Christian world, and for the brothers' "sibling rivalries"—their fractures leave them playing out different roles and conflicts among them. Young Goodman Brown seeks for truth about the nature of society, and the inner-workings of the complexities of the human heart. There is in all of these examples a profound search for vertical transcendence, an authentic striving for a "deep grounding" of reality. This profound searching reflects the fracture between appearance and reality, between the "images" of social construction and the truth that is obscured by such a set of confabulations. The dawn of Socratic philosophy, Plato's *Republic,* as reflecting the "theoretical imagination" begins with this distinction in the allegory of the cave. The dawn of sociological theory is historically placed within the emergence of novel. Within this genre, the problematized conversation (or even argument) is between the individual narrator and the emergence of the new social realities in modernity. Also present is the social chronicle, or the sociological conveyance of these changing ethics, moralities, and worldviews (Goldmann 1975, 4). The social chronicle is a precursor to the ethnographic method. Reinforcing Lukács, Goldmann observes in the sociological novel "the novelist's ethic becomes an aesthetic problem of the work" (Goldmann 1975, 6).

Additionally, each chapter of this volume reflects on the significance of the literary work in today's social and theoretical "problematics." The late twentieth to early twenty-first century indicates a secondary moment of the "End of" Fukuyama's conclusion about the "End of History." We are experiencing another lost center of the "nation" (Franssen and Kuipers 2015), endless identity politics, episodic violence within "civilization," civil and political strife, as a direct continuation of the problems of late capitalism, imperialism, sexism, globalization, and so on. These dynamics are described as rooted in earlier moments within these works of fiction discussed in this volume. Political and civic violence expresses a new form of authoritarianism. The erosion of civil society and the emergence of totalitarian dynamics within politics, reflect the modern *Zeitgeist* epitomized in the cast of characters of the crew and Ahab in *Moby Dick*. The new *Heart of Darkness* is now reflected in mass shootings in shopping malls, secondary schools, local civic centers, houses of worship. The significance of both *Heart of Darkness* and *Moby Dick* still holds as Wallerstein narrates the dark side of "Western progress" within World Systems Theory. The legacy of colonialism and imperialism still wreaks havoc in the continued problems of police brutality in "center/core" nations, and ecological exploitation, condescending development paradigms. This results in perpetual conflict in "periphery" nations, or between members of the periphery within "core" nations (Wallerstein 2004). Inheriting the questions posed by Gilman and Woolf, the #MeToo movement reflects the first wave feminists' elite white struggles coming to fruition, or at least a sense of manifest awareness. Also projecting from the early questions posed by a reading Gilman and Woolf's fiction, the establishment of LGBTQIA awareness and rights is a continued struggle for today's nonheteronormative community. Finally, with the trajectory of the decline of traditional forms of religion, even outright secularization, the observations of Dostoevsky and Boccaccio highlight the kernels of religion—communal spirit, collective conscience, and mechanical solidarity—in light of the question, "can man be good without God?" This question presses upon the very problem of a loss of the connective tissue and social glue in society, that of religious morals and value systems. In sum, this volume looks at key "fictional narratives" in Western consciousness to highlight both their parallels with classical sociological theory, and their significance to today's continued social problems and controversies.

ANTICIPATING A CRITIQUE

Past periods of literature should be approached from within their own moral, culturally normative, and aesthetic categories. But at the same time the reader might also acknowledge the weight of their historiographic-literary placement in a shifting context of morality (into modern categories), as well as the classic question of the character of "Great Books" that foster discussion about "human nature." By today's cultural norms (at least in most academic American contexts), the literary works discussed in this volume may be laden with ethnocentrism, sexism, homophobia, classism, racism, imperialism, and so on. In an important pause for critique, these particular *artifacts* of culture present the possibility of an aesthetic and moral order that should not be seen as an order to uphold today. This might culminate in an extension of Adorno's observations about the very nature of aesthetics and the problematic of aesthetic "enjoyment" of certain art forms after the Holocaust. How can we talk about aesthetics in the phenomenological experience of the general breakdown of the "projected" aims of "Western" civilization? But this is also precisely why these works of fiction need to be addressed; they are "classics" of Western literature and both relay and give their wider audience the problematic archetypes which serve as the currency of the social problems that drive the contemporary postmodern psyche. In this sense, the book is performing an archaeology of knowledge/archetypes that drive racism, sexism, homophobia, colonialism, and social breakdown.

WHY FICTION IS SIGNIFICANT TO SOCIOLOGY

There is a rich history of sociological observations being tied to or reflecting literary work. Before there was a proper sociology as an established academic discipline, Marx, in *The English Middle Class,* observed that the works of

Dickens, Thackeray, Brontë, and Gaskell uttered more "political and social truths" than all the professional "politicians, publicists, and moralists put together" (in Baxandell and Morawski 1973, 105). This is a great case for the significance of literature at the dawn of sociological theory. Echoed later by what W.E.B. DuBois noted in a great deal of early "professional" sociology—that of the car window, or the elite, armchair spectator. The call for organic intellectuals—so important to the realm of today's sociological discourse, hiring practices, and research methods—did not emerge in European or American contexts until long after Gramsci's case for it in the early twentieth century (Gramsci 1971). DuBois's 1903 statement against car window sociology (see Morris 2017) reinforces the theoretical case for engaging in deep ethnographic data gathering. But before "ethnography" was professionalized, sociologists have the work of novelists, though somewhat assumed to be "fettered" (for the "fact"-finders) by literary devices mechanisms that today's empiricists would shy away from in their pursuit of numerical truth, nevertheless Marx and Engels appreciated these methods of presenting the *emotional conveyance* of the social lifeworld.

The favoring of the "emotional" sense of social reality as the greatest deposit of truth is contextualized by a longstanding debate within the field of sociology. "What is the place of fiction at all?" the positivist might jab questioningly at this project. They may continue: sociology is a science built on the shoulders and postulates of Descartes to Comte to Durkheim. Wolf Lepenies has skillfully and comprehensively examined the roots of the Classical Sociological Canon in light of this debate in *Between Literature and Science: The Rise of Sociology* (1988). At the very founding of the discipline there was a methodological argument about the place of works of culture, and the writing of sociology itself as "cultural artifact." In this, Lepenies examines a basic conversation about the place of the Enlightenment (and the scientific method) and a reaction to it in an embrace of Romantic ideology, poetry, and literature. In sum, the French/English schools were dominated by pro-Enlightenment perspectives (rationalist), and the German schools by the reaction to the failures and incompleteness of science to capture the true sense of human existence via an embrace of the literary and the emotions. In American sociology today the tension between the "qualitative vs. quantitative" has shifted more toward the quantitative dominating. This has shifted even the qualitative away from the ancestors of postmodernism: Dilthey's and Weber's original hermeneutical methods of the cultural sciences are largely lost today through (again) the influence of neo-Kantianism and structuralist frames within qualitative domains of inquiry. Shocking for today's methodologists: Dilthey even desired to use poetry within the context of studying history as poetry revealed an culturally driven inner psychology (Lepenies 1988, 216). However, in today's academic divisions, within the social sciences, literature is examined in the fields of cultural studies, literary theory—but in 2021 rarely engaged by the average sociologist. Today Neo-Kantian dominance of even the qualitative school of thought has basically taken the examination of literature out of the question even in the qualitative branch of sociology—word searches, counts, coding, and the like where a quantitative research paradigm views texts' significance as numerically coded. As was commonplace at the time of the emerging mode of an "unmusical" Weberian method, today also one can look back to the very roots of the qualitative rationalized branches of methods. They are shadowed by an "outcome of the irresistible process of intellectualization" and an accompanying "increase in the significance of the irrational" (Lepenies 1988, 211).

This is why Lepenies's work on the origins of sociology's indebtedness to literature, and its method, is so important to revisit today. This mode of inquiry shows the original significance of sociology's engagement with the "literary" as it can be found in today's social, cultural and political climate. Whereby understanding schemas and archetypes as they surface within the social, cultural, and political dramas of the twenty-first century, sociologists should study literature again as a kind of archaeology of knowledge that defines the roots of contemporary social problems. As a reminder to the reader (perhaps the critical positivist sociologist), Lepenies states that one of the greatest cultural archetypes of Western Civilization—coming from *Faust*—was crafted by Goethe, both a poet and a scientist (Lepenies 1988, 4). But alas today more common in the profession of sociologists is not the broadly ranging scholar, cosmopolitan, or renaissance person, but rather is what Weber has referred to as "specialists without spirit" (Weber 2001, 124), and the late twentieth century's Michel Foucault has noted this shift from the "universal intellectual" to the "specific intellectual" (Foucault [1977] 1980, 126–128).

To address a more recent case for fiction and contemporary educational paradigms, in a 2019 *New York Review of Books* essay, novelist Zadie Smith reflects on the power of fiction as a vehicle for emotional identification—this is so potent, given higher education's battles with identity politics and the constant challenge of "relatability" for student-based curricular decision-making. Frequently the postmodern reader is a consumer looking to achieve consensus and agreement, whether it is news, opinions, pop culture, search for community on Facebook, and so on. Postmodernity is the simultaneous experience of multiplicity and the multitude in consumption patterns, as Kenneth Gergen has explored within *The Saturated Self*. It is also a kind of libidinal drive for the self's dissolution into the category of the same—any form of "otherness" must be connected into my own narcissistic realm, as reader. I need to "relate" to the author's conveyance of an experience or sentiment. In this realm language becomes the battleground for "containment" and "cultural appropriation" (Smith 2019, 4). Smith reasserts the importance of reading as "fascination with otherness"—imagination takes us to faraway places, even the inner workings of the psyche of the person sitting across the café. This is the post-post-modern *flaneur*. Is fiction supposition/presumptive/curiosity? Smith says, bravely, that fiction should challenge the current paradigm that authors can only write about people who are "fundamentally like us" (2019, 6).

Has not this level of solipsistic analysis also trickled into the social sciences? Or is fiction confessing a social-science envy? In the social sciences access to research subjects in communities for claims to gatekeepers make identity important as reflexivity. Additionally, inner/experiential knowledge presents good grounds for validity of conceptualization and gaining trust amongst research subjects. The end result, Smith observes: "embarrassed by the novel—and its mortifying habit of putting words into the mouths of others—many have moved to . . . the supposedly unquestionable authenticity of personal experience. . . . Stay in your lane" (Smith 2019, 6). Kantian freedoms and the triumph of the culture of public confessional via blogs, and so on, create a scenario where personal experience trumps all other categories for the possibility of knowledge.

Smith suggests fiction should give us something different; like early social scientific methods, it employed the heuristic of doubting surface images—this (assumed exercise of self-projection), folds back on itself into doubt. This level of reflexivity-moving-toward-compassion as a "quality of imagination" (Hector Abad, quoted in Smith 2019, 8) could easily connect with a Weberian mode of *Verstehen* with a dose of Edith Stein's sense of *Einfuhlung* (compassion/empathy) *fellow feeling*. This is somewhere between the functions of "escape" and "relatability" as an experience of fiction (Noble 1976, 221–223). On the one hand, this volume is a praise of fiction as a way into the sociological imagination. The unifying power of the novel through the very principle of relatability to the (even if somewhat broken or problematic) voice of the hero, or anti-hero, is a product of "Western" culture hearkening back to Faust, and perhaps even further to Odysseus (Moretti 1996). But contemporary literature's absence of a hero, and the novel of "rupture" is a commentary on the "broken promises of modernity, capitalism, and even to some extent those radical philosophies which sought to rebuild a world after the capitalist system.

This book is a departure from conventional sociology of literature, into the theory of the sociological imagination within the literary. Noble's (1976) and Dumont's (2018) apprehension about the impossible expectations and cultivation of elitist/specialized discourses in the vein of sociology of literature is duly noted. This text also takes into consideration the difficult task of balancing the questions of literary reception and audience versus the "intentions" of the author: "People find what they are looking for, in the sense that what strikes them is what touches on their own preoccupations" (Noble 1976, 221). Mary F. Rogers (1991) dealt with business of publishing and the book industry of British and American literature; however, this presents a unique contemporary discussion of the sociological imagination within authors who were contemporaries of the great classical sociological theorists. Goldmann (1975) integrated a concept of "ontology" in the novel, with respect to modernity and breakage, but did not integrate this discussion with the specific period, context, topics, and authors my manuscript is considering.

It is important to respect literature as literature, and not social science. This project is not attempting to make an assessment about readership, or reception of texts, for which Sociology of Literature conventionally may recommend other methodological tools and approaches. The monograph is less interested in the reader than it is in the worldview(s) (and critical appraisal) that contextualizes the author of each work of fiction. Both science and the artistic imagination are concerned with the "illumination of reality" and seeing below surface truths (Nisbet 2017, 10). As Nisbet notes, theory is a bridge between them. "Theory" comes from the same root as "theater" in ancient Greek (Nisbet 2017, 12)—theory is in this sense, a "spectacle" through which tendencies of the social world are drawn out into more clarity—both a performance and also, to pun, like a pair of spectacles that clarify our vision of the finer contours of the social world. With respect to this important hermeneutical stance that the authors critically interpret their world, this monograph is indebted to and a continuation of Lukács's project, and is in conversation with Goldmann's methodology. In dialogue with Goldmann it is concerned with the metaphors and images of "breakage" away from the past, that create an opening for an intellectual and sociological curiosity in late-nineteenth to early twentieth-century fiction writing. Some of these authors of fiction may be employing a certain level of fantastical-projection, but they also channel a sociological imagination to present how characters, less caught in the epic unfolding of divine forces, or tragic flaws and fates, are actually challenged and driven by psycho-social forces as a product of their contexts—including geographic/political, familial, social, historical, theological, and so on. The qualification for Zadie Smith is whether fiction "is a creator of compassion or a vehicle for containment" (Smith 2019, 8). The position of this book is that the authors discussed convey the power of compassion for individuals amidst a critique of the whole of society, fashioned through an empathic mechanism of reflective-critical, and Weberian interpretive understanding (*Verstehen*)—in the realm of feeling, motivation, and spirit (Nisbet 2017, 12).

I do anticipate this general critique of the monograph: "social science should concern itself not with fiction, but rather fact." Indeed, even the artistic form of realism, as described by Jameson (2013) in a hybrid concept that suspends a scientific category of "the real" even while trying to represent it (at least in all the variegated dimensions of experience). Jameson defines, "realism is a hybrid concept, in which an epistemological claim (for knowledge or truth) masquerades as an aesthetic ideal . . . if it is social truth or knowledge we want" we actually get ideology (Jameson 2013, 5). However, sociology of culture and aesthetics should communicate: as they are "both superannuated forms of thinking" (Jameson 2013)—perhaps in the categories of the famous Weberian "ideal types" or "social facts." They both seem to be suspended into the realm of the "non-empirical"—even within some analytics-driven social research today!

An added note, novels are constructions of language; and language is embedded in social realities. So therefore, we are able to read novels, both in terms of style but also plots, characters, and so on, all as reflective (or critical) of the relationship of the very social elements of "base and superstructure" (Williams 1977). An added note: this viewing of novels as a social product weaves nicely into the methods of intertextuality, as introduced by Bakhtin and Kristeva (Alfaro 1996). This implies the principle of the constructed and constructive sociality of the text. "There are always other words in a word, other texts in a text. The concept of intertextuality requires, therefore, that we understand texts not as self-contained systems but as differential and historical, as traces and tracings of otherness, since they are shaped by the repetition and transformation of other textual structures" (Alfaro 1996, 268). Thus, in the pages that follow, the "intertextual" discussions of each of the "case studies" of a particular literary work are enfolded in references to other works of the author under examination. Additionally, in the method of intertextuality, connections will be made to other authors, floating archetypes (products of the collective conscience and collective unconscious), theoretical themes and references. Thus, the sociological reading of these texts connects to the imagination of the authors, reflected in their writings, as a historical-social-cultural product.

Categorization is a human impulse—perhaps the scientific impulse (since Aristotle at least). But the other human intellectual drive is the poetic impulse: the imagination connects to categories, fuses emotions with nature and existence, and tries to understand, rather than dominate them through separating analytic and technical modes of control (see Ellul 1956). From the position of the ancient Greeks, this began in reverence at nature. The holiest places, like Delphi, were also wonders of natural landscape. In some modern fiction, there is a sense of an emptiness where space exists without the grounding place. This is perhaps the sacrifice to modern capitalism's domination of nature, or the conquest of an imagined and Romanticized "natural man"— heavily loaded in colonialist and other values since the dawn of "modern" novel as *Robinson Crusoe*. Though this volume stops its analysis prior to the postmodern element in fiction—it acknowledges that this is the natural next step in an analysis of the balance between "containment or compassion"—the absurdist/Dadaist perspective departs from any sense of coherent meaning or the act of story-telling as a complete whole.

One (albeit rather Christian) observation of the implications of Lukács's concept about the fracture leading to an opening of what I will call sociologically infused fiction, is the sense of *"ubi crux, ibi poesia."* The suffering of the world, the challenge of the distance between the "ought and the is" creates a possibility for the exploration of emotional and existential truths. This exploration requires a hermeneutical openness—much like the suspension of the everyday world and time that exists within the liminality of a seafaring journey. As suggested by a phenomenological reading of *Moby Dick,* the way in which mental categories of meaning both "appear" and are "constructed" shapes the way in which social science lends itself to a kind of interpretive openness, and continual narrative. This is a wholehearted rejection of the positivist tradition in the realm of sociology. Even within the realm of that tradition (or a spin-off) social facts (Durkheim) reside not so much in their connection to material observables, but in their social significances. Better said by the novelist Joseph Conrad: "Facts can bear out my story" (Conrad 1983, 382). Facts cannot explain the why.

This monograph also presents a warning to the social realm that rejects reason and fact entirely. Nostalgia for the emotional whole of the epic form is a function of postmodern politicized discourse; it is a reaction to it. Certain themes within Richard Wagner's music-dramas, and Thea von Harbou's (author of the screenplay for Fritz Lang's 1927 silent film epic) *Metropolis* tried to rescue epic unity as a response to modern fractures. These artforms were inspirational to the Third Reich, but these are desperate attempts to revive a unity that was not organically given. They hint at the experience of "ruins amidst the legends of castles" (Lukács 1971, 55). A running theme throughout the monograph is the concept of the "broken epic" and reflexive critique as a healthy form of the sociological imagination. At times of crisis, as historian John Mitcham notes, narratives of unified identity (especially a racialized one) created solidarity for Great Britain in World War I; forgetful of Scottish or Irish nationalism, the identity of "Briton" "emerges" just in time for a source of cohesion necessary to win the Great War. As a functionalist might suggest, the unity of the collective conscience creates strength, and casting nationalized out-groups galvanized support for the project of bourgeois nationalism—thus certain literary forms actually encourage the "mapping" of political geographies onto heretofore "imagined communities." But this is exactly what troubled social theorists like Rosa Luxemburg, who saw that war as a product of elite concerns and a bourgeois agenda. What is different about the novels I have chosen—novels which challenge or pose queries to these sociopolitical projections? These are both "epic" and "broken" narrations. This poses the potential for the opening of the reflexive sociological imagination in the very critique of the authors' contexts. This opening suggests an early experiment in the literary canvas of cognitive dissonance and the sociological imagination. As Said explored, the emergence of nationalism via novels and the age of imperialism are all united in the historical moment of the nineteenth century. As *Robinson Crusoe* launches an anticipation of the logic of "the beyond/the unexplored" there is an overlapping of explorers and novelists as they had explored the "unmapped" regions of the world. This links back to the way in which narrating a novel is also narrating the conceptions of symbiotic societies, and their concomitant identities at home and abroad—"nations are narrations" (Said 1993, xiii).

Looking back to ancient times, the philosophic age emerged, in the experiential rift between "outside and inside"; the incongruence between the world and the self (Lukács 1971, 29). The birth of philosophy (the Greek world) happened in a relatively small circle; whereas as Lukács observed (even in his time a century ago), the world in the modern and postmodern has become "infinitely large." Good art, good drama rejects this holism within the "greatness of the world"—the cosmos of drama ignores the contrast between wholeness and segment, event and symptom . . . drama must grasp its totality (Lukács 1971, 49). What these select novelists of the mid-nineteenth to early twentieth century also appreciated were the cracks in that totality of the project of "civilization." The fractures of social life and the incomplete ideological and utopic projects of democracy and capitalism present themselves in the tragic (and comic) gender relations in Gilman and Woolf, the hypocrisies and absurdities of Christianity in both Hawthorne and Dostoevsky, the failures of "civilization" in Conrad, and the underlying viciousness of modernity and American society in Melville.

A note on the abiding epic form. Beginning in late winter 2019–2020 the globe experienced the weight of an international epidemiological and social crisis in the COVID pandemic. In an American context, one could observe the desire to go back to "our" cohort/generational "epics" and "comfort tunes." Zombie apocalypse and dystopic films seemed to be less of a go-to for television viewers. For Babyboomers, GenXers, Millennials and beyond, pop radio and TV sought to provide ease and relief in "happy endings" from *Lord of the Rings, Harry Potter, Indiana Jones,* and enthralling "rock anthems" from Queen, Elton John, Springsteen, David Bowie, Journey, Coldplay. For the more highbrow, a popular YouTube clip offered the Rotterdam Philharmonic's Zoom performance of Beethoven's solidarity-conveying *Ode to Joy* from the 9th symphony. We were reminded to be kind and practice solidarity, in everything from Amazon.com advertisements to reruns from *Mr. Rogers' Neighborhood.*

In this critical time period, both mass culture and more elite versions of material culture worked like an "opiate," as discussed by the critical theories of Adorno, Horkheimer, and the Frankfurt school. Lukács was prescient about the "largeness" of the new world—especially with all our interconnections in a technologically driven globalized capitalism. Building on Lukács' observations, it seems as though in times of crisis there is less room for psychological opening and critique, and more of a need for culture to solidify and unify the human experience. In times of economic, social, political upheaval, an ideological orthodoxy is necessary to hold the fragments together—via the social glue of culture. The infinitely large and multiplex reduces to messages of uniformity, unity, covalence, rather than dissent, disorientation and reflexivity. But let us hope that this does not revert into an authoritarian cultural world system, where allegory is driven specifically by the dogmatic, as Gadamer's formulation suggests (Moretti 1996, 82–83).

Phase two of 2020—the Great Awakening of the Black Lives Matter movement after the murder of George Floyd. Our "hype" about solidarity was exposed. Media began to embrace the reality about how *fractured* American society really is. As a response, imagined utopias (both futuristic and nostalgic) became popular—the present "does not exist in epics" (Moretti 1996, 88). This, via Ernst Bloch's reflections on the "non-contemporaneous," is a symptom of capitalism's focus on projected futures and nostalgic pasts (Bloch 1977), but a suspended period of time is also a constructive response to both individual and collective trauma. Sometimes the response to rapid historical changes takes the form of cultural trauma. One example of this at the individual literary level is in the method of Dostoevsky's introspective "dialogues" and his own suffering of "epileptic fits" as an "amplification" of self-consciousness (Bird 2012, 129). The trauma of Dostoevsky's "mock firing squad" served as an existential "limit experience" in the sense of Maurice Blanchot and George Bataille—an opening to a sense of timelessness. This leaves the student of Dostoevsky to an observation that one can only know oneself in "instants of apocalypse" (Bird 2012). Therefore, by extension, society potentially comes to "moments of clarity" in time of crisis. It is an awakening within those episodes of dramatic events that gives birth to better visions of society. It is in this very opening that repeats the very essence of the birthing of the sociological imagination, from what Stephen Buechler (2011) has defined in "critical sociology"—a hope-driven lens for a better future.

These following chapters look at examples of literary "echoes of the past" (nineteenth to early twentieth century)—but simultaneously allegories of the disturbing consequences of capitalism's projected future into today. Watching the daily news, we confront these age-old archetypes, and "once dystopic futures" at work in today's current events. As in Faust's conclusion, "All that is changeable/ is but a refraction/the unattainable here becomes action"

(12104–12107). Appearing in the projections of society, but reflexively folding back upon itself, the "project" of literature in the dawn of sociology is to revisit the function of imagined worlds (in their projected dys/utopias and broken ontologies) in a time of political-social-economic change and crisis. All the while, a critical sociological read of aesthetics in social life should remind the reader, alongside George Steiner's observations, that the power of art is not "art for its own sake." Pressed to its logical conclusions, art for its own sake is a pure or "empty" aesthetic and leads to narcissism (Steiner 1989, 143). The poetic, narrative imagination functions through the processes of mutual empathy and recognition; it is a reception and encounter with both the sacred truths of a society and the very projections of the "other." In this way fiction is always and everywhere "sociological"—its connection through language, history, traditions, the very "ambient social" (Steiner 1989, 162–163). What marks this historical period of sociological fiction as perhaps the culmination, but also the conclusion of the historical period of "total art"—it must change our lives, as when the reader/viewer "observes" Apollo; at least so far as we take the metaphor in Rilke's poem, "Archaic Torso of Apollo." The departure point within modernity and capitalism is represented by the allegory of Faust—and this monograph begins with a Faustian narrative within an American application. The tragic nature of capitalism needs art as a kind of "metaphysical consolation" (Nietzsche 1993, 88). The modern theoretical and domineering man runs "nervously no longer wanting anything whole . . . so coddled by optimism" (Nietzsche 1993, 88–89). The sociological trend in today's literature (and even today's sociological literature) marks a departure from the very transformative power of discourse. Within sociological research sometimes the refracted discourse of on the one hand, the inane and tedious pursuit of the "empirical" descriptive, and the obtuse hyperboles of the politicized deconstructionist. Pollsters can't seem to get things correct, and today's identity politics are divisive rather than offering a hopeful criticism or vision. The energy of the sociological imagination has been lost through these fractured special interest narratives, and what Steiner critically anticipated as self-projections and "artificial feelings" (Steiner 1989, 143).

This volume, *Literature in the Dawn of Sociology: Community, Capitalism, and Critique* offers sociological readings of classics of Western literature within the historical period of the birth of social science as artistic forms exhibiting the changes brought forth by the cultural shifts in capitalism. As mentioned previously, we begin with an interpretation of *Faust* set in Puritan New England.

NEW ENGLAND SHADOWS: HAWTHORNE, FAUST, AND THE AMERICAN SPIRITUAL CHARACTER

In sociologist Andrew Greeley's *The Catholic Imagination,* the author surmises that religion is a kind of poetry. Greeley discusses this as the analogical imagination, via David Tracy's theology. The analogical imagination attests to the fact that God is revealed in creation—per the use of analogical language and God becoming incarnate—and this says something about the world being infused with spiritual potency. In the spirit of *"poiesis"* or Greek for "making," this chapter argues that the American fiction writers Herman Melville and Nathaniel Hawthorne, though influenced by Calvinism, created both a poetic and an anti-poetic of the American religious imagination. Interpreting the consequences of the psychological and sociological implications of the Calvinist doctrines of the elect, the total depravity of man, and God's absence from the world, "Young Goodman Brown" serves as an example of the American split psyche. The chapter examines the social psychology of characters in this work using sociological theory, psychoanalysis, and parallel literary consequences within the American religious landscape.

The sociological implications of these mental mechanisms point to the problem, however, related to the collapsing of the individual's relationship with the world and more directly, community. Reflecting back on the impetus and manifesto in Robert Bellah's *The Broken Covenant*, it is important to remember that, in the late portion of the classical period of birth of sociological theory and sociology of religion, R.H. Tawney first published his *Religion and the Rise of Capitalism* in 1926. This was in the resplendence and economic boom of the Roaring Twenties. Could the pursuit of self-interest in an unregulated fashion have led to the undermining of a pro-social ethic of care and responsibility for one's neighbor? As Weber warned in *The Protestant Ethic,* lurking in the Puritan attitude of the elect is the momentum toward this very individualism—and consumerism. This was, in Tawney's explanation, the natural consequence of the Puritan economic revolution. The implications of an individualist economic "ethic" meant that Puritan America had no true covenant to break, but rather it was undermined from the beginning.

A "SYMPHONY" ON A BROKEN ONTOLOGY: MELVILLE'S *MOBY DICK* AS MODERN EPIC

This chapter, building from observations on Calvinist theology/sociology in Hawthorne, travels "down the road" to New Bedford through Herman Melville's classic as an example of the epic responding to a "broken ontology."

This is in the context of the fractured world of capitalist mentality of obsession, domination and its resulting alienation. Classical sociological theory's literature on the relationship between theology and sociology, and their declining "contact" in modern "alienated" thinking, is applied in a discussion of the novel. The *Pequod* projects/anticipates a postmodern social experiment of community and hope, albeit on the verge of despair and destruction. The chapter also discusses Melville's use of a sea voyage as a liminal setting and multicultural/multinational characters within a post-modern allegorical tone. This reflects "portents of the transcendent" and glimmerings of the "divine magnanimities" of hope even while on the path to destruction. Ultimately this suggests the way in which "society" is ever incomplete, leaving room for the need for connection to a sense of "otherness." This chapter blends literary studies with queer theory, political theory, and sociological theory, entertaining a discussion of contemporary political, social, and religious implications of the "Great Book" via C.L.R. James's *Mariners, Renegades, and Castaways* (1953) Robert Martin's *Hero, Captain, and Stranger* (1986), Eugene Halton's *Meaning and Modernity* (1986), and a survey of literature in postmodern religion.

LITERARY *METANOIA* AND THE SOCIOLOGICAL IMAGINATION IN JOSEPH CONRAD: COLONIALISM AND WESTERN IDEALISM

The predominant scope of literary studies of Conrad's *Heart of Darkness* in the late twentieth century focused on its racism. Most famously, literary scholars like Chinua Achebe and Edward Said—both coming from a postcolonial perspective—staunchly defended the claim that the text was thoroughly, unapologetically, racist. This chapter gives a more nuanced reading of *Heart of Darkness* as a beginning of a coming to terms with, and an honest (and not Pollyanna style) rendering of an attempt at awareness of the brutalities of colonialism and imperialism. This turns a page forward in literary scholarship, but also suggests that the novel anticipates a form of reflexive sociological discourse.

Conrad may be called a "literary modernist" (Moses 2007), his creative work placed within the genre of an extension of naturalism, Romanticism, and realism. However, along with Giffin's (2013) observations, this text has a pivotal role in transforming "the 19th century classic realist novel, mainly based on authoritative and chronological narrative, into a 20th century modernist artifact challenging received notions of reality" (Spittles in Giffin 2013). The psychological turn in the novel, noted by Lukács, expresses a level of theoretical *metanoia*—presenting the possibility of self-reflective critique. This presents a conscious turn toward the reflective/inner monologue of conscience. Where Jameson describes realism as "the symbiosis of this pure form of storytelling with impulses of scenic elaboration, description, and above all affective investment" (Jameson 2013), at the conclusion of the novel Conrad leaves the reader to identify with Marlow, and with a sense of angst and Durkheimian anomie. From the point of view of a particular sociology of literature at the dawn of classical theory, *Heart of Darkness'* illumination of conscience shows that a sociological imagination is embedded. This is possible in the way in which authors use and manipulate time. The manipulation of time—also noted in Woolf's *Orlando* (chapter six)—represents a new stylistic epoch in literature, and one that is a) on the one hand ever present in the act of storytelling but b) on the other particularly evident in "modern" storytelling. What is unique about Conrad is the level in which his subject is located in sociological dynamics—those that are assumed in a false consciousness by those who live in those "sepulchral cities" of Europe, and, I argue, reflexively critiqued by Conrad.

Conrad honestly, but also reflexively, presents the latent theoretical worldviews of the nineteenth century's philosophers through narration: namely purveying the theoretical impact of Darwin and Nietzsche. But there are also latent critiques of these Western philosophical modes of domination. The question up for critical debate here is whether Conrad "receives or critiques" this reality (namely the Cartesian-Darwinian-Nietzschean-Freudian matrix of "Western" civilization). Conrad's philosophical conditioning and "anthropology" presents "man" in the character of the old Platonist split: mind/body; reason/feeling; ego/id; conscious/unconscious (Giffin 2013). There is a subtle level of critique, a progressive vision in Conrad's novel—this is in naming, and realizing "the horror" of Western civilization. Is the novel an artifice or a reflection of a new kind of consciousness? It presents the possibility of a seeing things *as they are and engaging in a critique of them.*

Heart of Darkness could be considered a kind of collective confession of Western imperialism: an honest, but dark, description of the brutality of the *European heart*, which says "Exterminate all the brutes!" The desire to bring love, truth, beauty, and "civilization" to the "Dark continent" reveals the barbarism of the force of civilizing: even more evil and savage than that of the "Dark continent."

WOMEN AND MEN: THE TRAGICOMIC

The war of the sexes and the birth of first wave feminism are discussed in the context of its distillation of unresolved age-old, but also current, issues in modern identity politics. This is reflected most recently by the #MeToo movement. Some of the impetus of the #MeToo movement may derive from archetypal feminist imaginings of utopia—popularized recently in films like *Wonder Woman* (2017). One hundred years before the #MeToo movement, a feminist utopia was envisioned in the novel *Herland* (published serially between 1910–1916) by Charlotte Perkins Gilman, a first-wave American feminist novelist and sociologist. This article explores the tropes of #MeToo's parallel mythological construction of shaming and exclusion of male characteristics in a literary scope. It suggests that Gilman's *Herland* reflects archetypal blueprints for the feminist impulse driving #MeToo. The conclusion of the essay argues that there are some weaknesses to this scope, in light of examples of heterosexual encounters in other artistic forms, through a contested conversation between Queer Theory, of social theory, and Catholic theology's views of sexuality.

SUSPENDING MODERNITY: GENDER AND TIME IN VIRGINIA WOOLF'S *ORLANDO*

This chapter examines the sociologically relevant theoretical contributions of Virginia Woolf, showcasing an analysis of the novel *Orlando*. It argues that there is a proven sociological impact to theorizing within the space of fiction. Some parallels are drawn to the theorist-fiction writer Charlotte Perkins Gilman to make the point that theory can sometimes best be articulated within the genre and audience of fiction. This is for both its theoretical technique and dissemination of ideas—Woolf and Gilman reached a wider contemporary audience of women (and men) by relaying their theories of sex and gender in literary publications. Using analysis from both sociology and literary criticism, the chapter describes the way Woolf exhibited the sociological imagination by deconstructing, and pushing the limits, of gender roles in post-Victorian England. Mid- to late-twentieth-century Queer theory is anticipated in Woolf's novel.

THE ABSURD CHRISTIAN: THE SOCIOLOGICAL IMAGINATION OF DOSTOEVSKY

How does religion relate to psychology? Is religion even relevant to those who live in a mostly secularized society in places other than the "Global South"? Dostoevsky's *Brothers Karamazov* provokes sophisticated questions about "postmodern religion" or "religion in a post-religious" context long before the disciplines of theology and sociology had come to terms with the social psychological impacts of such a complex historical development.

Weber wrote about "disenchantment" (2001) and Durkheim of "*anomie*" (1973) but how is this internal dialogue between the "ought and the is" conveyed at the experiential level, given this "breakage" in the subjective experience of modernization where forms of morality, norms, and expectations are fading? As C.L.R. James described the contributions of Herman Melville to so-called "world literature," the crisis of the modern world is reflected in the emergence of the form of the novel. The individual character at odds with or subsuming to society's wishes is the distinct theme of the sociological novel, wherein both individuals play out the dualistic pull of individual freedom and one's uniqueness with the need for connection and communion (James 2001, 160).

Durkheim and Dostoevsky both articulate how this very dualism of human existence reflects the split between the ego's desires and the community's needs. Dostoevsky poetically weaves these questions into a narrative with dialogues and conversations about how doing the good (the "ought") seems pointless in an increasingly absurd world (the truth of the "is"). Dostoevsky "did not write novels" (Lukács 1971, 20), but rather gives his reader philosophical-existential reflection in these "voices" of the individual and the "generalized other" of society (in Bakhtin's presentation). This "deep insight" is into the psychic worlds colliding between the pulls of what Durkheim named as "*les consciences particulier et collective*"; the reader knows that these struggles of morality/conscience and individual freedom are *only* a product of the loosening of freedom (and the potential for license) within the modern imagination. The imagination of *Gesellschaft* is an abstraction; that this "new world, remote from any struggle against what actually exists, is drawn for the first time simply as a seen reality" (Lukács 1971, 152). "It will then be the task of historical-philosophical interpretation to decide whether we are really about the leave the age of absolute sinfulness or whether the new has no other herald but our hopes: those hopes which are signs of a world to come, still so weak that it can easily be crushed by the sterile power of the merely existent" (Lukács 1971, 153). Dostoevsky reminds the reader that in response to secularization and postmodernity, faith and Christian ethics may be absurd, but they are most necessary as the all too human drama unfolds.

BOCCACCIO: ART DELUDES ITSELF

The anesthetizing power of art and narrative is hard to deny—but what happens when this mixes with a dose of reflexivity? This chapter looks to the early days of capitalism—its inchoate stages in fourteenth-century Florence, Italy. The Black Death ravaged this young city, causing much social-political upheaval. What can we learn amidst today's pandemic, and post-pandemic future, given the collapse of categories of meaning, the resurgence of religion, the challenges to science, the threats to solidarity, and detached isolation? Boccaccio's *Decameron*—whose voice some say mark the beginning of the Renaissance—pokes fun at the hypocrisies and impotence of religious authority, but from within the framework of a more authentic Christian ethic. Thus, the context of Boccaccio's interpretation of this social crisis ushered forth some of the modern categories we live with today. A reflection back on this important moment in literature and social history calls to mind the importance of community and responsibility in this, the new age of techno-capitalism. Or we will continue to be distracted by hype and the "sweet poisons" of culture's power to anesthetize and distract from realities and responsibilities.

Chapter Two

New England Shadows

Hawthorne, Faust, and the American Spiritual Character

INTRODUCTION

In Andrew Greeley's *The Catholic Imagination,* the author—a Catholic priest, sociologist, and Romance novelist—surmises that religion is a kind of poetry. Greeley discusses this as the analogical imagination, via David Tracy's theology. The analogical imagination attests to the fact that God is revealed in creation—per the use of analogical language and God becoming incarnate—and this says something about the world being infused with spiritual potency. In this spirit of *poiesis*, Greek for "making," this chapter focuses on the early nineteenth-century fiction of Nathaniel Hawthorne. However, in contrast to Catholicism, Hawthorne was influenced by the religious tones of Calvinist Puritanism, Unitarianism, and German Idealism's inspiration, Goethe. Hawthorne created both a poetic and an anti-poetic reflection of the American religious imagination. Given the religious roots of American culture, Hawthorne was well-suited to make sociological observations about the "youthful" nation and culture.

Nathaniel Hawthorne was born in Salem, Massachusetts in 1804, only a few years before Goethe published Part I of *Faust*. Hawthorne added a "w" to his ancestral name, Hathorne, as John Hathorne was one of the judges in the Salem Witch Trials. Carrying the existential burden, or perhaps even a superstitious belief in being cursed by one of the victims of the Trials, Hawthorne altered the spelling (Moore 1989). Through the power of allegory, Hawthorne's texts engage in a rich description of the psychological and sociological implications of the trajectory of modern religion. These implications include: alienation from the eternal feminine, the Calvinist doctrines of the elect, and the total depravity of man, and the absence of God's grace from the world. Hawthorne presents sophisticated "fictional ethnographies" of Puritanism in "Young Goodman Brown" and *The Scarlet Letter*. I use the term "fictional ethnographies" to evoke the sense that Hawthorne himself sees as "recounting" folktales—especially in his collection of stories, *Twice Told Tales* (1837)—twice told in that "he had heard them first before he had worked them out himself" (Moore 1989). "Young Goodman Brown" (1835) was published three years following Goethe's death and publication of *Faust,* part II (1832). Goethe, as both a literary figure and, like Hawthorne, a collector of "twice-told" tales in the reconfiguration of archetypes, is of supreme significance to Hawthorne's storytelling. Hawthorne innovates an aptly American application of Goethe's famed "ethic of the eternal feminine" (Eichner 1971)—a theme that was very important to the Concord authors, including Melville's *Moby Dick* (see chapter three). Goethe's *Faust*, especially Part I, was frequently discussed in popular British magazines and reviews such as *Blackwood's Magazine* and the *Edinburgh Review* during the early decades of the nineteenth century—all available for Hawthorne's review. Hawthorne himself likely read an essay on *Faust, Part I*, appearing in Blackwood's in June 1820 (Dameron 1994, 11).

In July 1833, Hawthorne was attentive to an issue of *The Foreign Quarterly Review*. This important publication included Abraham Hayward's essay on the second part of Goethe's *Faust* (published just in the year prior, the year of Goethe's death). Hayward invited the reader to "see what modes the second part presents of purifying the head and heart of a philosopher" (Dameron 1994, 12). Melville and Hawthorne used these Faustian tropes—meditation/action, feminine/masculine—to illuminate the American character. The tragic element of human nature comes across cloaked in Puritan value-systems and soap operas, for an American audience. Highlighting the social psychologies of characters in these works using sociological theory, psychoanalysis, and literary examples, this chapter suggests some lessons for understanding the *American Character* based on the contributions of these authors. These questions are addressed: A) reflecting God's absence from the world, how is American religion and culture anti-poetry? B) What are the economic, sociological and psychological consequences of this anti-world attitude? C) And finally, as a metaphoric link between the poetic imagination and the idea of the eternal feminine, how do these categories inform a sociology of gender in American religious life?

THE MELANCHOLY: ANTI-POETRY

Marion Montgomery's 1984 three volume study, *Why Hawthorne Was Melancholy,* presents a question that points directly to the essence of the

American character of the nineteenth century. It is cast in the term of a mood—melancholy—perhaps expressing more of a sociological spirit than exactly a psychoanalytically driven emotion. Montgomery refers to a quote by the American southern Catholic author Flannery O'Connor, "Why was Hawthorne melancholy, and what made Poe drink liquor and why did Henry James like England better than America?" O'Connor reflects on Northeastern Puritanism and its bleak side, perhaps causing melancholy, alcoholism, and a longing for escape. But why? What is at its root that would create such a psychic prison? Both a psychology and sociology of the American character as it derives from Puritanism—themes of the elect, sin, and the confines of and conformities of a repressive *Gemeinschaft* community (Tönnies [1887] 1961)—are at work in the writings of Nathaniel Hawthorne. It is important to put Hawthorne's work in conversation with his colleague and friend Herman Melville's novel *Moby Dick*. Melville presents the eternal workings of the tensions between frontier-and-fate and explores the problematic category of elect community as a possible solution to the failures of the American character. The larger question is on the failures of the American worldview as it is driven by the hypocritical juxtaposition of valuing freedom alongside the practices of slavery and genocide. This characterizes a Faustian bargain of sacrifice: a betrayal of one sense of the Rousseau-like conceptualization of the eternal feminine, Native Americans, African slaves, and nature herself for the success of the American project of capitalism. Melville picks up where his friend and colleague Hawthorne left off—when these themes play out directly in an allegorical reading of *Moby Dick*.

Montgomery makes the point that the philosophies of Transcendentalism and the figure of Ralph Waldo Emerson shadow over the work of both Hawthorne and Melville. All three were a part of the Concord, Massachusetts literary posse (Moore 1989). The Catholicism of Greeley and O'Connor, which call for a sense of "grace in the world," are in stark contrast with the harsh dichotomies and separations that define the Transcendentalist world. These fractures are both a product of but also a reaction to Puritanism (Montgomery 1984, 34–35). There are always sharp contrasts between nature-grace, and reason-imagination. Hawthorne's characters depict perceptions of black and white systems of morality, or the presentation of good and evil. However, Hawthorne is a critic of the American worldview, and his texts show him (the author) at work in the background using clever devices that grey this morality, or expose the posturing morality as hypocritical, especially in the classic, *The Scarlet Letter*. "Young Goodman Brown" expresses the darkness underneath the clean and perfect vision of a very bright and sunlit Salem. The light of the elect, or the "city upon the hill" of "New Jerusalem," however, suggests a simulated staleness compared to the bright sun of grace.

The light of the elect is an old trope in American religion; perhaps at the founding of the colonies aimed to be a "Beacon" to the world, hence the famous "Beacon" street in Boston, and the shiny-domed Statehouse at its "peak." Bellah et al. highlight it as a theme in *Habits of the Heart*. The sectarian church "sees itself as the gathered elect and focuses on the purity of those within as opposed to the sinfulness of those without" (1985: 244). The forgotten id-Dionysian pulses in the shadow and darkness of the forest and is explored by Brown's journey that is both "downward" and "inward." The complementary story to this is Hawthorne's "Maypole of Merry Mount" where he shows the loss of joyful excess (Montgomery 1984: 72). The celebration of the Maypole symbolizes sexual fertility and the excess and merriment of the new coming season—traditional English Morris dancers, drunkenness, celebration, and the like. From a sociological perspective what it represents is the debate between that thriving impulse of nature and the taming of human instincts in society (Freud 1930). Will the grisly saints of the repressed elect scoff at or awkwardly embrace the sexually liberated "sinners" at the margins of the society? Montgomery rightly observes that there is a Puritan hypocrisy behind this. Lingering is the power of the "dark secret" of embodiment—yet for the self-aware "sinners" it is no secret.

Carried forward to today, to the contemporary political environment, an alignment between the Christian Right and the political reactionary creates a new split between "intellectual" and "political" virtues. This new sense of the "elect" overlaps with the ribaldry of certain "non-presidential" behaviors in a way that reflects populism and fascistically absorbs both the pious and bold. The "silent majority" reaches back in American history, to Hawthorne's time as noted by Alexis de Tocqueville, who made important observations on the destructive implications of American populism. Again, the American project, imagined by both Hawthorne and Melville, dramatically plays out the larger contest of modernity—the tension between the "is and the ought," where individualism is kept at bay by the cultish normative pressures (the mob, in Plato's sense) of democratic society. The paradox of "democracy's wager"—the tension between liberty and equality and the coercive power of conformity—in the American project is that it seeks to throw off the fetters of tradition only to find itself embroiled in a more pernicious form of authority through anti-intellectualist authoritarianism (Tocqueville 1839, in Calhoun et al. 2012, 122–129). This actually *discourages* the cultivation of civil society and democratic values. Today's so-called silent majority paints itself as the elect but acts in a way in which the so-called "margins" would seem more respectable and genteel, practicing tolerance and graciousness in speech and displaying "statesman" norms/value systems. Langman (2020) highlights this as a characteristic of the contemporary politics of American populism, rooted in Tocqueville's observations. Today's new "right" perceives itself as marginal, acts out narratives of victimization, but yet it has the upper hand in political culture and economic status. To untie these present-day knots of political economy and its religious roots, the next section will examine some of the connections between soteriological categories of Puritanism and their social consequences.

TO BE A PILGRIM

The great sociological historian and Anglican socialist Richard Henry Tawney dedicated the writing of *Religion and the Rise of Capitalism* to the explication and rooted analysis of the origins of Puritanism. Every scholar of sociological theory or sociology of religion is aware of the Weberian thesis about the Protestant Ethic and the ascetic gloomy attitude that is its byproduct. Hence Hawthorne's melancholy partially explained. Weber's (in Talcott Parsons' famous translation) "specialists without spirit and sensualists without heart" evoke that dark trajectory into the future and that ominous Iron Cage of modernity (Weber 2001, 124). All this created by the Puritanical spirit, or what Adam Seligman has called "inner-worldly individualism."

R.H. Tawney is probably less familiar to most mainstream sociology scholars. Regardless, *Religion and the Rise of Capitalism* gives prescience into the social psychology of Puritanism and reflects on its consequences for both the American character and modernity in general. The Puritan image—ever-embattled—is cast by the hymn by John Bunyan "To be a Pilgrim."

> Since Lord, Thou dost defend us with Thy Spirit
> We know we at the end, shall life inherit
> Then fancies flee away! I'll fear not what men say,
> I'll labor night and day to be a pilgrim.

This sets the appropriate tone and is reinforced by Tawney's argument that mundane toil becomes a sacrament and there is a consciousness as to ultimate ends and an apocalyptic (Tawney 1998, 199–200). Hawthorne's characters are seen working. Idleness is sinful, thus leading to a new thrifty and efficient tone set for middle-class values (Tawney 1998, 213). However, Tawney has the tremendous insight for both Hawthorne and the American character that this sort of authoritarian regimented existence has as its alter ego expressed through self-interested, utilitarian individualism (Tawney 1998, 221–225).

When the individual is the center of the sacred, a solitary communion is the result. O'Connor again (quoted in Montgomery) reflected on the hollowing out of the sacred in American religion—"When Emerson decided in 1832, that he could no longer celebrate the Lord's Supper unless the bread and wine were removed, an important step in the vaporization of American religion was taken" (1984, 46). As it refers to the analogical imagination, something happened to the American spiritual impulse when elements from the physical world evaporated away. This move away from body-earth-corpus means nature becomes a doppelganger and not a brother (or sister!) in creation. From a Jungian point of view, nature is a dark *anima* to the human *animus* (Zimmer 1975). The isolated individual, with his private conscience, stands before nature as a temptress, illustrated in Hawthorne's "Young Goodman Brown," or as a wild spiritual mystery that is unknown, as in Thoreau's *Walden,* Melville's *Moby Dick.*

In a response to Emerson, Hawthorne/Melville/Thoreau theorize modes of the collective unconscious in the American spirit. To react to this split, each has a different response. Appearances in the world are to be doubted. Melville reacts positively, using the eye of the sperm whale as a metaphor for "catching the subtleties" rather than the vast magnanimities. In fact, the stylistic trope of the whale's surfacing throughout *Moby Dick* renders the message that nature and the potency of the supernatural are only briefly glimpsed, and never defeated or captured. Hawthorne's reaction is doubt and fear. But he uses the metaphor of "circle" to enclose but also "eternally return" to the paradox. In "Young Goodman Brown" the "waking up" from the dream sequence is the return. In *"The Scarlet Letter* the return/paradox is the sanctity of the individual soul. . . . We must see in these Transcendental ideals the ground of his religious and psychological faith and the source of his artistic strategy. His faith in the sanctity of the soul and in the ability of the imagination to perceive truth in the delusive shows of reality accounts in large part for the equivalence of his aesthetic vision and his moral vision" (West 1974, 322). Hawthorne reflects an original sociological imagination (a cultural layer of psychoanalytic insight)—one that sees there is a layer of truth below surface appearances. There is a retreat from "reality for the purposes not only of gaining aesthetic distance, but of attaining the testing-ground of truth and reality. This sacred ground is usually figured in magic circle imagery" (West 1974, 322). Here there may be an early appreciation for the method of alchemy, as it is linked to "magic" and the Faustian impulse: the pursuit of knowledge. In this way, West links the poetic imagination in Hawthorne, to the proto-scientific/magical imagination. Hawthorne, then, delved "into the depths of our common nature" and resuscitated archetypal ideas "for the purposes of psychological romance" (West 1974, 324).

One could also anticipate a kind of existential resignation in labor in Hawthorne as well—the old Pilgrim ethic (Montgomery 1984, 49). This is balanced by the sacramental enjoyment of nature—whose literary champion is Thoreau. The Concord authors' baptismal waters are in Walden Pond, a body of water whose mystical depths are unknown.

FAUSTIAN WAGER, AND A BROKEN COVENANT

The sociological implications of these mental mechanisms of division between male/female, mental/natural realm, point to a problem, however, related to the collapsing of the individual's relationship with the world and more directly, community. Reflecting back on the impetus of Robert Bellah's *The Broken Covenant*, it is important to remember that Tawney first published his work in 1926, in the resplendence and economic boom of the Roaring Twenties. Could the pursuit of self-interest in an unregulated fashion have led to the undermining of a pro-social ethic of care and responsibility for one's neighbor? Lurking in the Puritan attitude of the elect is the momentum toward this very individualism. This was, in Tawney's mind, the natural consequence of the Puritan economic revolution. The implications of an individualist economic "ethic" meant that Puritan America had no true covenant to break, but rather it was undermined from the beginning. To at least respect Bellah's trajectory, Tawney fashions a Durkheimian sense, albeit with Anglican shades, of the tension between the selfishness of the individualistic drive (almost a hungry "Id") and the need for communion and membership in society. These are the economic consequences of the Faustian wager.

As Stern (1991) points out, Hawthorne and Melville inherit a climate and audience of American arrogance and bravado. The victories of the War of 1812, the developing international spheres of influence (Matthew Perry et al.) and the manifest destiny Romanticism of the frontier all expressed a sense of limitless possibility. This however, left the Concord-gang pondering about those very human limits and consequences to expansion. Stern points out the resistance of these writers' audience, sociologically reflecting: "if, in God's country, everyone has the right to everything there is no development of which the self is not capable. To deny this is un-American, unpatriotic, and unworthy" (Stern 1991, 37). However, the role of the Concord voices was that of an outsider denying or at least questioning this position, or even perhaps like early critical sociologists of their time. "Young Goodman Brown" stands as an example of the greying of the moral principles of seeking redemption in toil and all-or-nothing thinking—these value orientations so common in Puritan psychology and culture.

The implications of a hollowing out the sacred, and the individualization of conscience, the loneliness of the Pilgrim, transforms into what Max Weber writes about a century later: the "disenchantment" or demystification and estrangement of modernity as a result of the Protestant ethic. The societal results are both crass commercialism and psychically, the famous "specialists without spirit" and "sensualists without heart" (Weber 2001, 124).

The message of Goodman Brown, particularly in Hawthorne's conclusion, reflects this. Mr. Brown sets out to understand the dark side of bright Salem and the inner workings of the human heart. His journey into nature shows the Black Mass—not a redemptive liberation in nature. What Hawthorne reveals is that this split gives us neither gaiety nor faith. Montgomery discusses: "the Puritans never denied the existence of evil, even if they confused it with an inclination to a pagan worldliness, making some of their descendants wonder that they had descendants" (1984, 73). Goodman Brown's "sin" was his excessive reaction to cast the whole world as fallen, becoming "stern, sad, darkly meditative . . . a desperate man whose dying hour was gloom."

HAWTHORNE AND THE AMERICAN TRAGEDY: FAUSTIAN "SHADOW FORTH THE SOUL OF THE AGE"

In a section of *Religion and the Rise of Capitalism* reflecting on Puritan ethics, the eclipse of theological attitudes of sacramentalism, Tawney reflects upon the role of Mephistopheles as a metaphor for modern economic life. "The shaft of Mephistopheles, which drops harmless from the armor of Reason, pierces the lazy caricature which masquerades beneath that sacred name, to flatter its followers with the smiling illusion of progress" (Tawney 1998, 283). As Zapf explores, the Faust myth employs "ruthless transgression of Biblical doctrines by intellectual pride, amoral hedonism, a 'relapse' into pagan forms of magic. . . . Symptoms of soul corrupting influence of the devil's power" (Zapf 2012, 20). Faust was a kind of antitype of Luther, both Georg Faust and Martin Luther coming from Wittenberg. Faust expresses the modern spirit: "constant overstepping of limits" that could lead to deeper insight and a deeper grasp of human experience (2012, 20). Though Doctor Faustus was a great heresy to American Puritans—pride and rejection of God going together in the pursuits of individual gain and knowledge—Faust's story was popular in late 1600s into the 1700s. Into the nineteenth century, a course of development in relation to the Faustian legend came alongside the change from the reification of human reason in an embrace of the concepts of the Enlightenment, to its semi-reflective rejection in the Romanticist reaction. The "magical" element of the dark underside of the human soul was appreciated, and the Faust parable was retold in light of that darkness. The diabolic becomes an internalized Promethean "other self." In Nathaniel Hawthorne's context, there was a "Faust renaissance" in the 1830s to 1840s New England (Zapf 2012, 23). In Emerson, Longfellow, and Fuller the "satanic" weight of Faust had been lifted—and the character could float high above the clouds on his intellect alone, without the drag of morality. His association with the demonic considered the point of turnaround and conversion, a *felix culpa*, "happy fault" (Zapf 2012, 24). Like Melville, Hawthorne moved away from a totalized "Puritan demonization of the satanic Faust and from the Transcendentalist idealization of the noble humanist Faust" (2012, 24).

According to Zapf, literary scholarship has relatively neglected Faustian themes in Hawthorne. This may be a lacuna in American literary and cultural studies scholarship in general, as described by Harry Dahms (2019). Why is an account of the contributions of Goethe's *Faust* as a sociocultural phenomenon important? Dahms reminds the reader, academics especially, of the centrality of the dramas between the archetypes within Goethe, which provides us with a window onto tensions at the core of modernity and modern society in general (i.e., in all modern societies). "*Faust* played a pivotal role, as an opportunity to address explicitly issues whose lack of resolution burdens us to this day, as well as who we moderns are exactly, and how we exist and coexist" (Dahms 2019, 9–10). Further,

> Thus, *Faust* is both a critique of emerging modern society as an empirically discernible world and a program for how this society should evolve if it would allow or encourage members of society to be active agents. However, Goethe did not frame this critique in a manner intended to translate into a novel framework for controlling an increasingly complex and befuddling reality, either via democracy or socialism. Rather, just as he was critical of established religion, he also was critical of efforts to propagate solutions to the tension-filled condition of human existence under conditions of emerging modernity that are purported to engender a happier world, while depriving individuals of what we have been referring to as agency. (Dahms 2019, 14)

Dahms makes reference to Safranski's discussion of how "the dead litter the course of Faust's worldly career" and that is the very price of his success, the destruction of others (2019, 14). The entanglement between Mephistopheles and Faust reveal the inevitability of the rapier and destructiveness of the "Dialectic" of Enlightenment, as also explored by critical sociological theory's Adorno and Horkheimer.

For Hawthorne's commentary on the context of colonial New England, the perversion of the eternal feminine (anima) plays out in the fraught relation with America's (animus) masculine/rational tendencies. The "Beacon to the World" and the "City upon a Hill"—not Jerusalem but the Massachusetts Bay Colony's cold, calculating *animus*—has a Jungian darkness. As the "Enlightenment" of Unitarianism's project, Hawthorne rooted out Transcendentalism's both fascination with Goethe and its own tragic lack of appreciation for the eternal feminine. Transcendentalism was a "claimed" revolt against the "rationalism" and the "corpse cold" Unitarianism of Brattle Street and Harvard College (Miller 1957, ix). Here is expressed the particularly American "mode" of Enlightenment—through a dialectical embrace with the Romantic literature and philosophical fascination with the contemporaneous idealism of Germany. It was precisely a protest against "modernity" via the Protestant Ethic and a rejection of the Faustian mode of existence. The next possible reaction was the idealistic romanticism of Thoreau's isolation in natural *Walden* as the rejection of society. And then, the celebration of a Proust, American style: Whitman's *Leaves of Grass*. From Thoreau's pen: "The ripeness of a leaf leaves the tree and never returns—only the genius of the past can pluck it" (in Miller xi).

Emerson sees Faust's political avatar in the "Napoleonic" figure—"spokesman for the impatience and reaction of nature against the morgue of convention" (Margaret Fuller, in Miller 1957, 152–153). Like Faust, the truly American character embraces the world of the new, of action, dominance, recklessness: the world of "vanity" as expressed in Dostoevsky's *Brothers Karamazov*. Even today, impatience and ambition are important values for the American character. We see it in Young Goodman Brown's youth-as-embracing-reactionary-politics, as opposed to the playful and reflexive sage-like Falstaff archetype's more relaxed "second youth." Goodman Brown's impatience is unable to grasp, or even appreciate, the delicate strength and contemplative nature of the eternal feminine.

Zapf sees "Young Goodman Brown" as Hawthorne's adaptation of "Faustian material into a unique, complex aesthetic response to the historical-cultural conditions and mentalities of his time and society" (2012, 25). Why Faust and Hawthorne? The "Enlightenment" and "American enterprise" both set forth masculinist trajectories. Hans Eichner (1971) illuminates the story of Faust as a reflexive ethical critique of the very dualities and projections of this experiment known as "modernity" and progress. One of the "ruptures" of modernity is the break between Christianity's fusion between "contemplation" and "action." Probably most famously inspired by Goethe, Marx addresses this choice, in modernity, between "thinking and acting" in the "Theses on Feuerbach" (#11, in particular, paraphrased: the point is to change the world, not interpret it). When carefully examined, the split between the contemplative and active life is not so much a product of the transition out of the medieval realm, but the choice of action without the restraint of ethics is certainly a product of the emergence of modern capitalism. Weber and Tawney note this in the transformation of Puritan economic ethics. According to Adam Seligman, Max Weber developed a thesis of the development of "the soteriological efficacy imbued to worldly actions" among the Puritan elect (Seligman, in Tawney [1926] 1998, xxxiii; Weber 2001). R.H. Tawney was concerned with the way in which this-worldly activities were "disengaged from soteriological processes," as a result of the advance of capitalism. As a force within theological history, capitalism caused the uncoupling of grace and the world, of spirit and economy. Goethe's *Faust* is describing this "uncoupling of grace and the world" by characterizing the doorway into modernity: Faust seeks "power and property" after he decides to perform "great deeds" (Eichner 1971, 623). Both Goodman Brown and the men (maybe even Salem itself) capitalize upon the domination of the eternal feminine, in both *Young Goodman Brown* and *The Scarlet Letter.* God-as-agent is not working, however, through the merit of any of the characters, but rather through the grace of the eternal feminine—this confesses a lurking humble "old Catholicism" (Fuller in Miller 1957, 158) that the American character denies. Mephistopheles takes up the dirty work so Faust can ignorantly enjoy the status achieved by these great deeds (Eichner 1971). Faust's reckless abandon of morality in pursuit of egoistic gains is another way of talking about the Weberian "instrumental rationality" required of capitalism. Archetypes within Goethe's *Faust* express the old poetic imagination of a "humble" Catholic Christianity, meeting its pagan roots in the constellation of metaphors and characterizations (See Fuller in Miller 1957, 158). These include a magnified sense of the "eternal feminine" in everything from the Virgin Mary, to Helen of Troy and Prostitutes, in the last scenes of *Faust II*. This "older," both contemplative but also embodied world of the eternal feminine is what, as the last lines of the play expresses, "draws us to higher spheres" rather than the cold, calculated action of masculinist principles (Eichner 1971, 616). However, in capitalist modernity the masculine-feminine connection, the "union of thought and action," is severed—this is the "tragic fall"—the result of the *hamartia*—of the Enlightenment project. This "enterprising intellectual" then takes a metaphoric journey through conquering first the "little world" of domination in the sphere of domesticity and the village, to the great one—what Goodman Brown aspires to, that is, the "Big Time" of science, commerce, politics (Jameson 2019).

Hawthorne's writings represent an allegorical reflection on these tendencies within a modernizing of America's economics and psychology. This is presented via a new characterization of the Faustian legend in *Young Goodman Brown*. It is paired with a triumph over these constraining categories of Puritanism through the presentation of the "angelic adulterer," Hester Prynne within *The Scarlet Letter* (Moretti 1996). One who, in the words of Beethoven, was a "soul that rose above the mud" (Fuller, in Miller 1957, 169). In historically early forms of Puritanism, "Faust represented the antitype of the ideal cultural self-image," while on the contrary, in the modernizing, instrumentally rational "intellectual" America of Hawthorne's time, Faust was the "ideal" self-image (Zapf 2012, 28). These images interact, presenting internal (and sometimes external) fundamental questions "of human life in the tension between moral and intellectual, conscious and unconscious, rational and irrational forces" (Zapf 2012, 28). These "unconscious" irrational forces are mirrored by the categories of Goethe's weighing of "contemplation vs. action"—"if the man of action is always devoid of scruples, [Goethe's] women emphatically have a conscience: they are all embodiments of an ideal of moral purity—the ideal of *das Ewig-weibliche"* (Eichner 1971, 618).

Faith, Brown's wife, relays through her allegorical name the power of the relational/connective aspect of the feminine, in contrast to a cold, harsh masculine reason's failed Faustian plans (Zapf 2012, 29). As Henry James (1879) noted, "Hawthorne, in his metaphysical moods, is nothing if not allegorical." Goodman Brown's "spirit" of capitalism—his cold, rational embrace of calculation and efficiency—are paradigmatic of a newly found Puritan individualistic and decentered social life. Max Weber was first to highlight this as an implication of the "protestant ethic" with its potential for creating specialization without spirit, and instrumental rationality (Weber 2001; Eisenstadt, in Weber 1968). Jacques Ellul develops this thesis further, in his theory of technique as it relates to "efficiency" and "method" as applied to instrumentalize social relations, and ultimately within the scope of industrialism assimilation to the machine (Ellul 1956). Also inheriting the legacy of Weber, R.H. Tawney reflects on modern economic virtues' triumphing in (especially) the American experiment: "economic efficiency is a necessary element in any sane and vigorous society . . . but to convert efficiency from an instrument into its primary object is to destroy efficiency itself . . . the condition of effective action in a complex civilization is cooperation" (Tawney 1998, 283). For Hawthorne, there are gendered dimensions to the cold, rational force of capital (as masculine). And the counterbalancing force is present within the feminine and nature. The recognition of difference, via the complex division of labor that begins in the household, presents itself as a kind of *Paradise Reclaimed*. It rehearses and attempts to restore the Eden-myth: the embrace of the first sense of "otherness" experienced as gendered difference.

"WALPURGISNACHT"

The Witches' Sabbath in *Young Goodman Brown* is an *anima*-embracing, ecstatic release from the cold rationality of Puritanism. Victor Turner (1969) lends categories to describe the *communitas*—power of connection and collective effervescence—and liminality of this ritual. This "witch ritual" is betwixt and between social structures and rejects the Puritan quotidian of stasis, daylight, order, individualism, work, and reason. The counterbalance in the anima of liminality would be "journey, flight, night, dream, chaos, rapture, and collective ritual" (Zapf 2012, 30). Perhaps an inspiration to Hawthorne, Goethe's version of the Faust interludes with a *"Walpurgisnacht."*

In Goethe's text, there is joy and release in the Witches' night—but in "Young Goodman Brown" it is pure nightmare. According to Zapf's analysis Goethe is incorporating the "Dionysian and mythopoetic elements" of pagan culture: the eternal feminine, as discussed above. Other links to the eternal feminine connect it to the realm of the "mothers," and the vast oceanic like experience of the Dionysian ritual (Nietzsche 1993). Connecting to the archetypes of *Faust* (II. 1): "the mysterious shadow zone into which Faust descends. . . . This is the everlasting sphere of womanhood, representative of the timeless abode of inexhaustible life, the well of death from which life pours forth in perennial rebirth" (Zimmer 1975, 82). Mephistopheles describes this reality within *Faust* (II.1): "Goddesses sit enthroned in reverend loneliness . . . they are the Mothers. . . . And had you even swum the trackless ocean. Lost in its utter boundlessness" (6213–6216; 6239–6240). The "oceanic" moment of pagan religion, or intense levels of ecstatic collective effervescence (Durkheim 1995) are contrasted with the experience of the isolated individual's inner-worldly categories of salvation within a Puritan context.

Illuminated by Hawthorne's retelling in an American context, this dense ritual and pagan moment also evokes the conflation between the "witch" and the eternal feminine/natural element absorbed, but also angelically triumphing, over the plot. As Zimmer's Jungian premise is extended: the journey into the darkness of death (underworlds of ancient mythologies) also makes possible the experience of rebirth. Also, for Faust: "that dim domain has been for millenniums the holy goal of all the great questing heroes—from Gilgamesh to Faust—for it is the repository of the spiritual treasure of the mystic wisdom of rebirth" (Zimmer 1975, 84). This is true in both "Young Goodman Brown" and *The Scarlet Letter*. There is a sense of rebirth in death. In terms of the confession of Hester Prynne's sin, by her publicly donning the famous "Scarlet A," converts her from "Adultress to Angel" throughout the course of the plot (Moretti 1996). Adultery was punishable by death in the Massachusetts Bay Colony (Dow 1988, 211). Though, according to Dow, that Mosaic principle wasn't frequently exacted, still the proverbial "noose" hung figuratively as a form of Durkheimian repressive law. And certainly, Hester Prynne suffered a veritable "social death"—the private existential and psychological burden taken up by her to protect her lover, Rev. Dimmesdale. But this social death delivered her to the angelic state through her channeling the forces of the eternal feminine, namely perpetual forgiveness (Eichner 1971, 624). As classical sociological theorist W.I. Thomas observed about the role of the repentant sinner, forgiveness is also a main source of social glue within society: "one of the functions of community, sometimes more particularly the function of the God of the community" (Thomas 1931, 68–69). The isolated American Puritan, with his private conscience, is ultimately conquered by a new version of "faith" which engages and incorporates the poetic imagination—the force that draws us "higher" through the reality of incarnation. In other words, the naturalism of the pagan, embodiment, and the eternal feminine.

Perhaps foreign to the American imagination, but not that "old Catholicism" as discussed by Margaret Fuller within the Transcendentalist circle, the medieval mind embraced the idea of the feminine in the pairing of the Magdalene alongside the Virgin Mary. The saintly virgin/whore dichotomy—familiar to feminist discourse today—was more mystical paradox for "everywoman" in the Middle Ages and the early moments of the Reformation (Bruenig 2019). In some medieval pageants, Mary is literally attacked (her social role being seen as pregnant out of wedlock), and then venerated for her thanksgiving, equanimity, self-confidence, and serenity in response to these attacks (Bruenig 2019, 25). Hester Prynne, along with Faith Brown, are representing the mix of embodiment and sainthood which characterizes the important role of scorn responded to with benevolence within the eternal feminine.

The Medieval folk spirit—perhaps in contrast to scholasticism—had no issue with the blend of body/spirit. It is a reminder that in Folk Catholicism, "Christ spent his time with people whose eros was very close to the surface—passionate people" (Bruenig 2019, 26). The symbol of the Magdalene presents an example of sexual embodiment connected to or redirected toward higher forms of virtue. However, this comingling diminishes within the context of the emergence of Puritanism. Hester Prynne and Faith Brown are, like Magdalene, "elevated to the status of Christ because they claim no status for themselves," and Hester, "making no appeal to her own merits, because she has none" (Bruenig 2019, 26). Hawthorne pokes fun at the haughty Puritanical sense of superiority. The heroines reflect the powerful universality of the sinfulness of man; and the hypocrisy of the Puritan male shows forth the hypocrisy of the entire American society.

DREAMLAND

At the end of "Young Goodman Brown" the reader sees a now familiar trope: "it was only a dream." Is the reader to take away the point of fiction or is Hawthorne signifying something more profound? In a more modern reading, is this story an allegory of the American unconscious? At the end of "Young Goodman Brown" Hawthorne departs from the dramatic renderings of Faust and the main character comes to the position of a kind of realism about the situation: his love is not the extremes of an "eternal feminine principle" nor a "hardened sinner" but something in between. His wife Faith is a human being, a "concrete personal presence as an intellectual and erotic partner in a shared life" (Zapf 2012, 31). Hawthorne's American Faust is not saved by the redemptive power of the force of the eternal feminine through the likes of a

Gretchen-Marguerite amalgam, but rather, more soberingly "is condemned to a life-long curse of misanthropy, loneliness, and depression" (Zapf 2012, 32). Hawthorne is both reflecting and critiquing the Puritan ideological systems of New England. He might also be telling a larger story about American social psychology, and gendered psychoanalytic dynamics. There is a reflexive message in this text. Zapf argues that it reflects both "Puritan condemnation of the Faustian pursuit; the story instead uses its potential for a cultural-critical purpose, i.e., for exposing the blind spots and inner contradictions of Puritan culture" (2012, 34). These two poles are never resolved. Present here is the sociological imagination's experience of objective "strangeness": cognitive dissonance.

FROM *FAUST*—IN THE PINK

The European Faustian paradigm is about the unfettered pursuit of knowledge and worldly success at the cost of those dear to the intellectual, namely the women around the ego-driven intellect. The American Faustian paradigm reflects the "shameful, sinful impulse of stealing away from official society to pry into its dark secrets and hidden crimes" (Zapf 2012, 33). Is there any mode of redemption in the American character? The eternal feminine as a communicational mode of engendered and embodied spirituality shines forth in a dismal world of Calvinism for Hawthorne. Faith's "pink ribbons" flutter as she walks into the street, reminding her husband not of the Platonic pedestal excellence of her virtue, but that she is of this world, a human-being: passion-and-virtue combined. Like Gretchen, of *Faust*, Faith in this scene is "disregarding Puritan correctness in her joyful acceptance of the natural forces of life" (Zapf 2012, 35). The binary "white" (purity) and "red" (passion) worldview—a binary consciousness that her husband ascribes to—is problematic, and her "pink" ribbon reflects symbolically the combination of passion/purity as a realistic human quality. The anima/animus is united in Faith, but not in her husband. That is why she fears for him in his "nights out." Goodman Brown's "lonely misanthropy leads him into irredeemable despair, and the communicational ethos of Faith remains an unrealized potential" (Zapf 2012, 37).

FINAL REFLECTIONS: HAWTHORNE AND TODAY'S "CANCEL CULTURE"

The power of the Puritan concepts of "individualism," "cold moralizing," "judgment," and "the elect" have a way of historically reverting to its toolkit and method within some contemporary discourse today. As *New York Times* journalist David Brooks (2020) identifies today's culture wars of "woke-ism" vs. "Trumpism," we must remember that both systems of thought are rooted in an American tendency toward the "red vs. white" (alluding to the symbols of "Young Goodman Brown") rather than the imagery of Hawthorne's "pink" ribbon of Faith. All-or-nothing thinking is a product of a unique modern flavor to religion, that which came with the Puritan/Calvinist sense of the "elect" (Weber [1930] 2001). The advance of "cancel culture" calls to mind the shaming and other elements of the old American Puritan moralizing tropes, albeit with a reinvented value system regarding "purity." It is fascinating that the method of judgment remains the same (shame culture), even while the mode of expressing it and the value systems it embraces are so embedded in modern paradigms and systems of social media and other communications technologies. American culture has ignored the lessons of "Young Goodman Brown," but still reverts to the categories it introduces. Hawthorne's themes in *The Scarlet Letter* illustrate how Puritanical forms of judgment prefigure shaming and cancel-culture in American culture today.

In a conservative magazine, *National Review* author Dan McLaughlin (2018) discusses the implications of "cancel-culture" within woke value frameworks:

> This is very much the same impulse that motivated the Puritans. Bigotry, [like adultery] is more a sin than a crime, but a sin that we subject to harsh moral judgment, and that we rightly see today as corrosive of society and a contributor to worse problems, like sudden explosions of violence. In other words, we see it in exactly the same terms that the Puritans saw adultery, which could trigger violence, blackmail, and produce illegitimate children who could face infanticide or become wards of the state.

Value systems still change, but the all-or-nothing coding of moral behavior still remains. McLaughlin continues: "People who say they don't want to judge sin invariably just want to judge *different* sins. They may denounce moralizers for hypocrisy in being against sin without being sinless, but theirs is the true hypocrisy. We have always needed moralizers, we have always wanted to be moralizers, and we always will" (2018). Ironically, the new paradigm of liberal categories of "woke-ism" creates a different, albeit veritably rigid status marker of moral absolutism. However, it is within different categories of taboo than Hawthorne and others saw in the "old" grey areas of Pagan-driven folk Catholicism. It has relocated Puritanical thinking to new all-or-nothing categories. But what is interesting is the very principled conflation of what Harriet Martineau might have distinguished: morals versus manners (Lengermann and Niebrugge-Brantley 1998). There is a lack of nuance in many of the "cancel culture" debates, and "woke-ism" replaces an openness for the possibility of the appreciation of different perceptions of taste, opinion, value systems. As society conveyed through the shame culture of social medias relies more and more upon both "belief in absolute moral principles formulated as rigid behavioral rules, and the resulting psychological reaction known as victimization. Both are clearly at play in the new debate. The energy released on both sides—by the inquisitors and the martyrs—feeds a cycle of recrimination that becomes self-perpetuating" (Isackson 2020).

Interestingly enough, capitalism and the "ethic of competition" fuels this juggernaut of cancel culture—everything from the over-supplied job market in academia, to other domains most impacted by the culturally elite discourses, like Hollywood, academia, and the arts industries. Cancel culture may be related somewhat to this dominant "ethos" that undermines ethics within capitalism: that of competition. "The duty of competition imposes on everyone the tool that obligatorily accompanies it: branding. Daily life, even daily intellectual life, becomes a war of brands" (Isackson 2020). Early on in the twentieth century, sociologically trained psychoanalyst Erich Fromm (1990) warned of the "marketing of the self" as perhaps the Janus-face of the shame-driven element of cancel-culture. Social media and other technologies make our self-presentations both increasingly vulnerable and therefore prone to be manipulated. As the classical theorist Charles Horton Cooley described it, the modern self is a looking glass, reflecting images only desirable to the outside world (Cooley 1902). But we are left with the message of Goethe-through-Hawthorne; Faith in "Young Goodman Brown" rejects the labels of all or nothing mentality, and its accompanying "branding" of acclaim or shame. Faith embraces the grey (or "pink") areas of moral complexity, and as we are reminded by Goethe, the eternal feminine of divine grace, tolerance and forgiveness functions gracefully to "lift us ever higher."

Chapter Three

Moby Dick as Modern Epic
"Symphony" in a Broken Ontology

INTRODUCTION

Numerous authors have explored the function of Melville's *Moby Dick* as allegory or social commentary. C.L.R. James (2001) suggests it is the story of America, and the *Pequod* is a microcosm of modernity. This chapter suggests, along with Moretti (1996), Sten (1996) and Grey (2004), the weight of the voice of Melville as "ancient/spiritual epic" amidst a turn to the modern as the novel's key significance. The novel itself has a simultaneously poetic/tragic and sociological imagination, suggesting the wholeness of allegory—or as Lewis Mumford called it, "a symphony"—within the broken world of an emerging modernity. This "broken modernity" then opens up into the novel's contribution to the American sociological imagination. Goethe's quote, "America, you have it better . . . you have no ruined castles" (Moretti, 1996, 35) hints at the lack of "ideals" and "grand narratives and the significance of American literature as a product of the "new." But as Sten's (1996) volume title hints, *The Weaver God, He Weaves: Melville and the Poetics of the Novel,* the method of the construction of "epic" with an all-knowing, creating God that creates a grand narrative within a broken situation, finds a parallel reference in Penelope's knitting, and unknitting, in Homeric modes of recounting. The elapse of time and the storytellers making and remaking of a journey are paralleled in the Western classic of the *Odyssey*. *Moby-Dick* is a commentary on the great human struggle to grapple with the transcendent amidst fragmentation—both cast in terms of God, and the hopes of a relatively young experiment of the democratic society. What Sherrill (1979) argues as *Moby-Dick's* "portents" of a (broken) transcendence, the opacity of that relation between "God and man" leaves humans with the need to create community. This is in response to the loss of the ontological security within the experience of Truth/God/Transcendence/Certainty, and the eclipse of that ontological unity in the failures and shortcomings of the democratic experiment. Richard B. Sewall described the sociological weight as an anchor: this "tragic vision" of Melville alongside that of Hawthorne (discussed in chapter two). This implies a vision "which pierces beneath the official view of any culture to the dark realities that can never be permanently hidden, and together they mark a recrudescence of the tragic spirit" (Sewall 1950, 692). This happens at an unlikely time and place—the inescapable shadows of human nature within the so-called "new" optimistic place of America, that is not haunted by the ghosts and ruined castles of tradition.

MAGNANIMITIES AND PARADOX

America's own sea-faring Homer, (within the author's own self-perception), Melville saw himself in the prophetic mode of *being spoken through* in the nineteenth century. Similar to Melville's contemporary Karl Marx (Fromm 2004, vi) the prophetic voice in *Moby-Dick* channels commentary, but in contrast with the mode of "epic" commentary, a critical protest to the status quo. As Erich Fromm might observe Melville within the prophetic vein, "the great prophets, from Isaiah to Marx also were critics . . . their main effort was to explain, convince, warn . . . and show new alternatives" (Fromm [1968] 2021, 121). The result was a grand book that matched up to its subject—the Great White Whale. In a letter to his contemporary and great friend, Nathaniel Hawthorne, Melville defines God like whale flukes: "in me the divine is . . . spontaneous and instantaneous-catch them while you can." Throughout the novel Melville explores questions addressing both the aims of skeptical and religious inquiry—namely in the text, there are only metaphors for and allusions to the divine: a) What is the supernatural, does it exist? b) Where is God/is God (if at all) in the world? c) What is the nature of justice, revenge? d) Is evil purely evil or does evil carry some goodness—in terms of perspective? For Melville, the perception of something evil is in a sense, that of "fate," or there is a final, providential ever-abiding good that emerges. In a Judeo-Christian-mystical mode of inquiry, one becomes evil in the untiring pursuit of what is perceived as evil. Addressing the aims of a religious and literary humanism—is man (and this book is most certainly about male character, masculine roles, and the possibility of gendered brotherhood) both small before a transcendent Deity and simultaneously the measure of all things?

Melville understood life as "an ambiguous affair" where the "deepest paradoxes in human experience resulted from man's inability to calculate the hidden character of the transcendent" (Sherrill 1979, 93). The extended metaphor for this is that the reader, along with the members of the *Pequod*, will go fishing for something that is elusive and paradoxical—a great white, lunged, warm-blooded fish. Or as Melville is here somewhat of a phenomenologist—both the reader and the crew seek that which cannot be caught, fishing for a fish that is not really a fish as the chapter on Cetology explores (Melville 1967, 116–128). If the Whale represents the "magnanimity" mystical theology is at work. That which is sought cannot even be described—the sea, and the whale are metaphors for a "totality" that cannot be obtained or described within the eclipse of the whole: in modernity. For Melville it is a metaphor for the human approach to the world, or the hubristic quest of power and dominance, or lack thereof, in the face of Being. This is somewhat like the Judaic-Protestant casting of God as inexplicable totality, *Otherwise than Being* (Levinas) or the *mysterium tremendum* evoking the numinous response to the divine as it is addressed in the classic text by Rudolph Otto. Caputo has evoked this as well in *khora* (1997, 36). But this fishing expedition, as is the case in all forms of searching or hunting, can be reflexive as the epic outward journey also refracts itself in an inward journey. Certain sentences evoke reflective inquiry for the reader, who throws out harpoons, searching for their cryptic internal and sublime meanings. The ones that hit the mark and strike deeply enough can pull the reader under into the indefinite deep, becoming the prey of a greater hunter with a greater, divine puzzle. As St. Augustine might have said, addressing the power of the "Western" philosophical intellect aimed at capturing through its faculty of domination: "I know the whale until I think about it." In this regard, with the search for Truth, reflecting Hawthorne's words about Melville, humans are to be "seekers" rather than "finders" (Sherrill 1979, 104). The search for the Whale is reflexive, as are the waters of the oceans are reflective. Melville might suggest the sailor faces an inner journey as he sets out to sea ("Loomings"). Halton suggests it takes the form of a liminal quest, a rite of passage (Halton 1986, 245). This, then is a metaphor for the novel as a journey of social-psychological introspection. The sea is, as Joseph Conrad put it, "a mirror" (2011 [1906]).

The historical moment of *Moby Dick* is important. It is before Nietzsche emerges philosophically, though his arguments dwell within the modern spirit. A reflective religious humanism admits a humility and the "unknown" where a secular humanism does not—in acknowledging our unfinished knowledge, the ultimate impossibility of knowing. In religious humanism, the search for Truth is chastened: an incomplete possessing cut off by the limits of the human mind/heart. The depths of Melville's ocean reflect both the depths of the divine and the demonic, and the incomplete abilities of the human heart/mind to fathom them. The book is full of religious imagery, characters, allusions, and at times alternating between a Miltonian/ Faustian frame. Melville's *Moby Dick* is also shadowed by the consequences of anticipating a postmodern absent, transcendent God—but unlike Mephistopheles of *Faust*, the White Whale never fully reveals Himself. The world seems somewhat empty and the reader must address human concerns on our own chastened incomplete knowledge as fellow co-sufferers in the trajectory of a secularizing world. In this shadowy world, the narrator Ishmael describes the "pagan" Queequeg as a member of the ultimate church and beyond (or before?) the confining consciousness of Western modernity, the "First Congregation of this whole worshipping world," that of humankind (Melville 1967, 83). This is a radical suggestion in a promise of a religious universalism and ecumenism that is a response to the failures of the (fallen) Paradise Lost of both the Judeo-Christian world and modernity. The social failures of imperialism, slavery, genocide, and environmental destruction are all consequences of the dominant Western rationalizing mind that Melville anticipated in modernization. This new "Congregation of the whole worshipping world" is a reorientation of the positive democratic experiment of Calvinism: "this is not the dignity of kings and robes. . . . That democratic dignity which on all hands, radiates without end from God; Himself! The great God absolute! The centre and circumference of all democracy! His omnipotence, our divine equality!" (Melville 1967, 104). In the words of Alejandro Nava, drawing a literary lineage from Melville to Ralph Ellison, here Melville ascribes "high qualities and exalted graces to the meanest of lives" (Nava 2017).

The spirit of the democratic highlights the divine imperative from this quasi-Calvinist worldview, overlaying American ethos (Geertz 2000). This is Melville's suggested reorientation away from the other dimension of the dark heart of calculation, obsession, capitalism. According to Melville's spiritual-historical psychology, this fragmented "spirit of capitalism," in the Calvinist consciousness—from competition/compassion & community—is brought about the evils of modernity. As Halton reflects, we are not "thrown together" in communion, but "cast apart" in the diabolic (Halton 1986, 244).

A PHILOSOPHY OF MIND-HEART

Melville, in another letter to Hawthorne, said, echoing his characterization of Ahab, "cultivation of the brain eats out the heart" (June 1851, in Melville 1967), defining one of the misfortunes of modernization and rationalization, and "I'd rather be a fool with a heart than Jupiter Olympus with his head." The seaman's concentration and ability to reflect on meaning and existence while at sea was a metaphor for the reflective integration of emotion into mindfulness. Melville, like other Romantics of the period, felt that in life everything had a "center," or an ultimate truth. The Transcendentalist vision encompasses this idea in the relation of Man to God and nature in an idealist ascendancy and perfection. But unlike the Transcendentalists, Melville was much more interested in heart as opposed to the "intellect and unity" of Emerson and others. He was disillusioned with the mechanization and intellectualization of the world around him. As highlighted in a review of Richard King's *Ahab's Rolling Sea: A Natural History of Moby Dick,* by John Loonam, Melville was well-read in the works of Emerson, "and *Moby Dick* is saturated with romantic naturalism. However, Melville had also read Darwin, "and was aware that the other side of the debate would dethrone God's benevolence and knock man from his place atop creation. Melville does not share Captain Ahab's certainty that the sea they sail on was the same as Noah's. King makes clear that assessing that similarity involves both science and poetry" (Loonan 2019). Further, Melville combines the "Darwinian perspective with the emotional, poetic, Emersonian perspective, pushing the reader to see nature as both dangerous and damaged. Here is King's main point: that Melville's novel can now be read as an introduction to environmental issues of the 21st century" (Loonan 2019). This encounter with the natural-as-analogically rendered in the whale takes on a new meaning or the power of reversal in the destructive power of the "eternal feminine," as described in tension with capitalism and its accompanying masculinist modern forces.

Though he never read German, Melville may have inherited the tropes of the tension between reason/emotion from the German Romantic school of thought through the secondhand interpretations and friendships with those steeped in German philosophy. Birgit Noll (2010) makes a case for Melville's contact with Schlegel, Richter, Goethe, Schiller and Hegel and his echoing of German tragic/romantic irony via George Adler and Thomas Carlyle (Noll 2010). Paralleling the emerging tension between science/reason and the literary in sociology's adolescence (something that is today is a complete divorce), like many within the German schools of sociological thought, Melville saw this bifurcation as a part of modern consciousness. *Moby Dick* is ultimately, then, a Faustian allegory (Eichner 1976; Jameson 2019). The classic "man vs. nature" presents a dualism more powerful than the traditional romantic novel; Melville's *Moby Dick* dives to the very heart of the ironies and hypocrisies of the idealization of nature in his Transcendentalist colleagues. The rational scientistic mind, and its resultant individualism, ultimately destroys everything. As even the "quite rational" Max Weber observed, "The thought structures of science constitute a subjective domain of artificial abstractions which think they can seize hold on the blood and sap of real life with their avid hands but are never able to catch up with it" (in Lepenies 1988, 245). Natural life always exceeds the domain of reason.

Both Protestant Transcendentalism and scientific skeptical humanism would probably emphasize "thinking" and "reasoning" more than Melville favored. Going out to sea is a metaphor for the new Rousseauian vision—where the "many merge into one" and where Ishmael's characterization is the "normal unpossessed human" (Sewall 1950, 696–697). But Ishmael's failure to prevent a totalitarian collapse and create a new vision reflect his naivete and privilege; ultimately the intellectual type radical fails to show alternatives (Fromm 1968 [2021], 121), instrumentalize the "masses" and play a part in the acquiescence to power. Melville seems to be driven by a sociological outlook in this regard (by later nineteenth-century ideas)—he wants to say that experience rather than learning or education is our great teacher. Marx's sense of this comes from the 1888 edition of the *Theses on Feuerbach* (in Marx [1888] in Marx and Engels 1978, 143–145): sensuous activity, not idealistic rationalizing knowledge, is what is favored. Melville might say in a Marxian voice, "we have to teach the teachers" through experiential modes. This may also have a somewhat *feminine* dimension and is not unlike Hannah Arendt's discussing of thinking-and-judging, but also acting to transform the world (*The Life of the Mind)*. In Arendt's outlook, moral considerations, conscience, experience, and relationships each have a way of shaping intellect in addition to pure reason. Though the book is definitively about male experience, this side of Melville reveals a social tenderness, and a sociologically informed thesis that relationships and caring are foundational to the human experience and are our great teachers. An "allergy" to abstract reason might also have been related to Melville's own relationship with formal status within the educational establishment—something his family's failed socioeconomic background prevented him from attaining. Perhaps he suggests, in the voice of Ishmael, the author of the novel, "a whale-ship was my Yale College and my Harvard" (Melville 1967, 101).

LOOMINGS

From an emerging brokenness away from a totality, toward the reflective discussion of mind and the mystical theology of the magnanimities, also comes the discussion of human relationships and action. The world, and the various manifestations of the whale working in some transcendent order, is something Melville defines as "weaver God." For the reader, the first question is the problem of evil. Where is God in all this chaos and suffering—"whither flows the fabric? What palace might it deck? Wherefore all ceaseless toilings? Speak to us [God our great] weaver!" (*Moby Dick,* 374). Melville frequently uses the metaphor of weaving and looms to (con)-textualize God. The first chapter is entitled looming and it is here where Ishmael explains reasons and calculations for deciding to sail on the ship. These are woven together to present the story and background of Ishmael, who, because of his given name has a great significance—in Hebrew, Ishma-el': God hears. Is not the God who is hearing looming in this chapter, creating a web, a textile? What is Ishmael but a witness—the only witness remaining from the tale: he is a Biblical saving remnant, like Noah. On the other hand, Ishmael is an eminently liminal wanderer, an outcast, like his namesake in scripture; in this sense he is not unlike the social thinker Simmel's description of *The Stranger:* someone who is both outside and inside the social landscape.

In this weaver image, there is a God who is certain and "weaves" all things. A text is a product of this weaving, perhaps a text, like the scars of the whale or the gash of Ahab's forehead. Meaning and a sense of order is also a weaving, a creation of a pattern. A sense of providence and order is a very comforting image of the Divine, and a widely accepted Protestant viewpoint. As reflected upon in Chapter 47, "The Mat-Maker," God, as a weaver of the world, underwrites all existence and control of things. This idea is conducive with the shepherd image—God is comforting, all-encompassing, omniscient and protective. But it is also less apt to be open to human freedom. In Melville's historical and sociological context, Calvinist theology comes with the coldness of predestination—fates are determined before individuals freely make any choices. Ahab has dropped any version of patient, spiritualized, waiting in Quakerism—he is a lapsed Quaker, a virulent anti-Catholic who spits on all things sacred—and has embraced "the [Promethean] religion of his age: material progress" (James 2001, 9). This is rooted in the mixture of both the individualist spirit of Luther's trajectory of the Reformation, combined with the Calvinist proposition that one had to prove oneself through worldly activity (Weber 2001, 74). Weber reflects on the power of material goods as a driving force for his contemporaneous economy (2001, 74). This is the "practical" position of a few members of the crew. Why not focus on the commercial aspect of obtaining the whale blubber—why focus on Moby Dick? Ahab's character takes Weber's thesis a step further toward the totalitarian implications of *The Protestant Ethic,* the Enlightenment, and the destructive power of isolated individualism mixed with pure reason (Weber 2001, 63). The progression here is the progression of human civilization as disenchantment: from an "enchanted" religious imagination, to materialism, to monomania. Weber highlights this potent force of monomania, but in the terms of the force of a technocratic rationalization and efficiency eroding a sense of (religious) obligation (Weber 2001, 36). Melville roots this "personality type" in the emerging Zeitgeist of the modern industrial age: Ahab's technocracy as described in the chapter "The Chart." And for Max Weber's sociological analysis, crediting the theological roots of the development of this dimension of the American character pivots the discussion of the origins to it as a psychological and cultural phenomenon, instead of just simply seeing the roots in economic/material culture, as Marx would highlight.

However, counter to Ahab, a force to be "reckoned" with—God is calculating, deciding, when and where his people have been and will be. Like the whale, God can see all around with eyes placed at the side and not in front or behind: "sideway position of the whale's eyes . . . two distinct windows" (Melville 1967, 279). On one level, a reckoning with things "beyond our control," God is in the whale, maybe in that blackness between the eyes of the whale. Or maybe, the whale floats in God, shapeless and deep as the ocean. Melville describes the sea as vast unconquerable depth—dark, indescribable. Perhaps Moby Dick the whale is His agent: God sees what the whale sees, and hears what the whale hears, feels what the whale feels yet curiously does not speak.

Humans of faith, and humans of doubt, may be able to hear this weaving God as a silent "spirit" spout, the whale's blowing into the human world's momentary glimpse, being the minimal entrance of Him into the world above the water. But within the emergence of modernity, the nature of this God does not allow humans to see (Him) fully. The whale is an animal too large to be seen in its entirety. This is a metaphor for both the (unpredictable) Holy Spirit and the (hidden) Father parts of the trinity. The spout inspires in this pneumatology (a definition of the Holy Spirit); humans can only make an incomplete phenomenology of the whale. The only glimpse one can catch of the great Leviathan is when it briefly surfaces. Categorically speaking, a whale's mass is so great that without the support received in water, it would be crushed by its own weight. A whale, by its structure, is not made to withstand its own massiveness outside of the ocean water. Its realm is, and must be, the vast waters of the deep. If a whale were to enter our land-world it would die, being crushed by its own body-mass and beached. This could be interpreted as a metaphor for the emergence of secular culture—God is not sustained in the world to come, for Melville.

Ahab is able, oddly, to perceive this trajectory (James 2001). Removing himself from the ravages of "civilization" and tossed into "the natural realm," the possibility for transformative vision only refracts back a more perverse domination of nature through desperate action. Advancing technologies present the power to both turn the body and spirit of humans into the instruments of modern industrialization—wherein labor loses all "individual character and charm for the workman. . . . He becomes the 'appendage of the machine'" (Marx and Engels [1848] 1976, 479). As C.L.R James describes, "men who are thinking like that," when faced with a "violent catastrophe that ruins them . . . they are going to throw aside all the traditional restraints of civilization" (James 2001, 11). Bitterness of resentment for the way things are *for them personally* is characteristic of the revolutionary class and the vanguard intelligentsia. Like the powers of revolutionary intellectuals, the crew, "savages and ragamuffins of the world" become a symbolic device for the instrumentalized and objectified "masses" of the world.

The reckoning with something greater is the force of the whale. In this theology, humans cannot see God fully. As is Exodus 33:17–24, "I know you by name . . . but my face shall not be seen." On a whale watch all we see is the "spirit spout" as the whale rises and its fluke as it dives back down. We only see this "magnanimity" when it subtly manifests itself as it takes a breath in our air. Or we see It as it dives deeper down into the ocean. For the religious humanist, humanity cannot have complete knowledge of the totality. Melville wants his reader to see the subtleties rather than the profound, when they appear before her eyes. When Pip goes into his "madness"—a schizophrenia with vision—he conjugates the verb, "to look." Pip also becomes a comforter to King Lear-like Ahab—the Shakespearean fool and soothsayer. Melville wishes us to see this in multi-vision, in every form and in every tense, as the whale itself has many layers to perceive. Little things have epic proportion. Knowledge is always incomplete. Ishmael believes and doubts in the whale, like religion, "in spite of his great ignorance of it" (Sten 1996, 190). Again, to parallel this limited knowledge in humans with reference to the piercing eyes of the whale, the eyes are small: "so vast a being as the whale should see the world through so small an eye . . . why do you try to enlarge your mind? Subtilize it" (Melville 1967, 280). Here we see Melville's criticism of some of the Transcendentalist and other intellectualist individualisms: movements to enlarge mind, expand reason, and a sense of limitless humanity. In words about idea construction, cast by Isaiah Berlin and Hannah Arendt, there are foxes and hedgehogs. In terms of theoretical construction, Melville seems to be critical both of hedgehog-like grand theory, or the limitless rationalisms of foxes.

THEODICY: THE QUESTION OF A BROKEN ORDER

Two theologies are in conversation in Melville—one suggests there is a weaver God with a Loom and a plan intricately designed. The other proposes the following—but this God, if He were there and if He were indeed weaving, wouldn't He protect the men of the *Pequod*? If God does indeed hear, as says in the name Ishmael, wouldn't the *Pequod*, a ship of decent men persuaded, by reason, into a diabolical oath, have been saved from its doomed monomaniacal captain? Yet the ship goes into the abyss. This is the diabolical will, a perversion of human community and cooperation—"entered freely and of [their] own will" (*Dracula,* quoted in Moretti 1996, 1). If this God hears, why is there no salvation for the *Pequod*? This God is a weaver God without a compassionate ear, "he weaves . . .hears no mortal voice" (Melville 1967, 374). This image is a God that contrasts with the responsive, protecting and providential weaver aforementioned—the comforts of religious holism. This God is beyond our reach or transcendence. From a Hebrew scripture perspective and Ahab's location, this God is a God of Job: "who wrote the first Leviathan? Who but mighty Job?" (Melville 1967, 100). Reading in a post-Nietzschean moment, the fleeting appearances of the all-seeing whale reflect a haunting God of what John Caputo might describe as the "perhaps" (2013, 5). This "perhaps" is not cowardice, in Caputo's definition, but rather "courage . . . for the dangerous perhaps . . . for the open-ended, for the fear and trembling before the uncontainable" (2013, 8). Melville's story of fate also illustrates a postmodern God to the members of the *Pequod*, who require a faith exceeding the simple "binary between belief and unbelief" (Caputo 2013, 5). The "perhaps" is the postmodern middle zone between the hermeneutics of suspicion and the suspension of disbelief: faith in a desert. It is faith within the culture of secularity. It is faith in the face of the evils of religion. Caputo suggests this space is older than a nameable God. It "insists as the immemorial in an ancient memory of an uninhabitable desert" (Caputo 2013, 259). Is the sea the *Pequod's* desert of the Patristics/Hebrew wanderers?

MODERN MIND: TOPMOST GRIEF

How can humans know this absent God and the desert of the "perhaps"? This question, in the frame of the story of the Great Whale, can be put in the human mediator's terms "how do we relate to Ahab?" Ahab's reflexive self-encounter, moment of clarity: "who am I for Moby Dick, who is Moby Dick to me?" and "is Ahab Ahab?" (Melville 1967, 445). Ahab easily answers his second question: "Ahab is forever Ahab" (Melville 1967, 459). He realizes his overbearing nature and accepts his similarity to the cruel (rendering of the) what was seen as the "Old" Testament. He goes on to answer his first question. "This act's immutably decreed. . . . I'll solve it!!" (Melville 1967, 459). Ahab is, for us, the epitome of a twisted heart, as we understand it. "Ahab never thinks; he only feels, feels, feels" (Melville 1967, 460). But when he does think, his thoughts are passionately monomaniacal. What Arendt might define as thinking, weighing in conscience as an obstacle to immoral action, is absent in Ahab. Ahab *obsesses* but does not think. To think, for Arendt, is to weigh mind and heart together—Melville would be comfortable with this relational, engaged, embodied and non-dualistic understanding of thinking. Ahab thinks technocratically throughout the novel—the means of reason as domination science is the management of things and nature, and politics the management of men, especially evidenced by *Moby Dick*'s chapter "The Chart" (James 2001, 15). Both forms of totalitarianism are linked in the narration of the story—there is a parallel here from Faustian resonances with Hawthorne's *Young Goodman Brown*: the "little world" of the natural realm (or domesticity) to the "big world" of politics (Jameson 2019).

In a final fleeting moment of self-awareness, Ahab cries "My topmost greatness lie in my topmost grief" (Melville 1967, 468). Emerging in Transcendentalism's perspective, mind and reason was the crowning achievement of "creation." The human mind has a power that is above all creatures: the ability to mechanically and rationally think. For Melville, however, the excessive development of the brain leads to the disintegration of the heart. Ahab recognizes his "mind" as his topmost greatness, the ability to think of the whale, will also be his ultimate grief. He develops here a new understanding of self-awareness and obedience to the weight of both the demonic and divine. As in the chapter entitled The Sermon, "And if we obey God, we must disobey ourselves" (Melville 1967, 45). What better articulation of the sense of the function of religion and civilization in relation to the individual's desires and urges, as it comes from both Freud's and Durkheim's definitions. In the voice of the clergyman's homiletic, God is not something we can touch intellectually or physically—it is the irreducible of the phantom of life. In the Job response, we weren't there at the "laying of the foundations," and Ahab never understands the tragedy and grief that results in the attempt to rationalize and play God. It would work with the controlling, righteous weaver and not the blank white whale. The eclipse of reason—the postmodern sense of *Moby Dick*—evokes the impossibility of the Faustian bargain. That destructive power of "nature" or the phantom of life is unleashed when the reason-driven ego seeks to dominate it. Thinking, then, is seen as the enemy of life, community, connection.

Monomaniacal thought-as-obsession, particularly monomaniacal thought, produces great suffering for Ahab and everyone aboard the *Pequod*. This monomaniacal defiance of the truth of fate he has seen in the white whale is Ahab's "electric with foreboding." He says in one of his own loomings, "Like curse like; and for this hunt, the malady becomes my most desired health" (436). This paradox holds a great light to Ahab's view of the whale. Moby Dick is the encounter with the Holy, the *mysterium tremendum et fascinans* to Ahab. The whale is tremendous, dreadful, daunting and at the same time fascinating, attractive and very much like himself. When he looks into the reflecting waters of the ocean—the dominion of the whale—he can see himself, and a Heideggerian being unto his own fate—death. But unlike Caputo's understanding of a Heideggerian death, which might be concerned with the others in the *Pequod*, Ahab's anticipation narcissistically singles out himself with the whale (Caputo 1997, 84). Both he and the whale have scars, and both have seen each other in their eyes. The whale inverts Ahab's world into a place where darkness becomes light, the insanity of men becomes heaven's sense and ultimately sickness becomes health.

This whale has dis-masted Ahab from that with which he had once stood, from humanity and community. Ahab's initial contact with the whale left this split in him, costing a leg and leaving a scar that "bled into his soul." Ahab, the split man, much like tree struck by lightning, is scarred for life with a maddening obsession and inner monitor that drives him on to hunt the whale, disregarding the rest of society. He hunts this whale, calling on that which had hunted him. Ahab's scar is a text. When Ahab encounters the whale for the first time, the whale leaves his mark, taking a leg and leaving a streak down his visage marking a schism. It not only tells of his "monomaniacal musings" but it also metaphorically acts as a set of directions back to that which left the mark: a scar and a map toward the hunted for the hunter. Ahab only calls upon and hunts the whale because the whale has called upon and hunted him. They haunt each other. In his final fated defiance he cries, "Thou all-destroying but unconquering whale . . . though tied to thee thou damned whale! Thus I give up the spear!" (Melville 1967, 468). The whale is in him, at "a little lower level," as the shipman Starbuck might say.

Sometimes an inner Western self, driven by the defiant Nietzschean cannot help but admire Ahab, even in his tyrannical state that was a "oneness . . . [directing the crew] toward that fatal goal which Ahab their one lord did point to" (Melville 1967, 455). His defiance in the face of a losing situation seems, at the heroic tragedy level, quite noble. He fights the whale with his last strength and curses the whale with his last breath. Ahab's fight is reminiscent of lines from a Dylan Thomas poem (1951) "Do Not Go Gentle Into That Good Night": "And learn, too late, they grieved it on its way . . . / Rage, rage against the dying of the light." As the poem mentions, in the interstitial lines, Ahab is a "grave" man—both serious and monomaniacal but also "being unto death." Ahab has seen the dying of the light but has learned "too late." His ship has gone down, but more importantly he is faced with his identity. He "sees with blinding sight," perhaps blinded from the whiteness of the whale. He rides the whale as his last hurrah. But he is not "going gentle," he rages. Originally, he thought "that a ship made by men . . . where God does not reign" (Melville 1967, 45) and he intended all along to rage against the all-encompassing whiteness, the ultimate truth, to the bitter end, knowing that "toil we may, we all sleep at last on the field" (Melville 1967, 445). He finally accepts death and pain—the white, stark, blank truth. He admits to God's control, but there is still the whiteness to be faced and he will not escape the confrontation. He sees the whiteness but is still driven on by a vertical force: "As if two antagonistic influence were . . . horizontal goal" (Melville 1967, 200). Ahab's tragically restless heart pulls him in these two directions—one on each side of his split visage. His scar marks his torn soul. This scar reflects the broken ontology of modernity.

THE DYING OF THE LIGHT

In one (rather Heideggerian) reading of this text, one must accept, as Ahab is forced to accept the white whale, the fate of suffering and death. Sometimes this eternal feeling of mortality and fate are suffered in pain or disappointment. Melville glosses on a psychology of trauma and loss. When in collective trauma, or meeting brokenness for the first time, the person of society searches for meaning. "Why," she may obsess, "did this happen?" She may ask the Job question—"how can the righteous rightly be punished by a weaver God who is seemingly concerned with justice?" Is there order at all with all these modern social ills and problem? Is this "God" attentively listening, as a shepherd tends his flock, or a captain watches over his crew? It seems as though in loss and social life are random, out of control—anomic as Durkheim describes modernity. In *Moby Dick,* "We are turned round and round in this world, like yonder windlass, and fate is the hand spike" (Melville 1967, 445). However, lurking in Melville's skepticism, there is a believer who embraces God as a good weaver—known from his vast creation and the being that all sense as good. But in his weaving perhaps this God is deafened from time to time. Melville is here both a sociologist of modernity, but also a harbinger of postmodern-like questions of the role of religion in society. The narrative evokes some of the conceptual plays on the death of God he also hints at the implications of this in a sense of late twentieth century's philosophical theology's definition of "religion without religion." Robin Grey highlights how Hawthorne once commented that Melville could "neither believe nor be comfortable in his disbelief, and he is too honest and courageous not to try to do one or the other" (2004, xxii). This honest belief *qua* agnostic desire is the perfect postmodern sense of what John Caputo addresses as "weak faith." It is a tempered passion—both desire and doubt.

THEOLOGY MEETS SOCIOLOGY

In the response to this skeptical-religious humanism, *Moby Dick* picks up as a sociology where theology fails in a holistic and ontological description of the world. This is very much in the spirit of a Buberian entwinement of the social and the mystical-religious. In brief, the theory of community is cast in the collective response to the experience of a loss of a theological ontology. Social life is thus a theodicy-response to the "universal thump of Fate's white fluke is rub each others' shoulder blades and be contented": supporting others in their hard times and letting them support us when our need arises. Nowhere is this "civil" affection more evident than in the examples of Queequeg and

Pip. Queequeg, a man of aboriginal nature, had "an innate sense of delicacy . . . treated me with much civility and consideration" (Melville 1967, 34). Symbolically Pip, a boy of "blackness" on the outside (opposite of the whale's whiteness), has great warmth inside and in a spirit of radical charity is the only one who is able to comfort Ahab in his ravings, like *King Lear*'s fool (Olson 1967 [1947]).

Though himself not a huge fan of Melville, Joseph Conrad expresses the way sailing ships fostered community and mysticism simultaneously—they fostered loyalty, determination, courage, commitment (Jasanoff 2017, 109). A sailing ship leads a "mysteriously unearthly existence, bordering upon the magic of invisible forces" (Conrad, 2011 [1906], 71).

Melville may be sermonizing that certain subtleties do lurk in everything—the remnants of the theological connection and providence amidst a hallowing out of old institutions. It is our job to "subtilize" our minds and then "Look, Look, Look," knowing we cannot conquer the "whiteness," but we rub each other's shoulders, getting to know the crew members on board while in the quest for the whale. As is appropriate for a transcendent phenomenology of God, in what Caputo has defined as a postmodern weak faith, "religion without religion," seeing is incomplete. Because of God's transcendence humans are left with completing social life in repairing the world together. One might have a sense of a New England spirit of a Hebraic *tikkun olam* at work here in Melville's phenomenology of allusions from Hebrew Scriptures. This incomplete seeing points to the ever-elusive problem of location and faith. In Vattimo's (2007, 28) account it is the Heideggerian question of the impossibility of objectivity and the question of the location of interpretation. Vattimo makes the point that hermeneutics does not begin with the New Testament, mentioning Jewish Rabbinics (Caputo and Vattimo 2007, 34). Perhaps Melville's genius is his Hebraic metaphors and names extending in the stories and characters attached to the *Pequod*. This is a nod to the original Hebraically infused interpretive tradition in distinctively American literature.

SO VAST A BEING, SO SMALL AN EYE

If God were an animal, would he be a great white whale with small piercing eyes, "so vast a being as the whale should see through the world through small eye" (Melville 1967, 280)? The mid-nineteenth century's use of the image of a weaving God is paradoxical in itself and provides its own opposition. *Moby Dick* emerges at the time within the currents of social theory and philosophical imagination was the description of the tension between individualism and community.

The contradiction of the American Project as a corollary of the English Enlightenment presents the idea that the more "individualistic" we are, the "more civilization progressed and the more men developed as a community" (James 2001, 50). From a theological and social-psychological perspective, humans are pulled in two directions: one toward the vertical, human obsession with fate, and one that takes us aside to the leeward portion of the ship that has a great view of the present, and community. The whiteness of the whale denies transcendence and may leave the reader with a blank feeling on the boundary of these dualistic directives, but who are humans to judge that which laid the foundations and that which is as undefined as the ocean water? And "to obey God, we must disobey ourselves" (Melville 1967, 45), for this God is completely foreign to the trajectory of modernity and undefined, impossible to possess, in that domain. God must remain in the vastness of the deep. With the question of slavery and agency, perhaps this is why Melville called this "an evil book" in a correspondence with Hawthorne.

Melville is ever the diabolical homilist with his view of the ambivalent character of life's joy and suffering. Ishmael is the hero here, but Melville is preaching to humankind in his journey that he must learn to recognize God's simultaneous presence-absence in the trauma of life's journey (Sten 1996, 197) in the modern. But ultimately the lesson is one of humility before the God of the whirlwind. Ahab's failure in an inability to love is that he cannot conquer his ego that fails to admit "there is an invisible power that rules over all" (Sten 1996, 211). The universal thump does hit, and when humans are faced with suffering, perhaps the best one can do is to simply be a comforter. Not to forget Bildad, one of the *Pequod*'s agents and more importantly a not well-regarded comforter of Job in the Hebrew Scriptures: "Something of the salt sea yet lingered in old Bildad's language, heterogeneously mixed with Scriptural and domestic phrases" (Melville 1967, 85). There is some merit to scripture and hope in its comforting qualities, but mixed in is a little of what keeps the boat afloat—"the salt sea." In the context of a modern or post-modern death of God, in an "absent" theophany, what the voyagers on the *Pequod* find comfort in is the community of the boat. Theology in skepticism fades into community of doubt, but this is an adult form of faith. Love and connection happen despite the presence of doubt. In the chapter, "The Chapel" "faith . . . feeds among the tombs, and even from these dead doubts she gathers her most vital hope" (discussed and quoted in Sten 1996, 144). This is the world's "chapel": faith-with-doubt with its intention toward the responsibilities of community. In Melville's genius anticipating the postmodern turn, an absent God and the warnings against a monomaniacal unbridled reason points to the sociology of solidarity, of a community of mariners, renegades, and castaways (Halton 1995; Sten 1996, 162). The sociological opens up as the result of the doubt of God and absolutes, this temptation of the conflicted. It is a dance between the one and the many: "the imperative to be single-minded, to affirm one thing, one God . . . and a world that seems to offer many paths and to invite us . . . to search for other meanings" (quoted in Grey 2004, xxvii). The transformative possibility of egalitarian friendships also suggests the power of a pragmatist spirit lurking in Melville's sociology. Though there are some sexualized readings of the relationships on the *Pequod* (Martin 1986; Halton 1995), at the baseline, even of a metaphorically interpreted significance of homosexuality, is an understanding of human relationships that could be radically different from one cast in power, dominance, and inequality. This is the critique of the authoritarian power of Ahab or the blind, hypocritical faith of the preacher in the chapter, "The Sermon." Martin reflects on the transformative potency of this type of friendship in the oppressive historical context Melville was living in and perhaps commentating on—American slavery, genocide, and imperialism. These elements constitute what the American sociologist Robert Bellah called evidence of the dark implications of the American social experiments of the religious overtones of the colonies—the "broken covenant." Ishmael's intimacy with Queequeg is an idyllic interracial, anti-imperialist connection across what W.E.B. DuBois called the "color-line." This erotic alignment is a transformative type of religious, ethnic, and political egalitarianism; it is a metaphor for a new kind of universalist friendship, the basis for a vision of community.

LOST EDEN AND "FIRST CONGREGATION OF THIS WHOLE WORSHIPPING WORLD"

As discussed above, Queequeg's significance in the story symbolizes a new vision for friendship, and a sociology of a universal community. Martin's text (1986) places the relationship between Ishmael and Queequeg in opposition to the solitude of Ahab. In this he deflects two Narcissus-like figures, and a Miltonian allegory of an America alienated and an image for paradise regained. Queequeg's coffin—the remnant of the mystery of the universe—will emerge to save the solitary misplaced intellectual aboard the *Pequod*. Queequeg embodied "the mystery of the universe and the attainment of truth," yet he was just another anonymous crewman (James 2001, 35). It seems that truth matters little in the overall destructive pattern of world civilization. The notion of the "noble savages" presents a counterpoint truth to the destructive power of money and ego-driven Western consciousness, and "the intellectual and emotional self-torture" that is the primary condition for the survival of modern society (James 2001, 30). Ishmael is no pure hero, however. Ishmael, in James's reading is the "rebellious son of the middle class" who sets out on his "personal avant-garde adventure—like so many real Marxist intellectuals of the twentieth century . . . Ishmael is a proto-totalitarian of a generic kind, Nazi and Stalinist" (Pease, in James 2001, xxiii). Ishmael, again, reflects both the interminable quality and the desire to escape from that condition particular to the intellectual—a raging sense of disaffection from the contemporary sphere and anomie. The disastrous effects of this were explored extensively in Durkheim's *Suicide* (Bellah/Durkheim 1973). Ishmaels are definitely urbanites. Their ultimate submission, though suggesting a glimpse of the value of "authenticity or self-actualization," rather comes in the reality that Ishmael-Ahab form a sado-masochistic authoritarian symbiosis (Fromm 1957). Ishmael is the intellectual enabler and counterpart of Ahab.

Ahab's reflection is akin to Narcissus (also obsessed with reflections): the only character on the *Pequod* who is so incredibly imprisoned by his power-mongering freedom. But this freedom, as a Hegelian might critique, is utter license. In Nietzsche-meets-Marx's parsing it is a capitalistic will-to-power. Ahab is "free" because he is not in community or responsible. He is reckless, destructive, and this Narcissus' stare at the waters of the ocean causes destruction (Melville 1967, 14). This reflects "will-to-power" more than freedom, per se. The diabolical nature of Ahab's quest is the pursuit of not communion with the whale, but the domination of the "phantom" of life. Ahab and the officers represent "the science, knowledge, technical skill" and force of domination in "world civilization" (James 2001, 34). This is a nod to the hypocrisies of modernity and colonial powers, as discussed in the next chapter on Conrad's *Heart of Darkness*. Alluding to William Blake, "he who would cast aside all human bonds for freedom would soon find himself the most bound, constricted and unfree of all" (Halton 1986, 246). The novel gets to the "heart" of the violence in the Western soul as the megalomania of mind. The captain and officers of the Pequod are then the "specialists without spirit" within the iron cage (Weber 2001), and the bureaucratic technocrats of world civilizations that are heading for the ultimate crisis (James 2001, 34).

Franco Moretti's description *Moby Dick,* like other classics of Western literature, inherits some archetypal categories from Goethe's telling of *Faust*—even more Faustian than Faust himself. Where *Faust* has an incredible redemption in terms of the "claimed" victory of the eternal feminine through the Gretchen/Helena amalgam's forgiveness of Herr Rationalist-Cad, the intellectual Faust, *Moby Dick*'s conclusion parallels its victory in the destructive power of the whale, something akin to Wagner's *Götterdämmerung*. Ahab's monomaniacal masculine persona approaches the eternal feminine-cast-as-whale. The eternal feminine absorbs the Pequod, captain . . . all but Ishmael in *Moby Dick*. Paralleling the power of nature, the whale—with its connective, Rousseauian function of spermaceti—symbolizes what Richard King has called, "proto-Darwinian decentring of the human and the elevation of the whale" (Burrow 2020). Mentioned in a review of King's text, *Ahab's*

Rolling Sea: a Natural History of Moby Dick, Colin Burrow further articulates that the novel is "an ecological fiction that not only displays sympathy for whales but sets acquisitive human perspectives against the wide and impersonal horizon of the sea." These acquisitive, isolating powers of the human, particularly driven by the unbridled spirit of capitalism are another play upon metaphor of nature as a final, conquering metaphor for the eternal feminine in the story's dramatic climax. It metaphorically counters the power of human domination and rapier of the earth, especially through the natural images of the womb-like sea.

Ahab's madness is so enthralling that its power of isolation separates itself even from the economic system that "launched the Pequod"—the "captain of industry" splits and the captain becomes more dangerous than the shipowners (Moretti 1996, 32–33). Ahab is a pivotal character in the emergence of the "modern epic" in the dawn of sociological theory—captain-as-capitalist—and as an archetype that is part Faust, part Mephistopheles (Moretti 1996, 33). The hidden violence is internalized, and in the modern epic, concomitant with the birth of the classical period of sociological theory, we see the emergence of solitary image of the (anti) hero at the center of his world, a reflection of rationalizing narcissism.

Counter to this, is an archetype which inspires the works of Marx and other thinkers: Melville's character Queequeg. He represents is a Rousseauian moment of the desire for exotic innocence, community and egalitarianism—and he intimately connects with Ishmael. Martin eloquently observes the circular writing style at the parts of the novel concerning this topic (1986, 70–71). This circular stylistic represents the opposite of Ahab's phallic, linear, and imperialistic drive toward exploitation of the crew. Ahab represents monomaniacal consumption and destruction. The harmony and brotherly connection between Ishmael and Queequeg run counter to Ahab's lonely obsession. Ishmael's reflective Apolline/*ephebe* like Narcissus is caught between two poles of action—Ahab's and Queequeg's, again symbolizing the divide of the color line. Ahab's modern railroad train language of conquest is "the prose of a civilization gone mad" (Martin 72, 85). Ahab's pursuit of the whale is a metaphor for modernity individualism, and alienation. Martin refers to this as "Progress-Logos as rapist" type of knowledge, where lonely technical power is valued over human affection (1996, 94). The counterbalance to this is egalitarian friendship as seen in the metaphor of the "monkey-rope" in the text (Melville 1967, 270–273): signifying human interdependence and fellow workmanship, without Ahab's rope's likeness of a top or bottom (Martin 1996, 94). What the monkey-rope represents is the fragility of society when trust breaks down—in the weakening of the ontology that is modern life. The narrative describes Queequeg's life in Ishmael's hands as he precariously leans over the sperm-whale they've harvested, dangling from waist to waist and connected by the rope. Much like a rock-climber depends on her spotter or the patient depends on the skill of her doctor, Melville uses this nautical apparatus (knots-as-ties) as a metaphor for the subtle dependence and trust that constitutes the social. This resoundingly anticipates the same sociological thesis of Durkheim, coming a generation after Melville, writing in the French school of social thought. If the doctor misguides or mistreats the patient, the system would break down. A recent exhibit (Summer 2015) at the New Bedford, Massachusetts Whaling Museum noted the role racial and ethnic diversity played in both the New Bedford, and the Whaling Industry itself. Cape Verdean and Portuguese communities were showcased, and on the *Pequod* Ishmael notes how Africans and Pacific Islanders held higher ranks than him, counter to the societal trend. This was different from the legacy of racism in Melville's contemporaneous America. The whaling excursion is a moment of Durkheimian society and organic solidarity within the division of labor: both highlighting diversity of ethnic origins of the crew and the deep levels of intimate trust among them.

A universalist solidarity of cross-cultural intimate brotherhood is suggested as the counteraction to the legacy of American genocide, slavery, imperialism, and conquest. Eugene Halton (1995) also suggests Melville's vision is the solution for the Western theoretical mind's tendency toward alienation and abstraction and its result, domination. Halton argues that without community and solidarity postmodern thinking leads to a dark path that is "bereft of reason." The social theorist Gillian Rose highlights this "rationalism without reason" as a symptom of postmodernity. Thus, Melville's epic offers itself up as an incomplete definition of living in the world amidst a response to the broken whole, with only short glimpses of a totality, a Divine reality. It is both a call to American reform, and a social statement on the need for a "First Congregation of the Whole world." It suggests a reversal of the Calvinist American roots of the elect—the diverse "communion of sinners" as a response to the alienation of the Western monomaniacal mind of exploitation and imperial conquest.

Chapter Four

Literary *Metanoia* and the Sociological Imagination in Joseph Conrad

Colonialism and Western Idealism

INTRODUCTION

Focusing on *Heart of Darkness* by Joseph Conrad, this chapter highlights the sociological themes present in his (relatively) early criticisms of colonialism/ globalization through the method of literature as reflexive *metanoia*. Joseph Conrad (1857–1924), born in Poland, Józef Teodor Konrad Korzeniowski, was writing in a historical period where the novel was more far-reaching in its audience than an inchoate-stage "scientific" sociology. Edward Said observes that Joseph Conrad is important in contemporary discussions of policy in the Developing world in that his narratives shaped "Western" ideas of such places. Conrad was both "criticizing and reproducing" the imperial ideology of his time (Said 1993, xx).

This chapter argues that the novella's unique contribution is its reflexivity within the genre of "colonial" novels—that for his time period, Conrad should be highlighted as a contributor to the project of postcolonial critique as he was engaged in reflexively exposing imperialism and colonialism's brutalities. Conrad, in the words of John Orr, was a witness to the "tragic irony" (Orr 1977, 99) of the British Empire, as its semi-outsider; an immigrant. Considering this biographical fact, this chapter begins with, but goes beyond, the claims of Edward Said's and Chinua Achebe's interpretations of the novella as inherently ethnocentric. Using the inheritance of the philosophical-ethical frame of *metanoia,* a change of heart as a result of mental awareness, Conrad's sociological imagination is represented by the narrator's voice (Marlow's) stepping back and reflecting via mechanisms of stylistic "disorientation" (Moses 2007). The techniques of irony, disorientation, metanoia, and reflexivity all show evidence of Conrad's sensitivity to emerging cultural and political contradictions evident in the broken promises and hypocrisies of imperialism, Western political ideologies, and "Western culture." In Franco Moretti's description in this form of "epic": "culture wounds and disintegrates" individual subjects (1996, 195). The violence of the main character Kurtz, and the wounds of the "nameless Africans," in *Heart of Darkness*, and, as briefly mentioned, Stevie and Verloc in *The Secret Agent*, both reflect the way Western idealism is accompanied by corpses. In *The Secret Agent*, Conrad is haunted by the ghost of his father's political idealism, which perpetually endangered his family, but also by a larger question of the hypocrisies of idealistic value systems in the West.

The predominant discussion of Conrad's *Heart of Darkness* in the mid- to late twentieth century focused on its racism. Most famously, established literary scholars like Chinua Achebe and Edward Said—both coming from a postcolonial perspective—staunchly defended the claim that the text was inherently racist. Today there are calls to expunge *Heart of Darkness* from the Western "great books" canon as "It's done so much damage in fashioning savage notions of Africa," according to a recent statement by Michael Eric Dyson (quoted in Tamaki 2020). Additionally, Achille Mbembe has illuminated the way in which the "normless"—as in law/nomos-less—continent comes across in Conrad as barbaric and the anti-Europe (Adepitan 2003). However, along with Adepitan (2003) and Marzagora (2016) I argue that this Africa/Europe dichotomy—the obsession of the "posts" discussions (Marzagora 2016)—is unproductive. This chapter contests that Conrad also reflexively and critically reveals to the reader a self-criticism of European consciousness, and an articulation of the moral ambiguities of racist beliefs which, understood in historical context, was *progressive for his time*. Forgetting this dimension of *Heart of Darkness* points to the very reification of the split between an idealized Africa/Europe that scholars like Mbembe and Achebe seek to transcend. This chapter highlights a more nuanced reading of *Heart of Darkness* as a realistic self-appraisal and the beginning of (historically, as a first moment in the movement of literary Modernism) coming to terms with the brutalities of colonialism and imperialism. The novel confronts the reader with what was for the time, and even remains, an unusually honest awareness of the savage violence at the heart of Europe's self-proclaimed "civilizing" colonial enterprise. The novel represents a form of critical reflexive awareness that is devastating for the comfortable illusions that Europeans enjoy, unconscious, asleep in their "sepulchral" cities. In making this analysis, Conrad's novel should be understood as an early form of reflexive sociological discourse. The very moral murkiness of the European characters presents a moment of literary realism; but it also serves a point in a sociological critique of the ideals of Western civilization.

RACISM IN CONRAD

The critique of Conrad as "inherently racist" is well-known. A trenchant critique by Achebe, notes his use of "N-----" and other racial slurs. But this deserves a closer look. There are two "obsessively" repeated words in *Heart of Darkness:* "N------" and "ivory." How do both of these words "ring in the air"—"one was shouted, one whispered?" For Conrad, the two words are intimately connected to each other. Their pairing signifies the great irony and hypocrisy of civilization and the attempts at the globalization of Christian consciousness and Democratic Enlightenment. Below the surface truth, the "White Man's Burden" was a project based on the devaluation of a race of humans. Another play with language is important. Marlow describes Africans with a double negative, which, again, is a grammatical thing the reader "trips" over, representing a stylistic mechanism for a reflexive consciousness for his time: "but they did not appear inhuman." To say either "they were inhuman" or "they were human" stylistically does not grab the reader. "Not inhuman" reflects the power of the introduction of a notion of reflexive consciousness; an admission of a crack in the iconographic sculpture of European racial superiority. There is a psychological inversion that is introduced by the use of the double negative, and an opening for reflection. The point of observation then leads to how the reader can begin to grasp how the dehumanization of Africans by colonialism was driven by the madness for the pursuit of a luxury material good, ivory.

Chinua Achebe's critique of *Heart of Darkness* rests on this very duality—or maybe continuity—symbolized in the ornate decorative flair of European cultural items and the nullification of the humanity of Africans. "Africa" as a concept is set up as a "foil to Europe" (Achebe 1977, 337). Africa is the negative, the absence of civilization. According to Achebe, Africa is depicted as the darkness to the light of "Europe's spiritual grace" (1977, 337). Further, by defining *Heart of Darkness* as a part of the canon, as a "classic" in Western literature, Achebe claims that this has reified such racist categories about Africa and Africans—both in the sphere of intellectual discourse, and more widely in the domain of "Western" culture and psychology, via its place in the curricula of secondary and post-secondary educational systems. Africa is set up as "another world" (Achebe 1977, 338) and therefore Africans are seen as aliens to civilization.

But could there be another interpretation? Conrad, in the voice of Marlow, by pairing these two words ("n—" and "ivory") illuminates the realities of the connection between racism and imperialism. In Achebe's concluding thoughts, "Conrad saw and condemned the evil of imperial exploitation but was strangely unaware of the racism on which it sharpened its iron tooth"

(1977, 349). My observations on Conrad's text reflect not only an admission of racism within *Heart of Darkness*, but also a criticism and acknowledgment of the hypocrisy of civilization, and of racism's link to imperialism in European consciousness and ideals.

In a 2003 conversation with *The Guardian,* Achebe claims how Conrad sets up Africa as the "other world" so that he might examine Europe. "According to Achebe, Africa is presented to the reader as 'the antithesis of Europe and therefore of civilisation, a place where man's vaunted intelligence and refinement are finally mocked by triumphant bestiality'" (Phillips 2003).

> The overarching question is, what happens when one group of people, supposedly more humane and civilised than another group, attempts to impose themselves upon their "inferiors"? In such circumstances will there always be an individual who [like the character of Kurtz], removed from the shackles of "civilized" behaviour, feels compelled to push at the margins of conventional "morality." (Phillips 2003)

Chinua Achebe defends the claim that there is inherent racism in Conrad, while acknowledging a modest confession in his appreciation for the critical perspective on the part of the Polish-British author: "Towards the end of the nineteenth century, there was a very short-lived period of ambivalence about the certainty of this colonising mission, and *Heart of Darkness* falls into this period. But you [Europeans] cannot compromise my [African] humanity in order that you explore your own ambiguity. I cannot accept that. My humanity is not to be debated, nor is it to be used simply to illustrate European problems" (Phillips 2003). What is fascinating is that Conrad drops hints at the existential awareness that Europeans might reflect—not so much as a self-indulgent exploration of psychological ambiguity—but as the problem of the mental construction of civilization itself. There is an inherent paradox in the thrust of Western "civilization" in that it is built on brutality. This subconscious awareness does not produce a Narcissus gazing at himself in the therapist's office—at least not in the nineteenth century. Perhaps this is for later generations. For Conrad, "What makes mankind [civilization] tragic is not that they are the victims of nature, it is that they are conscious of it" (in Freedman 2014). The unconscious awareness of the hypocrisy of civilization—its rootedness in violence—is supported by a social-psychological, religious, and political superstructure that is ideologically driven (Marx, in Williams 1977, 75). This defends and justifies what W.E.B. DuBois noted as the "color line," and how Conrad describes the brutal exploitation of Africans. "Society" requires the "sleep" of "saving illusions" (Freedman 2014, 36)—once these illusions are exposed, or these "opiates" no longer work (Marx [1844] in Marx and Engels 1978), disruptions occur. This is why, for Marx, the beginning of all critiques starts with the most potent form of ideological distractions, the inverted consciousness of the world: religion (Marx [1844] in Marx and Engels 1978). Religion is the ideological mechanism of justification; Conrad alludes to religion in *Heart of Darkness* as the very superstructure that legitimates the course of colonialism: "The conquest of the earth, which mostly means the taking it away from those who have different complexions or slightly flatter noses . . . is not a pretty thing when you look into it too much . . . what redeems it is the *idea only* . . . something you can set up, and bow down before and offer a sacrifice to" (Conrad 1899, 7).

The "redemptive" illusion of Christianity justified imperialism to the point of creating a false consciousness. Conrad makes evident and lays bare the hidden will-to-power as the modus vivendi of that naked imperialism—Kurtz's character is then an exposé on the power of capitalist imperialism, that reaches "to the corners of the globe." Edward Said uses this very quotation at the dedication page to his *Culture and Imperialism* (1993). The link between capitalism and imperialism was first hinted at in Marx & Engels *Manifesto of the Communist Party*, but it was developed further in the opus of Rosa Luxemburg's *Accumulation of Capital:*

> The need of a constantly expanding market for its products chases the bourgeoisie over the whole surface of the globe. It must nestle everywhere, settle everywhere, establish connections everywhere. The bourgeoisie has through its exploitation of the world market given a cosmopolitan character to production and consumption in every country. (Marx and Engels [1848] 1978, 476)

Conrad, according to Said, exposes the way imperialism is a "system" but that also the schemes of civilizing never succeed but are the hallmarks of the delusions and cultural constructions, including religion and psychology, of a notion of the hegemonic, racialized "West" (see also: Said 1993, xix).

ADDRESSING COLONIALISM AND BLACK LIVES MATTER

In addition to Edward Said's reflections, Chinua Achebe's observations on the intrinsic racist assumptions and actions in *Heart of Darkness* are key to understanding the historical and literary context of today's social movement of Black Lives Matter. In the narrative of the movement, the problem of police brutality from Freddie Grey to George Floyd (and, of course, before and beyond) is that it stems from these culturally pervasive modes of dehumanization of African identity and blackness that were cultivated by readings of *Heart of Darkness,* among other texts. As a kind of "primal violence in the origin" as Rene Girard describes in ancient civilizations, the death of black and brown people is the ground upon which European modern capitalism is founded, and the philosophical and literary moments of existentialism illegitimately emerge. Albert Camus's *L'Etranger* stands as a political critique of itself but is also, ironically a popular successful literary product of colonialism. Perhaps what Achebe would contest with *L'Etranger,* unlike Camus's existential rendering in the story, the violence against racial minorities and marginalized populations is beyond the banal. In Camus's novel, for Meurseault the murder just "happens." Like the "others" of *L'Etranger,* the Africans do not have names, but the death of the "Muslim" is responded to nonchalantly. In Conrad's narrative, the dehumanization of the "other" exists at a much more blatantly grotesque and instrumentalized level through the very categories of what DuBois has called "the color line"—the relation between the white and non-white "races"—it objectifies, brutalizes, and kills non-white *humans*.

However, even considering the damaging effects of the social construction of race in literature, as former president Barack Obama encourages, we should "still read Conrad" (Jasanoff 2017, prologue). It is vital to address *Heart of Darkness* for its insight into that very process of the social and psychological constructions of whiteness, blackness, capitalism, colonialism, philosophical idealism, and modernity.

In some ways, Joseph Conrad's *Heart of Darkness* is a literary harbinger of what Charles Thorpe has articulated the way in which a culture of capitalism, or a unique, repeating, leitmotif of capitalism in the tendencies of *necroculture* (Thorpe 2016). The link between the fetishization of commodities and capitalism as destruction of life was first observed in the early texts of Karl Marx, namely the *Economic and Philosophic Manuscripts* (1844), then reintroduced in the West by the work of sociological trained scholar of psychoanalysis and member of the Frankfurt School's Erich Fromm, in *Marx's Concept of Man*. Thorpe's observations bring these two theoretical contributions forward into the postmodern context, and by applying Thorpe's theories, the reader can see what Conrad's novel "echoes of the future" in the literary imagination.

Conrad's meditations on "ivory" ringing in the air uses the object as a symbolic fetishization of death in a luxury item—both the death of nature (elephants), and the death of Africans, whose heads were displayed on spikes in Kurtz's compound. As Thorpe eloquently, but horrifically, describes: "Capital is the power of the dead . . . it . . . draws sustenance, energy, and power from its exploitation of the living" (Thorpe 2016, 2). Life in capital reverts to the dead things and falsehood of the worship of commodities—paralleling them with "idols" in Erich Fromm's parsing of Marx's prophetic language (Fromm 2004). What are we left to worship in capitalism? What mode of sovereignty gives way? Fromm, via Thorpe, and Conrad converge in their observation that personal relations at the cultural level become infected with "envy, resentment, aggression, contempt" and all for the sake of the driving force of technical achievements and glorification of "efficiency" (Ellul 1964; Thorpe 2016, 4–5; Conrad 2006, 6). This is the (anti)value system of capitalism. It creates a tension between instrumental rationality and value-based forms of decision-making. Conrad uses textual imagery to describe racial categories that make possible the instrumentalizing and dehumanization of the Africans in the story—all of whom are nameless—but this might be a stylistic point to make a larger frame out of which the reader must "critically reflect" on the opacity of these characters. Is it their namelessness or the very action of the dehumanization of the characters in the novel, juxtaposed with the narrator's statement that they were not "inhuman"?

At the political level, one could discuss the realm of bio-politics, from Foucault and Agamben, as the logic of capitalism (Mbembe 2003). One way of rendering the *realpolitik* of colonialist and imperialist politics of death, sovereignty is parsed in:

> the generalized instrumentalization of human existence and the material destruction of human bodies and populations. Such figures of sovereignty are far from a piece of prodigious insanity or an expression of a rupture between the impulses and interests of the body and those of the mind. Indeed, they, like the death camps, are what constitute the nomos of the political space in which we still live. Furthermore, contemporary experiences of human destruction suggest that it is possible to develop a reading of politics, sovereignty, and the subject different from the one we inherited from the philosophical discourse of modernity. Instead of considering reason as the truth of the subject, we can look to other foundational categories that are less abstract and more tactile, such as life and death. (Mbembe 2003, 14)

By naming the very *heart* of darkness of colonial powers, and the *realpolitik* lurking behind the guise of "civilization," the unique contribution of the author Joseph Conrad was that he offered a departure from his contemporaries in "colonial" literature. Said addresses this briefly: Conrad was ahead of his time in that he recognized what was addressed as the European prototypical framing of "darkness" was reflexive; it "has an autonomy of its own and can reclaim what imperialism had taken for its own" (Said 1993, 30). For this reason, Conrad stands as an important example of literature driven by a critical sociological imagination. He even anticipates the delicate nature of the "social construction" of society—that fragile balance between perception and reality. Conrad is able to anticipate that very "fracture" that Lukács and others frame as the key to the sociological novel. According to Said, "if Conrad can show that all human activity depends on controlling a radically unstable reality to which words approximate only by will or convention, the same is true of empire, of venerating the idea" (Said 1993, 29). "The idea" which redeems everything is just that—a socially constructed convention. The very "chains" that man finds himself in, according to Rousseau. The world is then, "made and unmade" (Said 1993, 29). Everything is unstable—today's police brutality is then the same as the "brutish savage."

Conrad's contemporaries who lacked that reflexivity glorified and celebrated the achievements of colonialism. Conrad was prescient here in relaying a new literary technique, perhaps anticipating the modern turn in literature. Orr addresses it as "tragic realism/tragic irony." Another way of accounting for this form of literary realism is as Conrad's voice providing an aperture to the sociological imagination. *Heart of Darkness* in an exercise of the reflexive epic novel within the dissonance between the hype/reality of a broken system of emerging colonialism.

Heart of Darkness also anticipates the departure into the modern anti-hero, in Kurtz. Adorno's interpretation of Lukács renders modernism emerging as the breaking of ontology: the modern antihero is "asocial, solitary, and ontologically incapable of entering into relationships with other human beings" (Adorno et al. 2007, 158). In the tense "dialogue" between Adorno and Lukács there is a general conversation about holism versus fragmentation, and whether or not there was even a whole to be broken. Lukács protested the irrationalist element in modernism but was wholly insensitive to its positive disruptive moment; Adorno had disdain for Soviet optimism (Adorno et al. 2007, 149). What is interesting about Conrad is that he articulates, within the projected conversations between Marlow and Kurtz, both sides of this response to modernity.

Another interpretation of colonialist categories is that Kurtz is "*conquistador and guerillero* rolled into one" (Orr 1977, 113). And further, Conrad's writing predicted these dialogical tendencies, but through the lens of a pathetic character, Verloc, within *The Secret Agent*. As Phillips in *The Guardian* observes, "Oddly at the same period war and genocide all seem to be eerily prefigured by Conrad, and Heart of Darkness abounds with passages that seem terrifyingly contemporary in their descriptive accuracy" (Phillips 2003). *Heart of Darkness* is a literary harbinger . . . life then imitated this *Heart of Darkness* as history moved forward within the twentieth to twenty-first century, where imperialism and nationalism reverted back into Europe itself in the two World Wars, and the Cold War. Today, Conrad might mention the legacies of imperialism in the instabilities of regions of Afghanistan, Libya, Iraq, Rwanda, Democratic Republic of Congo, and so on, whose colonialist interests' and haphazard borders' effects still linger today. Applying also, a technique of what Naomi Klein (2008) has named "shock doctrine capitalism," developing nations are introduced to neo-liberal capitalism as an anesthesia to colonial violence: shop so you don't "drop." Neo-liberal ideologies of democracy-qua-capitalism save the day only after Western military powers unleashed a newer, vicious campaign of violence. "Enter now terrorism and barbarism" (Said 1993, 27) and the relativism of history's freedom fighter becomes terrorist: Osama Bin laden for example, as Eqbal Ahmad (in Barash 2018) has described. Just to mention a few recent examples: Operation Iraqi Freedom/ Operation New Dawn, Operation Enduring Freedom, and the authoritarian aftermath of the Arab Spring, for three twenty-first-century examples of the importation of "democracy"—from both above, with bombs, and below with selective grassroots mobilization Democracy and freedom, "hype," have become the new force of imperialism and colonialism. As Achille Mbembe describes the lingering effects of colonialism and, and its concomitant spread of "democratic peace":

> Colonial warfare is not subject to legal and institutional rules. It is not a legally codified activity. Instead, colonial terror constantly intertwines with colonially generated fantasies of wilderness and death and fictions to create the effect of the real. Peace is not necessarily the natural outcome of a colonial war. In fact, the distinction between war and peace does not avail. Colonial wars are conceived of as the expression of an absolute hostility that sets the conqueror against an absolute enemy. . . . Here, the fiction of a distinction between "the ends of war" and the "means of war" collapses; so does the fiction that war functions as a rule-governed contest, as opposed to pure slaughter without risk or instrumental justification. (Mbembe 2003, 25)

Again, when the hype speaks through the words "Freedom" as hypnotically distracting, the brute reality reveals colonial interests, as colonial influences of the *Heart of Darkness* are projected into the twenty-first century, as a "wilderness" and death reflect important archetypes, with an added sense of awareness of the real and the suspension of the categories of civilized/uncivilized.

Colonialism operates as a pathological function within the text of *Heart of Darkness,* according to Lorenzo Servitje (2016). European colonials were seen as the source of what Servitje notes, "coloniopathy: the physical sickness in the Congolese is caused by colonialism," and contributing to the fog of morality of colonial violence is the fog of disease (2016, 132). "Illness in the Africans both demonstrates the pathogenic effects of colonialism and reflects Western notions of Africa as an unwholesome environment. Even while Conrad critiques the morbid effects of empire, he is unable to avoid using its tropes, such as primitivism" (Servitje 2016, 132). This is a strength for praising Conrad's display of critical sociological insight, even though he represents the point of view of a "racist" perception within identity politics in the opinion of today's discussions within literary reception and theory. Even Said acknowledges that the historicity of the text (and Conrad's personal history of being a Polish expatriate should be respected, wherein it represents the very method of ethnographically embedding the story about colonialism within colonial value systems. This gives the text a narrative authenticity within modern, albeit tragic sense, of realism.

MODERNISM

Conrad may be called a "literary modernist" (Giffin 2013)—an extension of Naturalism, Romanticism, and Realism, however suggesting, alongside Giffin that *Heart of Darkness* has a pivotal role in transforming the reflective sense of modernism. *Heart of Darkness'* sociological imagination, "into a twentieth-century modernist artifact challenges received notions of reality" (Spittles in Giffin 2013). The discomfort that Marlow exhibits hints at a psychological turn in the novel, noted by Lukács, which expresses a level of theoretical "metanoia." Marlow represents a self-reflective critique about global capitalism, and an especially "problematic/unhappy consciousness" in the example from Marlow of Francis Ford Coppola's *Apocalypse Now*. This presents a conscious turn toward the reflective/inner monologue of, for Conrad, a sociologically informed conscience, beginning with the awareness that brutality in Africa makes "European civilization" possible. The "wisdom" suggested by the Lotus/Buddha position of Marlow suggests a psychospiritual transformation.

CONRAD'S USE OF THEORY AS SOCIOLOGICAL METANOIA

What is the nature of sociological inquiry via the novel? Reflecting on one's social context, social roots, is an expression of the sociological imagination (via a later contribution of C. Wright Mills). What is unique about Conrad is the level in which his subject is located in sociological dynamics. Conrad uses Marxian theories of ideology, and metaphoric language to describe the way in which only "surface truths" of those residents of "civilization" are able to be stomached. Without direct reference to the early texts of Karl Marx, Conrad employs theories of historical materialism, false consciousness, ideology, and base-superstructure (Williams 1977). Those who live in those "sepulchral cities" of Europe, are reflexively critiqued by Conrad, wherein they reflect the essential elements of "bourgeois consciousness" and as Marx put it in *The Eighteenth Brumaire*, "a whole superstructure is reared . . . peculiarly shaped feelings, illusions, habits of thought and perceptions of life" (quoted in Williams 1977, 76).

The concepts of truth vs. ideology are a running theme throughout *Heart of Darkness*. The latent theoretical worldviews of the nineteenth century's "everyman" (at least according to philosophical discourse)—expressed in the agon between a fading Christianity and the ideas emerging characterizations of the human impulse for selfishness and survival of Darwin and Nietzsche—are presented in the inner monologue of Marlow, and dialogues of the characters. But as in a therapeutic confessional mode, as soon as these thoughts appear on the page, the absurdity becomes apparent. Embedded in these statements, and exposing them, are also latent critiques of these expressions of "will-to-power," the relativism of a genealogy of morality, and the survival of the fittest "for a few francs," "exploitation of those with flatter noses," and so forth.

The question up for critical debate here is whether Conrad receives or critiques this philosophical idiom—mainly the Cartesian-Darwinian-Nietzschean-Freudian matrix of "Western" civilization. Or does Conrad in a kind of naivete embrace the Rousseau-like element of primitivism in the fact that Kurtz "goes native" and is absorbed into the land with a raw human nature and rudimentary souls (Achebe 1977, 341)? Conrad's philosophical conditioning and "anthropology" presents "man" in the character of the old Platonist splits: mind/body; reason/feeling; ego/id; conscious/unconscious (Giffin 2013). Najder (1976) presents the case for Conrad's core contribution to the sociopolitical philosophies of the late nineteenth century. The concepts of "man and society" emerge as a new theme, in the context of literature at the dawn of sociological theory. Conrad was labeled a "conservative" in the 1930s by the likes of Irving Howe and others (Najder 1976), placing him within the traditions of Burkean thought. Discussing Conrad's response to Rousseau's *The Confessions,* Najder presents this summary of Rousseau, via Conrad's interpretation:

> Rousseau boils down to this: I am unlike anybody else and therefore I should be judged by special standards; I am well-intentioned and sensitive, therefore I cannot do evil. Any account of the moral principles advocated by Conrad must include the exact opposite of Rousseau's position, and the moral stance of many Conradian heroes represents the antithesis of Rousseau's peculiar "great moral lesson"; "to avoid those situations of life which bring our duties into conflict with our interests." This, Conrad would say, is stark moral cowardice. (Najder 1976, 79–80)

This suggests that the novel is either an artifice or a reflection of a critical framework of consciousness. Like the main idea of a dramaturgical self, borrowing themes from Mikhail Bakhtin and Charles Horton Cooley, the author reflects creates a world unto "himself." The role of confession here is in tension with Rousseau's sense, and may revert back to a Catholic trope, shaped by Conrad's Polish upbringing. But the ironic thing is that the "confession" of Kurtz is not exculpatory, but rather self-indulgent. It is almost as if Kurtz is a mockery of Rousseau and the narcissistic inflections of self-absorption and indulgence. "Conrad's ethic of fidelity and constraint, of duty, honour, and human solidarity, was directly opposed to that of Rousseau, and was rooted in a fundamentally different concept of human nature" (Najder 1976, 81). Humans are free insofar as they live within the conventions of society—a direct contrast to the inheritance of Rousseau's stripping away of the "chains" of conventions. In the idea of the "unsettled settlement" (See Williams 1977, 176) Kurtz's compound presents a literary social experiment in the "unbound" lack of conventions. When stripped away from norms, restraint becomes superfluous. But that is not the moral of the story—it is rather that to live in society is to be within the realm of norms—though capitalism and imperialism expose their hypocritical nature.

If Conrad was a moralist; a conservative in that sense of the word, it certainly did not extend to modern day equivalent with the defense of capitalism. To expand on Najder's mention of Aristotle's observation, "man outside society is either god or beast, Conrad adds in Heart of Darkness that a man who wishes to be a god becomes inevitably a beast. Kind emotions and good intentions have a limited ethical value" (1976, 82). This is on par with some of Conrad's contemporaneous philosophical and sociological observations, from especially the early works of Karl Marx, on how the pursuit of Capital presents the "god—or idol—of modernization" (Fromm 2004). However, Conrad pierces the soft underbelly of the paradox of nineteenth-century socialism as it points to its inheritance from Rousseau. Namely in a literary drama about license, liberty—the suspension of norms in the pursuit of capital—Conrad exposes the contradiction between individual liberty and the social glues of norms, values, and cultures. This is what Catholic Social Thought harmonized in the writing of *Rerum Novarum* (Pope Leo XIII, 1895). For Rousseau society is simply the sum of human wills, in the "general will"—but Rousseau misses the "before" experiential aspect of what Durkheim noted in society as "sui generis." Society is not merely emergent from the sum of wills; it exists in a kind of rootedness in those very conventions that Rousseau saw as "chains." If we were without customs and conventions, we would be without rootedness or a common life to begin with, including the elements of language, a necessity for the articulation of that very general will—so essential to collective life. Conrad may have been conservative in that he rejects the embrace of the "intemperate" revolutionary complete overhaul of the cultural layers of society in an embrace of the "new." But he certainly brings to the table a critique of capitalism, property, and commerce in "an attitude as scornful as a revolutionary" (Najder 1976, 87). The logics of Capital and material interests, locally and globally, have disastrous and unethical effects. Conrad's politics should be recovered from the said "conservative label" wherein he passionately rejected autocracy and authoritarianism as contrary to all that he valued most in man" (Najder 1976, 89). However, he was critical of democracy for its atomistic implications and material interests.

The entryway into the criticism of capitalism is for Conrad not the social system and structures of Marx, but however, that very atomistic principle introduced by the modern psyche in capitalism. This comes from the stripping away of responsibilities and restraints—so in this regard, Conrad does embrace a semi-traditionalist understanding of the way in which conventions prevent self-interest. But it is also present within the terms of organic solidarity/mechanical solidarity and implied in the more (cultural) socialism of Durkheim.

METANOIA AND CRITICAL REFLEXIVITY

The balance between on the one hand, an atomized selfishness and the other hand, social altruism and solidarity, requires inner conversations and the engagement of conscience. The type of dialogical "inner conversations" that exist on the level of the fiction of Dostoevsky (Wiley 2016) are somewhat muted and transferred into the creation of a dramatized, theatrical world of strong symbols within the Kurtz compound. Is it fantastical, or a vivid confession of the realities of capitalism? With a sociological lens, one could refer to the observations of Geertz on the "construction" of and the narrative structure, and the device of time ellipsis and framing, as parallel to the way an ethnography explores layers of truth and meaning—interpretation always has a frame, and endless mechanisms of reinterpretations. Geertz's (2000) metaphor for this is, turtles on the backs of turtles, on the backs of turtles *ad infinitum*.

However, Conrad's is a critical imagination that goes further than just "spinning a sailor's yarn." As with the works of his contemporary and counterpart in "domestic" British literature, Thomas Hardy, there is a subtle level of critique, and an emerging progressive (or at least critical) vision in Conrad's *Heart of Darkness*—this is in naming, and realizing "the horror" of Western civilization. It is a moment of grounded, this-worldly sociological metanoia—whether or not it results in otherworldly soteriological realities deserves another mode of inquiry. But it presents the possibility of a seeing things, *as they are, and engaging in a critique of them.*

Heart of Darkness could be read as an introspection and confession of Western imperialism: a dark Augustinian reflection of the brutality of the Western heart which says, "Exterminate all the brutes!" The lengthy passage that begins with Kurtz's directive from the "International Society for the Suppression of Savage Customs" and ends with the "extermination" mandate reflects the hypocrisy of discourse in the Western context. "Western civilization—what a nice idea" was Mohandas Gandhi's famous quip. The desire to bring love, truth, beauty, "civilization" to the "Dark continent" reveals the barbarism even more dark, evil and savage than that of the "Dark continent." The implications of Conrad's observations spin off into global capitalism's integral crises today—everything from a constant war on "terror," to environmental crises/conflicts over resources, to the issues faced in the COVID-19 pandemic (Thorpe 2016, 132). As Jasanoff states so succinctly, "The issue for Conrad wasn't that 'savages' were inhuman. It was that any human could be a savage" (Jasanoff 2017, 225). As Mark Twain observed the perversity of white consciousness, "There are many humorous things in the world . . . among them the white man's notion that he is less savage than the other savages of the world" (Quirk 2007, 225). White consciousness has convinced itself that it is not savage, but Conrad, while acknowledging the belief itself, undermines it by exposing white savagery.

Is Edward Said's labeling Conrad as a typical "closet imperialist" fair, or do we read this story on the level of tragic realism and metaphor? Is it a warning or a description? Is it even fair to Said's and Achebe's discussion to include *Heart of Darkness* in the canon today? Reading *Heart of Darkness* today may be the sunlight of Western civilization's coming to terms with its own Jungian shadow-self. The Thames, a seat of European imperialism, was the once (in Roman times), and then again, the truly dark river of the world. And perhaps today the Thames is now the Potomac. Do we long for something lost in the construction of civilization, or was it ever there in the first place?

Giffin, quoting Erdinast-Vulcan, connects these elements to the concepts of virtue in Mikhail Bakhtin and Alasdair MacIntyre: "Conrad was by his own fidelity to a lost cause, impelled to formulate an alternative code of ethics in a world where virtue has disappeared." The birth of the "modern" may begin with this 1899 publication. Conrad's innovative method both elucidates and obfuscates the exploitations of "savages" by the true savages—the hypocrites of civilization. Franco Moretti highlights this turning point, also shared (a bit later) by Mann, Kafka, and Joyce—"all writing stories about *Bildung* [formation] where it does not occur—where objective culture, institutions and conventions, wounds individuals" and does not help construct a "better" world (Moretti 1996). The whole has perforations.

Lukács deals with this "disappearance" of a whole in modern literature. Bridging with a discussion of (an assumed) holism of literature in the ancient, modern literature parallels the movement of Greek: from the Homeric epic, to the tragedies of Sophocles, to the emergence of the Socratic/philosophical. Moving to the contemporary, modernity's broken, tragic *weltanschauung,* the "closed totality" has disappeared and been inverted into alienated, fractured life. In the ancient world, then, the "journey" is from epic to tragedy to philosophy. But this is also a journey of the "European self"—a Jungian-like shadow self runs as a current theme through the course of the river of history . . . as Jasanoff uses the metaphor (2017, 237), "the Thames" reminds the reader that it was once like the Congo.

The parallel journey is reflected in key moments for Marlow, and the result is the alienation and tragic: the homelessness of the *Nellie*, the discomfort of Marlow, the tragedy of Kurtz, his sickness as reflecting the sickness of the entire enterprise of society as a whole—his "only health is his disease" (Eliot 1943)—and ultimately Marlow's Buddha-wisdom (the emergence of the philosophical solution in an "alternative" non-Western Culture).

CONRAD AND THE SOCIOLOGICAL METHOD

Conrad may be an ethnographer (storyteller) who engages metaphysics—on the other hand he is an author who appears at the historical *end* of metaphysics (within philosophical discourse). Is it not mere coincidence that sociological and ethnographic analysis begins to emerge at this time, especially with the publication of Durkheim's *Elementary Forms of Religious Life* (1912), an armchair examination of another "dark place" of the world? What can a reflexive reading of Conrad reveal for sociology today—in both reading it and employing its vein of moral hermeneutic? Like Durkheim's study of the "primitive" religious impulse refracts back on religion's function in more modernized contexts, Conrad's storytelling of Africa points to the darkness of the European heart. One can connect today's research in social science professions. Are ethnographers and sociological storytellers today "journalists" or "rhetoricians" or something in-between? This story may just be a "seaman's yarn" (Watt 1976). There may be little distinction here between "knitting a story" and science—would this make ethnographers closer to Platonist theorists, or even in the storytelling realm, the holism/organicism of the Homeric epic? What are the gaps between the artistic imagination and scientific method of the storytelling enterprise?

Connected to this question of "objective journalism" in tension with the "literary imagination" the critical theory of aesthetic walks a tightrope. Art is not a mirror to reflect reality but a hammer in which to shape it—in the formula of Brecht. But this "reflects" a modern sentiment, post-Conrad. Conrad stands in between these two points. Artistic creations are both in tension with but products of the worldview out of which they are borne. Broken-modernity is in this sense a redundant statement: the artistic expression of Conrad's broken narratives between Africa and the so-called sleeping "sepulchral" city illustrates the disjointed gap between different peoples' appreciation for "truth" in "modern capitalism": the colonized and the colonizers. This dichotomy is especially evident in the distinction between the worldliness of Kurtz's African mistress and the naïveté of his European "intended," or fiancée. This presents the two levels of consciousness: reality and hype. One reading of the reflective historical-sociological consciousness in Marlow, plays out in contrast to his observation that the rest of the world is unaware/asleep. Marlow has a sense of annoyance and disenchantment (alienation) surrounding their lack of awareness of the "reality"—so in some sense this is the *unhappy consciousness* of the "enlightened but burdened" sociological imagination. But the work of "civilized" society is to prop up the "lie": and white women are the epitome of civilization in this regard. As Freedman explains, quoting the conclusion of the novella, "Women are out of it—should be out of it. We must help them to stay in that beautiful world of their own, lest ours gets worse. Oh, she had to be out of it" (Conrad, in Freedman 2014, 40). Freedman notes a progression:

> the slippage from the declarative ("are out of it") to the judgmental ("should be out of it") to the self-serving ground of that judgment (we must help them stay out of it for our own sake) to the climactic imperative ("had to be out of it"). The sequence reveals not only the source of Marlow's insistence on woman's exclusion from the truth, but also an important cause of truth's banishment from much of Conrad's work. The simple absence of knowledge gives way to the subjectively grounded desirability of such ignorance and in turn to an insistence on its urgency. (Freedman 2014, 40)

Will-to-power runs alongside "will-to-ignorance": society must be propped up by the lie, though it is in no way noble; but a sloppy necessity. But the truth will out—whether in its manifestation in privileged neurosis or outright revolution from the "margins." The "civilized" will be seen as "primitive." From a sociological point of view, ideology distracts society from knowledge of its own brutality, passion, and desire. "The nearer one comes to the heart of darkness, the instinctual self that, libidinous, passionate, and uncontrolled, responds unresistingly to the seductive whispers of the savage wilderness it consorts with, the more one welcomes the surface as a refuge from these depths" (Freedman 2014, 60).

"UNSETTLED DISORIENTATION"

This dis-ease with the colonial project is hinted at by Edward Said. The voice of Marlow is hesitant and reflective, "unsettling the reader" in a fragile world dominated by capitalism that is essentially a social construction being "made and unmade" on the burdens of exploitation of those in resource-rich colonies (Said [1993], 428). Michael Valdez Moses (2007) describes this unsettled, "enlightened-but-burdened" imagination as "disorientalism." The power of the use of metaphorical descriptions and settings like the experience and the purposeful use of hazy and obfuscating language: "fog," "vertigo," "dreamlike," "nowhere," "inscrutable." As Conrad (via Marlow) comes to grips with the moral ambiguities of colonialism the descriptive language is conveying a sense of *disorientation*. Here is where, as Moretti (1996) describes it, a sociology of literature must dance between the literary form and the "world" conceived by and informing the writer. The form itself conveys a sociological message: the broken and foggy images reflect the moral clouds of the ambivalences and hypocrisies of colonialism. The method of metaphors and stylistic delivery relay the conflation of these different emotional and ethical swamps of meaning. It is also a literary metonymy for the power of ideology as distraction and obfuscation (Freedman 2014, 39). Like the "haze" of the opium of cultural forms of distraction. What this fog/haze represents is the tension between reality, and a false social construction. There is a broken ethic within the story—as Moses describes (2007, 6), presenting a key moment in the dawn of modern literature. In Moses' parsing the "Thames and the Congo form a continuous waterway" (2007, 67) just as there is a literary link between the disjointed narrative voices in Conrad's novels, postmodernism, and postcolonial literature. The postcolonial literary voices of the "periphery" and the fringes of empire "write back at" Conrad, as a result of Conrad's metanoia-like reflexivity and questioning (Moses 2007, 61, 67).

Another key use of the metaphor here is the "suspension of the real" in liminality and fog. This is a time and place "set apart" so that the reflexive conversation might be isolated from "living in the quotidian." To consider the context of the ship, the *Nellie*—like the *Pequod* of *Moby Dick*—the sea offers the sailor a moment of liminality, betwixt and between civilization and the savage, in the "unmapped" places of the world, across and aligned with borders. As Conrad biographer Maya Jasanoff stated, "on a ship you're in motion without moving . . . you're never alone, you're always isolated" (Jasanoff 2017, 90–91). Isolation and reflection are important in both the place of conscience and the ethnographic space. As the ethnographer engages in "storytelling," Conrad's novels describe people in strange and faraway places as "un" or "de-civilized." Conrad himself stated in *Almayer's Folly* (cited in Potter, 1943):

> The critic and the judge seem to think that in those distant lands all joy is a yell and a war-dance, all pathos is a howl and a ghastly grin of filed teeth, and that the solution of all problems is found in the barrel of a revolver or on the point of an assegai. And yet it is not so. . . . The picture of life, there as here, is drawn with the same elaboration of detail, colored with the same tints. Only in the cruel serenity of the sky, under the merciless brilliance of the sun, the dazzled eye misses the delicate detail, sees only the strong outlines, while the colours, in the steady light, seem crude and without shadow. Nevertheless, it is the same picture. (Conrad, in Potter 1943, 66)

The creative aspect of the "art" of the ethnographer is similar to the novelist . . . in that they deal with bringing "darkness into consciousness" (Potter 1943). *Heart of Darkness* is then a fictional projection on the act of storytelling, or commentary on commentating. In an essay on Henry James, Conrad comments:

> This creative art of a writer of fiction may be compared to rescue work carried out in darkness against cross gusts of wind swaying the action of a great multitude. It is rescue work, this snatching of vanishing phases of turbulence, disguised in fair words, out of the native obscurity into a light where the struggling forms may be seen, seized upon, endowed with the only possible form of permanence in this world of relative values the permanence of memory. And the multitude feels it obscurely, too; since the demand of the individual to the artist is, in effect, the cry, "Take me out of myself" meaning really, but of my perishable activity into the light of imperishable conscious-ness. (Potter 1943, 53)

Could this also be compared to the meaning of the dramaturgy of theory, of its "clarifying spectacle," displaying higher order concepts of theory as theoria? Novels are inscriptions, codes, and forms creating a reality—much as theory brings certain forms and tendencies into focus. Novels are also mappings of social realms. As the knight sings in Wagner's *Parsifal* "time here turns into space"—or even the domination through ordering of *place into space*. Space is significant in that it is grounded in the experience of geography of "ordering" a sacred/set apart or unknown mystical place "not an inert container, not a box where cultural history 'happens' but is an active force" (Moretti 1999, 3). Franco Moretti discusses how cartography is a kind of domination—and method—of the novel's inscribing of "blank spaces" or places of the earth. To name a place is to situate it within ordered space through language. Metaphor and geography are mutually reinforcing here: they "express the unknown we must face, and yet also *contain it*" (Moretti 1999, 47). Said makes this point as well: "Conrad's point is that like narrative, imperialism has monopolized the system of representation" ([1993], 425). "Africa" as a concept engages a kind of colonial romance between the force of masculine light, truth, civilization, and the feminine, the association with the Garden of Eden's metaphors and symbols, an unknown prelinguistic darkness: "the snake had charmed me" (Conrad 2006, 8; Moretti 1999, 58–59). The Congo stands as a "mighty big river . . . a snake uncoiled." Moretti reflects upon the "linearity" of the journey of the Nellie into the *Heart of Darkness*. One reading here is that it is a narrative of descent—the boat presses on into the chaotic realm of brutality—but does the darkness take over Kurtz or is Marlow's reflection a metanoia or call to conscience in recognizing a common humanity/animality within the European? Is there a touch of cynicism and critique in Conrad? As with Dostoyevsky, the novelist appears as a vehicle for the liminal zone of participation in and critique of society. Perhaps inheriting an Eastern/Russo worldview here, Conrad is both dubious of, while engaged in, the "project" of Western civilization. This is a common theme in the Russian school of novel-writing: "Western ideas embody the cynicism of modernity but also its greatness" (Moretti 1999, 32). Where in Dostoyevsky the individual characters—Ivan Karamazov, Raskolnikov—are "great" because they are divided within their own psyche, representing the "split" or "fracture" within modernity between past (tradition) and future (freedom), in Conrad the split is between the Doppelgänger pairing of Kurtz/Marlow. The reader can see the "Western" self as reflected in either tendency—toward force/domination in Kurtz, or the power of reflective, contemplative consciousness and awareness as Marlow (albeit sitting in an *Eastern* metaphor—a Buddha position).

Adam Hochschild's "new" classic on the history of Belgian colonial presence in Africa, *King Leopold's Ghost,* presents the theory that the character Kurtz is an amalgam of actual historical figures Josef Teodor Konrad Korzeniowski (birthname of Joseph Conrad) encountered in his journey into the Congo, beginning in early 1890. Conrad had every hope in King Leopold's intention, in the nineteenth century's cultural understanding, to "bring light of civilization to the 'Dark' continent." But according to Hochschild, what Conrad viewed so horrified him that his "view of human nature was permanently changed" (Hochschild 1998, 141–142).

The framing and writing of history is like creating a map. The play between present and past creates an ambiguous moment where history is interpreted through the present moment of the weighing of choices, of individuals looming large and small in the course of history. "No history can possibly relate the past as it really was because our histories will always be influenced by our present perspective. Furthermore, histories are written in language; the rhetoric the historian adopts shapes and determines his representation of the past" (Thomas Brook, in Niland 2005, 172). For the individual character of Marlow in *Heart of Darkness,* this moment, a metanoia, also presents an example of Conrad's use of sociological imagination. Presented with the puncturing of the illusion of civilization: reflexivity is born. Kurtz-Marlow is the ultimate Doppelganger: one embedded in the horror and one reflexively making an account of it all. Kurtz: perhaps a synthesis of Edmund Barttelot (an associate of Stanley, who went "mad with brutality," and eventually murdered), Arthur Hodister (a Belgian with a famed African harem), Georges Antoine Klein (an ivory-trader agent), and Leon Rom (a swashbuckling head of *le Force Publique* with a collection of African heads) (Hochschild 1998, 144–145). Kurtz is a Jungian amalgam of "Western civilization": both a butcher and an artist. Are global solidarity and revolution the antidote to poisons of capitalist civilization?

CONRAD THE IMMIGRANT

There is a moralizing diptych: a natural pairing of *Heart of Darkness'* narrative about the exploitative nature of global capitalism with that of Conrad's fictional exploration of the radical sociological and political theories of his time in *The Secret Agent.* They are point and counterpoint. Conrad had a disdain for the "hard absolute optimism of the revolutionary spirit" (Jasanoff 2017, 52). The "sea" for a transient immigrant, stateless person, offers a Romantic opening—the unchartered places have an allure. But these dreams turned into nightmare for Conrad the person. Edward Said acknowledges Conrad's morally imbued anxious self-consciousness as the once "Polish ex-patriate" turned (reluctant) employee of the imperial system (Said [1993], 424, 427). The darkness of London—the darkness of civilization—was exposed as much as the seafarer wishes to escape the very boredom of the quotidian. Jasanoff notes that after this African sea/Congo journey, Conrad attempted suicide in Marseille—perhaps he was suffering from post-traumatic stress, having witnessed the "darkness," the reckless brutality of those who are sent to tame the brutes.

Heart of Darkness and *The Secret Agent* suggest both capitalism and its alternative create such strong points of ironic entryway into the hypocrisies of Western Civilization. *The Secret Agent* defused anarchism and radical political philosophies by reflecting it within a family soap opera—not unlike the tragedies of the ancient Greeks—but it hides a deeper, political statement about the vacuity of political idealism. It is a commentary on growing up out of fading radical dreams (Orr 1977, 102–103). *Heart of Darkness* was really about the darkness of Europeans, rather than the "Dark continent." In *The Secret Agent,* anarchism delivered "more punchline than punch" (Jasanoff

2017, 80). The tragedy of anarchism, "lies in its complacent betrayal of the anonymous and desolate who have no voice to express their suffering" (Orr 1977, 104)—thus Verloc's brother-in-law Stevie is a casualty. These two extreme ideologies form a philosophical-literary diptych with a potent moral lesson: (1) When we pursue the taming of others for capital conquest, we unleash the brutes in ourselves. (2) When we seek to change the world, we destroy those who are nearest and dearest to us. Both capitalist civilizer and revolutionary anarchist are hypocritical shams. Conrad rejected the "dream world" of utopic imaginings. He embraced anomie, at least as a kind of literary ambiance (Orr 1977, 103).

Conrad was a depressive, once suicidal, but finally settled into a semi-contented home/marriage later in life. Throughout his work, his characters and contexts were a window into a person who, parallel to his life, rejected any "pretenses" of the imaginary land of the elite salon-discourse of idealism. Hypocrisy and disillusionment are the moral backdrop of such "idealists" in modern life. Jasanoff accounts for an exchange of a common parlor game of "confession-questionnaire"—"What would be your dream of happiness?" to which, Conrad replied, "Never dream of it; want reality" (Jasanoff 2017, 157). This is a great contrast to the famous documented parlor game entry of Karl Marx's *Confession*—"doubt everything" "my idea of happiness=to fight." The realism inherent as an awareness of the givenness of the world—versus the radical's rejection of it—is what characterizes Conrad's *worldview*. In some ways Conrad's fiction is a more "objective" and balanced interpretation than the radical's projected and sometimes clumsy misapprehensions about the possible negative consequences of a utopia. Conrad's writings are a commentary on the very idealism present within the Western mind. Had he lived later into the twentieth century, he might have rejected both "catastrophes" of socialism and capitalism as equally "barbaric," as described by French Christian phenomenologist Michel Henry. Conrad's skepticism about ideological solutions presents a kind of fatalism—the individual and their single acts of virtue and justice were more important than any movement of liberation (Jasanoff 2017, 286). There is hypocrisy in idealism. T.S. Eliot expressed this in the poem "The Hollow Men": the civilized are really empty (a phrase lifted from *Heart of Darkness*), "behaving as the wind behaves" (1925)—"Between the idea, And the reality. . . . Falls the Shadow." The shadow of darkness suggests the juxtapositions of violence and civility—mysterious as the human heart. Or perhaps this reveals the powerful hypocrisy of the intentionality of how famously, in the text of *Heart of Darkness* "the suppression of savage customs" comes through "extermination of all the brutes." Thus, the paradox of "global interconnection and manifest division" is felt even today (Jasanoff 2017, 285). The sociological vision of Conrad is a description of how the individual is caught up in social forces—expressed contextually as tragic, divine, and universal forces, as described by H.L. Mencken (Jasanoff 2017, 307).

Learning from his father, Apollo, Konrad the stateless person, immigrant, refugee, could find the best places for political and social expression in the poetic imagination. His advice to his son was, "If you had no power in politics, you could use the power of poems" (Jasanoff 2017, 21). Fiction is both a product of history, but it is also more than that—it is an emotional and cultural rendering of reality of an imagined critical projection. It is driven by the imaginative, yes, but also empathy and Weberian-*verstehen*. Conrad argued that fiction "stands on firmer ground, being based on the reality of forms and the observation of social phenomena . . . whereas history is based on second-hand impression of documents" (Jasanoff 2017, 11).

CONCLUSION: SOCIOLOGY MEETS THE POETIC

Conrad's father, Apollo, liked the saying, *"ubi crux, ibi poesia"*—where there's a cross there's poetry (Jasanoff 2017, 18). The sufferings of those on the margins—not always well-represented in their interests by some of the hypocrisies of the radical philosophies surrounding them—find more transformative hope in the power of the artistic, provocative, subtle forms of dissent and challenges to the social order.

With the use of metaphoric language, *Heart of Darkness* paints an impressionist image in a way the theorists of his day could not quite render (Watt 1976, 37–38). Like Simmel's method of "impressionist theory" (Lepenies 1988, 240–241), Conrad's literary paintbrush, like Simmel's descriptive power of theory stressing the importance of the sociological eye, uses the delicate balance of Form and Life through hues of background, character interactions, and symbolic forms. The use of fog and obfuscation of the description of "Africa" renders the flip between impressionism and expressionism—the evocative emotional realities inwardly, in verbal form, from what for Conrad was a short-lived but traumatic experience in the Congo. The artistic need to create unity to overcome this trauma is fragmented. As Jameson describes this (in Adorno et al.), in the conversations between Bloch and Lukács there is a tension between unity and fragmentation. The "old" impressionistic artistic form would pull toward this unity of the social whole, but the unity was irreducibly *contradictory* (Adorno et al. 2007, 14). In *Heart of Darkness,* Conrad artistically paints this contradiction in the moral—and visual—fogs of imperialism.

Chapter Five

Women and Men

The Tragicomic

INTRODUCTION

The lingering theoretical problematics of the Classical Period still reverberate with today's social issues, especially regarding gender relations.[1] Some of the inspiration of the #MeToo movement may derive from feminist imaginings of utopia—popularized recently in films like *Wonder Woman* (2017). Roughly a century before the #MeToo movement, a feminist utopia was envisioned in the novel *Herland* (published serially between 1910–1916) by Charlotte Perkins Gilman. Gilman was a first-wave American feminist novelist and sociologist writing in the later portion of the Classical Period. Gilman's theory encompassed several key concepts including themes relating to: gender-identity, feminism and the sexuo-economic relation, family systems, sociality, evolutionary theory, and utopianism. The focus of this chapter is on her multivalent theory of androcentrism and its utopic critique via a society run by empowered women. This theory of androcentrism, and an evolutionary response to such an orientation, is embedded within the #MeToo movement. The major contribution to this theory of androcentrism comes from Gilman's book *The Man-made World, or Our Androcentric Culture* (1911). Chapter five here explores the eclipsing of the *Eternal Feminine* and its accompanying concept of androcentrism within the inchoate stages of sociological theory's critical appraisal of gender and sexual roles.

THE ETERNAL LIGHT, THE ETERNAL FEMININE

Taken from E.M. Forster's *Howards End*, a contemporaneous vision of the "eternal feminine" is important for contextualizing Gilman's *Herland:*

> He remembered his wife's even goodness during thirty years. Not anything in detail—not courtship or early raptures—but just the unvarying virtue, that seemed to him a woman's noblest quality. So many women are capricious, breaking into odd flaws of passion or frivolity. Not so his wife. Year after year, summer and winter, as bride and mother, she had been the same, he had always trusted her. Her tenderness! Her innocence! The wonderful innocence that was hers by the gift of God. Ruth knew no more of worldly wickedness and wisdom than did the flowers in her garden, or the grass in her field. Her idea of business—"Henry, why do people who have enough money try to get more money?" Her idea of politics—"I am sure that if the mothers of various nations could meet, there would be no more wars," Her idea of religion—ah, this had been a cloud, but a cloud that passed. She came of Quaker stock, and he and his family, formerly Dissenters, were now members of the Church of England. The rector's sermons had at first repelled her, and she had expressed a desire for "a more inward light," adding, "not so much for myself as for baby" (Charles). Inward light must have been granted, for he heard no complaints in later years. (Forster 1921, chapter X)

In post-Victorian English literature, there was a lingering (yet also semi-eclipsing) assumption on both sides of the Atlantic—even in the most utopian manifestations. This was mainly the characterization of an "inward light" as a feminine principle—untouched by the brashness of masculinity's dominance, power and spoils. This assumption carries across the Atlantic into the American novelist/sociologist Charlotte Perkins Gilman's depiction of a woman's utopia, Herland, a bright light whose hopes for civilization shone above the shadows of World War I's destruction. *Herland* (completed in 1916) portrays women in light of that "unvarying virtue" described above and renders an image of utopia as a society made only of women. *Herland* is a novel about American male explorers venturing into a land (Herland) governed and populated solely by women. It is a utopic imagining of a flourishing society without disease, conflict or war, and without men. Three male explorers discover this area—somewhere mysteriously in a tropical South American context—and attempt to carry through with "traditional" relationships with the women of Herland to (somewhat) tragi-comic effect. These three men are eventually expelled.

The implications of *Herland*'s "pacifism" through gynocracy reflect Forster's rendering of Ruth's proclamation in *Howards End*, "I am sure that if the mothers of various nations could meet, there would be no more wars." (One could only wish if the mothers ruled the world, war and conflict would actually cease. The Irish under the thumb of Margaret Thatcher might disagree.) Gilman's *Herland* is a fictional escape from the historical coincidence of World War. The root problem, then, extended in both examples from the quoted Forster passage, and Gilman's entire plot, is the problem of men (and the masculine). As Robert Sapolsky's (1997) discussion of the cultural assumptions about testosterone, violence, nationalism, and hormonal masculinity, and a long streak of feminist ideology asserts: masculinity= power=force=destruction of the "other." Yet Sapolsky challenges these naturalist assumptions as somewhat misguided and suggests an approach that might open up to the social construction of gendered outcomes and roles. This leads us to an analysis of the conceptual and cultural assumptions that led to the imagining of the utopia in the country of Herland.

In *The Man-Made World, or Our Androcentric Culture* (1911), Gilman defines key historical/evolutionary processes and theoretical schemas that operate in a male-dominated society. Her key thesis is a grand theory of the possibility of a common humanity lost to the particulars of reified categories of gendered identity—namely the overemphasized distinction between masculine/feminine (Gilman (1911), in Lengermann and Niebrugge-Brantley 1998, 144). This is the source of a kind of "original" sense of loss. An emphasis on masculinity, according to Gilman's systematic narrative of biology and history, brought about alienated consciousness and destruction. This is not unlike Marx's theory of capitalism, as Gilman's theory offers a root cause of social problems. Like Marx, for Gilman the solution is utopic. "Union, organization, complex interservice . . . is the joy and health of social life. . . . But so far as men combine in order to better combat; the mutual service held incidental to the common end of conquest and plunder" (Gilman (1911), in Lengermann and Niebrugge-Brantley 1998, 148). This solution is presented imaginatively within the gynocracy of the serial novel of *Herland*.

Lester Frank Ward, a correspondent and colleague of Gilman, reinforced Gilman's critique of androcentrism. Ward defined the concept of male "efflorescence"—projections of evolutionary categories of male superiority, and as Gilman (1911) notes this elevates the vices of competition and destruction (Lengermann and Niebrugge-Brantley 1998, 148). Andocracy was a function of not so much "natural" selection, but the misused power of male dominance (Bender 2010, 69). Ward supported Gilman's work and presented a scientific case for female superiority as a critical natural history.

Similarly, another contemporary of Gilman, Edgar Rice Burroughs "linked the primitive emergence of male superiority as the precursor to industrialization and colonialism" and noted that *Herland*'s setting "within tropical spaces" reflects the themes that "both contemporary domesticity and the industrial system had emerged from mishaps of evolution that had led to male primacy" (Bender 2010, 64). Both Burroughs's and Gilman's worldview, though consonant with a critical theory for the historical context, failed to engage a larger colonial and race-based critique. Their ideology was driven by the assumption that industrialization and development were the "gift of temperate races," lacking in an account for the way in which the difficult nature of "primitive" humans' labors constituted the blood, sweat, and tears of the foundation of "civilization's" structures (Bender 2010, 64). This is alluded to in the globalized contexts within the novels of Gilman's contemporary, Joseph Conrad (*Lord Jim, Heart of Darkness, Nostromo*). Further, as Daniel Bender rightly claims, their imperial frame provided a frightening historical context even as it claimed industry as the racial mark of the civilized and assigned women a pioneering place in the industrial progress (Bender 2010, 64).

From the genre of literary theory, Kim Johnson-Bogart observes that one element of a utopian strategy is the elimination of one side of a dichotomy, where the undesired element is the source of all the problems in the present state of existence (Johnson-Bogart 1992, 85–92). The mental constructs of utopia operate in such dichotomies—good/evil, light/dark, poverty/wealth, public/private, Christian/atheist, finally for Gilman—female/male. "Life for the male mind is a fight . . . there has never been a democracy . . . only an androcracy" (Gilman (1911), in Lengermann and Niebrugge-Brantley 1998, 146). On the one hand, there is an immense hopeful imagining of something different in gynocracy. But on the other hand, this mental process of elimination has a difficult time creating a healthy positive construction of a world—it is easier to critique and eliminate than to build. As Johnson-Bogart observes Herland's society knows "no war, no killing or other ship, disease, poverty, crying, but is 'a half-country'" (Johnson-Bogart 1992, 86).

GENDER AND CHARACTERS OF *HERLAND*

Upon arriving in Herland, we are presented with three (archetypal male) explorers—Van Dyck (an "innocent" and student of sociology), Terry (the brutishly, toxically masculine), and Jeff (the condescending "nice guy"). These men enter a "paradise" world geographically "lost" but somewhere in South America. And interestingly enough, we see, through the (female) author's perspective, a male narrative stream of consciousness inner dialogue between male expectation, and surprise at how well this society is run, by women even. Repeated throughout chapter two of the novel, the men articulate: "surely there must be men here somewhere." The assumption is that otherwise things would not be going so well. But as the character development unfolds, there is also a collective confession amongst the male characters that the paradise is thus because it is organized and constituted by women who violate traditional gender expectations and essentialisms. This is both surprising but also endearing to the men: these women are over forty years old *and* beautiful; they are beautiful, athletic intellectuals (Gilman 1998, 17–19). In other words, these women are not the usual nineteenth- to twentieth-century archetypal dichotomy of fishwives and beauty queens. This society that women built sustains ecological balance: they are also connected with nature—"civilized yet still arboreal" (Gilman 1998, 14). In one reading, this encourages ecofeminism, rejecting male categories of both objectification of the feminine and dominance over nature. Gilman suggests that there is a latent connection between masculinity, noise, industry, and here gives a vision of feminine development as driven by a kind of Gaia/earth mother principle—"no noise, no smoke. . . . Everything was beauty, order, cleanness, and a sense of home over it all" (Gilman 1998, 16). This sense of "home" or domesticity is different than the classic "separate spheres" thesis (Godwin and Risman 2001). Domesticity here has an organic characteristic (perhaps a *Gemeinschaft)* and is connected to nature and community, rather than the prison of the isolated household.

The male characters each fall in love with their complementary female archetypal characters—and of course conflict ensues, even violence. The way this violence is depicted is as an essentially male characteristic—foreign to the natives of Herland. And the ultimate results are the male element—violence, toxic masculinity, and its enablement—which first are quarantined, and then eliminated or expelled.

Another reading of *Herland* is possible. More subtly, Christensen sees *Herland* within the tradition of not a pastoral, feminine utopia, but a technological scientific dystopia (Christensen 2017). The elimination paradigm, along with population control and eugenics presents the feminine domination and environment; not a harmonious symbiosis with the "given" or "thrownness" reality of the human condition (of the paradoxes, tensions, complexities of elementary "particles" of existence within the messiness of real life outside of utopia, or the diversity principle of *Gesellschaft*). After all, Gilman had racist, nationalist, and eugenicist views—they present an elitist flavor to feminist thought, expressing the elevated bourgeois contours of early twentieth-century American white feminism/liberation movement.

SIGNIFICANCE OF UTOPIA

The origins of the "utopian novel" are suggested in Gilman's presentation of the narrative of the scientist/explorer (in the *dramatis personae* of "amateur" male scientists):

> More interesting is the way Gilman engages science and literature at a meta-critical level in setting up a sort of experiment in Émile Zola's sense . . . "provoked observation." The idea goes back to the origins of the novel, found nowhere more conspicuously than in *Robinson Crusoe*, in which Defoe embeds

experiment and observation in his narrative at multiple levels. With the island his laboratory and Crusoe his subject, he sets out to find out what might happen if you took a Puritan, middle-class merchant and stranded him on a desert island with a limited set of tools and supplies. Gilman does something similar in her thought experiment designed to "test" the range of female capability against contemporary gender stereotypes: If a geographically isolated group of women somehow managed to reproduce without men, what sort of civilization might result? (Christensen 2017, 288)

There is a quintessentially pragmatic, and probing, agenda to the "scientific" encounter with the "other"—"They knew just what to ask, and just what use to make of it" (Gilman 1998, 66). This approach to "science" is discussed by Christensen, in a gender-role deconstruction (Christensen 2017, 289). This element of pragmatism in the scientific utopia suggests an element of a rejection of frivolity—perhaps this is Gilman's rejection of a "projection" of male perceptions of "quasi-Victorian" feminine gender roles. The functionality of the society is interesting—it works like an intentional machine. Here, Gilman is rejecting bourgeois male assumptions about women: that they are creatures of adornment and dependence, enjoying only the trivialities and *rococo* of fashion, and the like. Additionally, Christensen highlights that the religion of Herland is rational, not emotional—one could think of a kind of Platonist/Aristotelian *"nous"*—but another dangerous element is lurking behind this over-rationalism. Poetry seems absent in Herland—is this the dark, dystopic side of functionalist basis for society (recalling the absence of poetry in Plato's *Republic*)? This, then, is not an overly genteel "feminine" utopia, but rather a rationalized mechanization of society via the claims and worldview of science.

What are the aims of *Herland*'s scientific utopia? It aims to progress toward the "improvement of the human condition, to render the universe comprehensible, and to provide a sense of order" (Christensen 2017, 288). There is an assumption that technical acumen and science can build the "perfect" society. Nature is dominated in order to improve upon it. The Herlanders aim to construct a perfect world: progress and improvement are implied here.

Why are the human sciences absent in the country of Herland? There is an elimination of the "masculinist" version of science via its power of domination: "genetics is applied not through the traditionally masculine values of hunting, competition, and individuality, but through the traditionally feminine values of nurturing and, more generally, creating an environment where no one will be hurt" (Christensen 2017, 290). Is this domination of nature—as opposed to harmonizing with nature? Science is compared to marital rape, by feminist philosophers of science like Sandra Harding, "forcing nature to 'man's' wishes" (Christensen 2017, 291). If nature is seen as exclusively feminine (and not masculine), is this not an objectification of humans and nature alike (not to mention gender roles)? This potentially reifies categories for nature, confessing the legacy of capitalism and the exploitation of nature/Mother Earth/Gaia as commodity (Badiner 1990). Gilman's utopia borrows categories from Francis Bacon, whose utopia is the colonialist harbinger of political geography. Bacon's utopia prefigures its economic counterpart in (one interpretation of) Adam Smith's individualist focus of division of labor, self-interest, and competition. Geography and anthropology are absent in Herland, presumably because they are unnecessary? Or is Gilman's presentation of the feminine reinforcing the reified sense of categorization, its primacy in the division between masculinity/femininity? Again, this reflects the gender roles echoed in the opening quotation from Forster's *Howards End:* the sense of the feminine as precisely *a-political*. Gilman's vision is "no less than the scientific management of all human labor, be it industrial, agricultural, or reproductive" (Bryson, in Christensen 2017, 289). Christiansen further argues that the famous Malthusian variables echoing his argument about overpopulation—"disease, hunger, and war—have all been eliminated in Herland, and given the geographic limitations, the population problem becomes all the greater. Gilman's solution, beyond that of cultivating the whole land like a garden, reveals the tendencies in the scientific utopia that would soon become bases for the modern dystopia," namely that of eugenics—control over nature ripples into control over humans (Christensen 2017, 296–297).

Whereas Karl Popper, in *The Open Society and its Enemies,* and others had described the effects of power in scientific utopias becoming the dictatorship of a sovereign or the scientific elite, the logic of domination in *Herland* is rendered in the voice of uniformity and conformity through the consensus of the population of its citizens (Christensen 2017, 297). However, one important principle of postmodern feminist political theory suggests a potential problem: what about dissent and nonconformity? Dissent and difference seem to be absorbed in Herland. To bridge to the contemporary situation, there is parallel movement here in a mode of contemporary discourse that drove the #MeToo movement, but hidden behind it is a level of utopic naiveté. This includes the assumptions that women will agree with each other, and with a kind, nurturing, mothering, and charitable character. This innocent assumption suggests that is *only* men who disagree, fight, wage war (recall the Forster quotation above). This assumption is very dangerous—alongside the expectation of the elimination of dissidence and disagreement. It also ignores the historical, psychoanalytic, cultural, and other roots of women's competition and hostility within their own female to female relationships (Chesler 2003).

CRITIQUE OF WHITE FEMINIST ISOLATIONISM

The hidden punchline of *Herland*, also driving Perkins Gilman's main theory in the sexuo-economic relationship, is that "meaning resides neither in a term nor its opposite, but in the relation between the two. Though the world is filled with men and women, for Gilman their meaning lies in their humanity, the term of which both are a part and through which both relate to and are included in one another" (Johnson-Bogart 1992, 86). As the famous joke goes, "Nobody will win the battle of the sexes. There's too much fraternizing with the enemy."

There is a bridge from *Herland* to the discussion of #MeToo—evidence of this can be found in an essay by Nora Caplan-Bricker, "Leaving Herland." She notes the ambivalence felt with both the thrill of a kind of utopic and revolutionary liberation within the call to "end sexual harassment" and the simultaneous hesitation about the construction of utopic binaries:

> But even after I overcame my instinct for detachment, I remained wary of the movement's language, which was a language of binaries: *women* and *men*. I resisted the pressure I felt, from nowhere and everywhere, to think of myself at all times in terms of *womanhood*; to espouse a solidarity both too narrow and too broad; to foreground my gender. (Caplan-Bricker 2018)

Gender is potentially a prison rather than a prism on the world when it isolates itself from the opposite gender. What lessons can the #MeToo movement take from this projected utopia in *Herland*, but also a critique of it? The accusatory, *J'accuse* method without due process, investigation, evidence, is perhaps an angered reaction to generation upon generation of victim-blaming/slut-shaming. The current way out, "#Believewomen," could be understood via the above analysis. Utopias create binaries in language and psychic structures—the latent Jungian component to our construction of female/male, good/bad, victim/perpetrator should be muddied in some cases of co-responsibility. Furthermore, the aims of a utopic purging like #MeToo is counterproductive; in the realm of identity politics, it has created a backlash from men of ethnic and racial minorities who play a reverse persecution card—with claims of racism, ethnocentrism/antisemitism, ageism, "sex panic," or other games in identity politics (Gessen 2017; Hamblin 2018). Critics of #MeToo's white elitist feminism can find fuel in the paradigms of *Herland* as well. To begin, consider the "savages" who surround *Herland*: although the women are aware of the indigenous tribes in their vicinity, they ignore them, at best, assuming them to have no valuable knowledge, ecological or otherwise. "Many critics have engaged with the racism inherent in the novel, but I have yet to see anyone consider the grim possibility that the explorers' indigenous guides might be telling the truth when they say that 'a good many' had gone to Herland but they never came back" (Christensen 2017, 293).

There is a eugenicist *Gemeinschaft* tendency in *Herland,* and other titles within Gilman's corpus of writings. This image of a purist and purified homogenous society, without flaws, is ultimately a violation of other forms of feminist "welcome" of difference. This element of her thought puts Gilman's vision in tension with diverse class, racial, ethnic, and potentially other forms of solidarity. It is important to also note another critique of #MeToo as a product of white bourgeois feminism: much like *Herland*, it diminishes categories of racial and ethnic differences in experience. Further, it leaves out the important question of race/class-based privilege in white women whose experiences of fragility and perceived "discomfort" have a long legacy in mythologizing the black male rapist, the vampire Jew, the eroticized Arab, and so on. The encounter between racial/ethnic categories and the hysterical, fragile white woman on a pedestal is a dangerous trope, with latent historical baggage. This is so especially in an American context. As Bender explores white women's imperialism in a particular flavor of gynarchy, Herland, like #MeToo, forgets a larger vision of solidarity. Gilman worried not about the larger questions of oppression and exploitation, "but that the artificiality of male superiority had come to threaten future racial progress of white women" (Bender 2010, 68).

Giving credibility to the diagnosis of a social hysteria, Laura Kipnis has written a trenchant, muckraking critique of the collective panic element within the #MeToo movement as a kind of "feminism hijacked by melodrama." Kipnis suggests an "open narrative" quality of masculinity-femininity today. For some in postmodern life, these gendered scripts and roles are open, and negotiated, not set in victim-perpetrator prisms: "there aren't fixed truths about sex. All we have are fluctuating emotional colors and tendencies" (Kipnis 2017, 13). From Kipnis's perspective, gendered stories are narrated differently across individual experiences and the life-course. Though some would acknowledge serious trauma and injury—the stories we tell to ourselves can change over time. Even in a musical expression from pop icon and "sparkplug" of the #MeToo movement, artist Ani DiFranco's song *Pulse* expresses this potential for open roles and reflexivity in narration of personal and relational "disappointments" quite well. In DiFranco's lines we seek, but fail, to save ourselves "from the quaint tragedies we invent and undo / from the stupid circumstances we slalom through" (DiFranco 1998).

If the #MeToo movement were to listen to its musical icon, DiFranco, women and men, too, end up "slaloming through" life experience, especially the deeply embodied ones, inventing and undoing tragedies like reinforcing or undoing of a dysfunctional *Gestalt*. Kipnis highlights that today the #MeToo prism drives home the point of the vulnerability and trauma of sexual experience in the utopian elimination paradigm of shaming perpetrators, via vindication for victims. On the one hand, it is important to expose what feminists call a "rape culture" and the objectification of women in the media industry. This pervades not only college campuses, but also reflects a wider culture of both idolized and dehumanized sexuality playing out sex myths and objectification in advertising, film, and other media (Kilbourne 2010). On the other hand, one must recognize that media myths create false expectations for *both* women and men, and both women and men then have the capability to internalize a general disregard for the *sanctity* of the body and the human sexual bond as they should be experienced: shared, mutual caring, and interrelation. The solution, however, is not to make all men "perpetrators" and kick them out of the utopia (either metaphorically or literally, as is the destiny of the three male scientists visiting Herland). There is a level of infantile isolationism in wishing to eliminate one part of the gender dichotomy.

The fundamental question that #MeToo has not addressed is, a problematic still unsolved and lingering from the Classical Period of sociological theory: How are we to be together in a complementary fashion as embodied beings in the complex and sometimes improvisatory realm of gender roles, identities, and narratives following the Sexual Revolution and Feminism(s)? The answer does not reside in a naïve embrace of femininity as victimhood on a pedestal (as a reversion back to a latent Victorian image of the eternal feminine). However, it could engender an attitude of gentility, respect, mutual vulnerability/concern and, most importantly, not treating others as means to ends. So frequently men and women are objectified, and boundaries of consent are blurred in the hook-up culture. With alcohol and drugs often involved, women, and men, are compromised in their ability to make truly consensual, mutually affirming, and loving choices.

LEAVING HERLAND

#MeToo has a noble aim—to call out predatory men. There are some horrible cases of gendered bullying, violence, and victimization. But here we must pause—to see where a kind of "reign of terror" has produced a canvass of shame/blame spirals. First, we must acknowledge that the culture industry plays a strong role in the warped roles that men and women have taken since the 1960s and the Sexual Revolution. The result of what Giddens describes as "plastic sexuality"—sex divorced from the natural outcome of procreation—the "pure relationship" emerges in the context of romantic love. Giddens observes that this could potentially lead to possessive domineering of women. The unintended consequence of Feminism(s) and the Sexual Revolution is actually the backlash of violence against women and an unleashing of a "compulsive character of male sexuality more plainly revealed" (Giddens 1992, 3). Cultural messages (especially media images) are lacking a purveyance of a basic ethos of love and concern for sexual partners, and need to build in a level of respect, kindness, regard for the other. This means working against the cultural seeds that have been sown, and the consequences have taken root: a rampant culture of abuse (emotional and physical), objectification, infidelity, recklessness, "love 'em and leave 'em" mentalities, disease, unwanted pregnancy, and so on. Their consequences alone should point to the fact that sexual encounters are not to be taken lightly: they are literally a product of concrete life or death decisions—not a vehicle for irresponsible fantasy and selfish enjoyment.

The underlying assumptions of #MeToo via *Herland* are misguided in that they play an essentialist card that still reflects some of the baggage of gendered realities from the founders of sociological theory—men and women. The way out is educating men and women about the dignity of their bodies and mutual interdependence, with an impulse toward care and approaching sexuality as an action of giving, rather than what can be "gotten" or "gotten away with." Sexuality is not about what is conquered or possessed, as the men visiting Herland became domineering in this way. This essentializes men (as it has happened so disastrously in the #MeToo movement when it swiftly moves to convictions in the court of public opinion).

Postmodern culture is obsessed with sex yet appreciates very little about the profoundly complex psychological reality of sexuality, and therefore the large responsibility that should come with it. This is why, at the moment, our culture vacillates between victim-blaming/shaming and victim-praising. There are real perpetrators, not all conjured up by hysteria, but they should be made responsible and given consequences through due process. And we need a vision of some system of restorative justice for the "battle of the sexes"—perhaps not just at the individual level, but at the cultural level through educating young men and boys to empower women and give them choice, and not shame them for taking initiative, or alternatively shun them for saying no (avoiding the classic whore/virgin dichotomy).

Where *Herland* is misguided is to assume that all masculinity (or essentialized "masculine") traits are toxic. This is mistaken—but our academic and cultural discourse should move beyond the assertion that the mere education and elevation of status of women (only) necessarily improves gender relations. Women's liberation may be at the expense of future generations' battles with a backlash of sexism. The issue is complex: powerful socioeconomic shifts "have a lot more to do with male unhappiness than the latest sexual harassment ruling" (Hochschild 2018, 13). This "toxic masculinity" surge against feminism results, ironically, from declining contact between boys and their fathers—a side effect of the high American divorce rate. Discussing the (lengthy) book *The Boy Crisis: Why Our Boys are Struggling and What to do About It,* by John Grey and Warren Farrell, sociologist Arlie Hochschild presents (perhaps counterintuitively for the goals of women's liberation) an argument for how divorce reinforces a hostile world for future generations of women. When boys have fathers present, it encourages a heightened ability to empathize, delay gratification, and avoid taking on bullying behaviors (both on the receiving and giving sides of bullying) (Hochschild 2018, 13). The backlash against women can take different forms and responses, not only from reactionary religious and political spheres, but also from men who feel "left behind" in the wake of women's liberation or success. The men who are left behind sometimes coming from families or educational contexts which encourage women's education and achievement. What Hochschild makes a case for is the idea that overall, what we need to move beyond is the elevation of victimhood, or the zero-sum approach to the #MeToo crisis vs. the crisis of men/boys. The legitimization of victimhood creates a mimetic cycle of victim-perpetrator-victim, an infinite loop of sexual politics' reactivity and *ressentiment*. To move beyond that cycle, we should channel the concepts of gender complementarity. "New feminism" (Gawkowska 2012) is a movement within contemporary European Catholicism that absorbs the best of both feminism and religious narratives. It does this by granting the dignity of independence of women—in their bodies, freedom to work outside the home—but also recognizes what Simone de Beauvoir affirmed, but Charlotte Perkins Gilman failed to recognize: an all-women utopic vision is unviable and untenable. New Feminism calls for co-responsibility, mutual respect, mutual vulnerability. Men, and women, in capitalist cultures may approach sexual and romantic relations with a sense of "what they can get away with" or "what they can get." This is reflected in a long legacy of cultural analysis in criticism of capitalist values, but most notably in R.H. Tawney's *The Acquisitive Society*. As discussed by the humanist Marxian and psychoanalyst Erich Fromm, Tawney's book highlights that what drives capitalism's insanity is the quest for, and thus being dominated by, things (Fromm 1955, 192). Sexual activity, then, if we follow this logic, becomes detached from the relational aspect in the pursuit of the "thing" of the experience rather than connection with the other person. It is driven by the acquisitive nature of the modern capitalist ego, rather than a collapsing of ego boundaries, or overwhelming of the ego in traditional cultures (Giddens 1992, 37). We might connect this to Giddens's observations on the commonplace addictive mentality within romantic relations today (Giddens 1992, 73). Fromm's reconstruction of the concept of alienation implies the objectification of sex-relations, whereby, like its effect on all aspects of human life, capitalism instrumentalizes sexuality. The other person is secondary; they are disposable and merely fill a limitless void for a displaced orientation toward yet another form of consumption.

However, a different approach is possible which reverses this objectification, or at least rejects the notion of sex as separate from true encounter with another person (rather than simply the abstract physical power of arousal). Inspired by the teachings of John Paul II, "New Feminism" sees sexuality as "gift"—it proposes: What can we *give* to another, in a reflection of the gift of divine love, rather than what we can *take* from one another. This is not inapplicable to secular or non-Catholic persons of faith. In the true sense of Catholic as "universal," John Paul II's teaching recognizes the deep profundity of the universality of the relation between the sexes and the way in which there is a tragic play of psychological dysfunction, chaos, and pain when the transcendent and spiritual nature of sexuality is disrespected or denied (John Paul II 1997). As queer theorist, Jane Ward, notes, however, the "tragic" is the dominant reality in today's heterosexual relationships, and that "people persist in these attachments . . . because the fantasy object provides a 'sense of what it means to keep on living and looking forward to being in the world'" (Berlant in Ward 2020, 70). Perhaps religious discourse, as a transcendent goal, creates such a "hype amidst tragedy," alongside other products of the culture industry like the average romantic comedy. The mode of "queer" fantasy of *Herland* seeks, through science fiction, to surmount this tragic situation for women. The tragic realism here, presented in Gilman's contemporary, D.H. Lawrence, in the inner female's voice, during the boating/swimming scene in *Women in Love:* "And she knew it was all no good, and she would never go beyond him, he was the final approximation of life to her. . . . She wanted connection with him" (1922, 206–207). As Ward describes it, the "no good" is supposed to make women happy but the dominant straight culture "fail(s) to name the contradictions and miseries of [itself]—the entrapment, the disappointment, the antagonism, the boredom, the unwanted sex, the toxic masculinity, and the countless daily injustices endured by straight women" (2020, 16). Gilman's solution is escapist, with another form of utopic fantasy—gynocracy. Greater versions of art, however, may expose, and triumph over, the tragic.

HERLAND AND OTHER ARTISTIC CONTEXTS

The tragedies of slighted, used, objectified, and discarded women have ripple effects involving grandiose episodes in society, and even the world (or the natural realm) within certain examples of literature and the arts. A few examples include *Anna Karenina, Faust, Clarissa, Madama Butterfly, Götterdämmerung, Hamlet, Tosca, Norma,* the women of Thomas Hardy novels, and so forth. These feminine tragedies are actually triumphal, in that they derive sympathetic responses from the audience. *Herland*'s weakness (as is #MeToo's dysfunctional origin) is that it evokes more pity than sympathy, as the story "achieves" an unreflective utopia. *Herland* is not great art—not tragedy drawing out bathos, or pathos. Nor is *Herland* comedy creating reflective self-knowledge about gender-relations, as found in Aristophanes's *Lysistrata,* or Shakespeare's *Twelfth Night* and *Taming of the Shrew*. As Charlotte Perkins Gilman presented in her other (sociological) works, there is an important dynamic in the sexuo-economic relation: men do not realize their dependence upon women (Gilman 1898). *Herland* does not realize or evoke awareness in this important dual dynamic—the (perhaps psychoanalytic) rendering of the dependence and resistance wherein the male clings to the mommy/servant figure, even while he tries to leap free from her oppressive bosom. Gilman is trying to resolve what Jane Ward calls the "misogyny paradox," "wherein boys' and men's desire for girls and women is expressed within a broader culture that encourages them to also hate girls and women" (Ward 2020, 65). *Herland* attempts, but fails, to reorient this dynamic into a loving, mutual sexual union (per the narrative voice of the male character):

> These were women one had to love "up," very high up, instead of down. They were not pets. They were not servants. . . . I found that loving "up" was a very good sensation after all. . . . It was like coming home to mother . . . it was a sense of getting home; of being clean and rested; of safety and yet freedom—a love that didn't irritate and didn't smother. (Gilman 1998, 120–121)

There could be a latent interpretation of putting women on a Goddess-like pedestal here—or is Gilman (through the voice of male narrators) suggesting something with more subtlety? In the paragraphs leading to the meditation on "loving 'up,'" Gilman inserts reflection on the confining of women to the household, the kitchen, "in their place." But loving "up" doesn't seem to work out in the end when the men are asked to leave Herland.

Similarly, in #MeToo the shaming and guilt-tripping of men comes from the internal interpretations of the victim and the audience, and the public claims of the accuser. However, great art is different as—for one example—in Puccini's opera *Madama Butterfly*. In the final Act of the opera, the used, objectified, and rejected Butterfly's ritual suicide, driven by shame responding to the strictures of Japanese culture, creates tension and guilt in the mind of the perpetrator. In the final scene ("spoiler alert!"), American naval officer Pinkerton concludes the opera on a terrifying unresolved chord, shouting "Butterfly!" Pinkerton's is an act of (musically conveyed) contrition. Pinkerton may be a cad, but he does have a heart that winds up breaking—perhaps this was more evocative in Puccini's (earlier, more chivalrous) generation's audience.

In contrast, the images and archetypes of *Herland* are parallel to the #MeToo movement and they suggest that men are to be cast out and expelled rather than encouraged to come to an action of contrition and the valuing of women: collective accusation and purging replaces due process. In *Herland*, there is the assumption that men are heartless, and have souls that are irreparable. Regarding the "court of public opinion," Lionel Shriver (2019) in February 2019's *Harper's Magazine* stated it well: "Most judicial systems distinguish between high crimes and misdemeanors. Trials in the court of public opinion appear to do no such thing." #MeToo has the tone of Arthur Miller's Salem in *The Crucible*, convicting through public opinion, and conflating assault with an awkwardly rejected flirtation. Neither unwanted advances nor assault are good things; but there is a great degree of distance between the intents, and outcomes, of the two actions. The problem exists in the subjective realm of the construction of reality left to the isolated experience of the interpreter. Rather than a wholesale, utopic rejection of one element of the dichotomy in casting out the "male," a corrective is necessary for those men who violate women's boundaries and objectify women: an admonishment and reminder that *women are not objects.*

Relatedly, but also ironically, the epistemological problem of #MeToo complaints and charges is rooted in the historical and philosophical inspiration of feminist freedoms: a Kantian sense of autonomy. Contrary to a Kantian sense of self liberation, freedom, and autonomy, humans are always and everywhere interconnected beings; meanings and morals arise contextualized by universals and experience—but not individualistically. This is the main point of Catholic thought as it inspires New Feminism. Nowhere is this sense of the problematic approach of autonomy as a category for sexuality more powerful than in the sexual relation: we are responsible for each other when boundaries of pain/pleasure are crossed intersubjectively. This shows that most conventional feminisms are really in the service of male interests when it comes to defining sexual "liberation": freedom from responsibility, emotional attachments, and the lonely atomized search for stimulation and pleasure. This is one of the hypocrisies of conventional feminisms as it unleashes what Giddens calls "plastic sexuality." However, psychosocially, there is a great deal of emotional baggage, evolutionarily speaking, still attached to the sexual encounter. Why else would there be such strong responses to mere "unwanted advances" if the nature of sexual encounters were mere trifles? This is where liberated feminism has built a castle on a foundation of sand, washed away by its raging waters of the psychoanalytic roots in the violation of the eternal feminine.

Based on a conceptual and logical fallacy, conventional feminism creates its own impasse in #MeToo. As explored here, and to conclude, a new (but also ancient?!) paradigm for sexuality is necessary. Gawkowska, author in the "New Feminism" movement within Catholicism, explains that in sexuality, "[e]xistence is always already given and already meaningful. But for this gift [sexual submission], to be realized, calls for the generosity of another gift; for the meaning to be made clear, the collaboration of other freedoms is called for" (2012, 178). Sexuality is a mutual gift, and other (soft) Catholic teaching expresses this eloquently: Vincent Genovesi, S.J. (1987) describes modern relationships via Medieval definitions of love, *caritas-via-eros*, stressing the importance of "mutual vulnerability" in the sexual union.

EPILOGUE

In 2017, Garrison Keillor, popular novelist, host of NPR's *Writers Almanac* and *Prairie Home Companion,* and winner of the Mark Twain prize, was tragically (in the sense of Greek tragedy) brought down by his flaw in the #MeToo movement. In a charitable read of the situation, Keillor, noted for many failed romances and marriages, seemed to be the "emotionally needy man" in the workplace. In his *The Book of Guys* (published in 1993, long before the #MeToo movement), the author offers a confession of sorts in many vignettes about famous "guys." These stories include titles like "Don Giovanni," "Lonesome Shorty the Cowboy," "Zeus the Lutheran," "Mr. St. Paul," and "The Midlife Crisis of Dionysus," among others. In the introductory chapter, the voice of one "guy" observes that "Monogamy for men is like a bear riding a bicycle—it's possible but the bear would rather be in the woods doing what bears do" (Keillor 1993, 14). Male authors, artists, actors, and so on, the masculine side of the creative class, may sometimes idealize and simultaneously deride, use, and objectify their muse, all while paying homage to "the eternal feminine." In the concluding chapter of *Herland,* in the male character's voice, Gilman reflects: "we [men] honor them [women] for their carefully enforced virtue, even while we show by our own conduct how little we think of that virtue" (Gilman 1998, 120). This paradoxically painful and comical relation is older than poetry—an artform that is relatively absent in *Herland,* but so essential a mode of expression of the human predicament. The gift of the literary imagination, and by extension the poetic, is incommensurable when it comes to understanding gender roles. What literature can do—through soliloquy, dramaturgy, setting, metaphor, and so forth—is evoke the key subjective reality of gender, namely through the display of emotions and roles. It is not a surprise that Charlotte Perkins Gilman used the genre to convey these ideas. Both for the power of the method and the ability to reach her audience, Gilman's *Herland*, may not have been "high art" but it was sociologically significant in the later stages of the dawn of sociological theory. Next is a discussion of the novelist Virginia Woolf's broad reaching works out to the realm of sociology for women, through fiction and essay.

NOTES

1. Parts of this chapter were previously published in *Soundings* and used with permission. MacMillen, Sarah L. 2020. "From Herland to #MeToo: Utopia or Dystopia?" *Soundings* 103 (2): 243–263.

Chapter Six

Suspending Modernity

Gender and History in *Virginia Woolf's* Orlando

INTRODUCTION

This chapter examines the contribution of Virginia Woolf's sociological imagination through a close analysis of her novel *Orlando* (1928), along with brief intertextual references to other works. Employing the method of "disorientation" akin to Conrad's literary impression of imperialism and colonialism, Woolf first "muddies" the categories of gender. Her key hermeneutical tools—for both author and audience—are of gender disambiguation and androgyny (Piggford 1999). As such, we can see in Virginia Woolf's writing an early form of "queering" aesthetics and self-narrative—not only a unique contribution for her context, but an important hint at the suspension of sociological categories. This reflects a narrative voice of objectivity, or at least a literary aloofness when it comes to the categories of gender. This anticipates much later theories on the social construction of gender in today's mainstream sociological sphere.

Relatedly, Woolf suspends and mires another important "modern" category in narrative—that of time (Esty 2007). Building from the observations of her historical contemporary, theorist Ernst Bloch (1977), Woolf describes non-contemporaneity in modern capitalistic artistic forms. Non-contemporaneity reflects both the experiential element of timelessness, and the suspension of the course of chronology via projected futures or nostalgia. In *Orlando,* this is an important plot device. Woolf's character Orlando "does not age" and the refusal of chronology is a critique of modernity's juggernaut of industrialization, colonialism, and imperialism—an "eternal" character unaffected by the course of time is a rejection of constant change and claims of "progress."

GENDERING

Within the theoretical corpus of mainstream sociology, gendering—or the performance of transitory gender roles—is a relatively new concept. Women's lives especially were not regarded with interest or understanding. Women were usually denied the opportunity to express their experience of gender and class structures within sociology, a scientific field composed almost entirely of men. A few sparse voices—albeit marginalized—form a small set of critical positions on gender roles in early sociology. As American sociological theorists of the early twentieth century, who were by no means embraced by the "mainstream" at their time, Jane Addams and Charlotte Perkins Gilman articulated the experience of "bifurcated consciousness" of being a woman. This consciousness reflected that double reality of living in a woman's body in a man's world. The "twoness" of being African American was also discussed in the concepts of "double consciousness" by W.E.B. DuBois (1903). That duality of identity is especially pronounced for marginalized groups within the mainstream society. It is very different from the "normal" claims of the split experienced, and negotiated between a Durkheimian sense of "individual" and collective conscience. Additionally, unlike today, the concepts of "sex" and "gender" were seen as equivalent and though gender roles were critiqued, they were assumed to line up in natural and biological terms (as discussed in chapter five). An additional item to consider: the voices of women and minority social thinkers were largely left out of the construction of the canon in mainstream sociological theory (Wright 2020; Lengermann & Niebrugge-Brantley 1998). So, given this observation, alongside the fact that most women did not receive post-secondary education, a much wider audience had to be reached via fiction.

THEORY: FACT AND FICTION

Virginia Woolf, a twentieth-century British female intellectual, used imaginative fiction to purvey a sophisticated understanding of gendering and societal norms long before sociology adopted the theoretical approach that it does today. Charlotte Perkins Gilman, like Woolf, wrote creative fiction, as well as more direct nonfiction commentaries on gender. The critique of a system like gender is well-suited to presentation in fiction over against theory. As Charles Lemert has suggested in Blackwell's *Companion to Classical Sociological Theory*, the boundaries between "theory" and "fiction" are properly blurred. Bridging fact and fiction, the work of a theorist and a novelist are similar. Just as Joseph Conrad outlined the moral intricacies of the social philosophies at his time through his fictional account of anarchism in London in *The Secret Agent,* or articulated the soft underbelly of Social Darwinism in *Heart of Darkness,* so too do Gilman and Woolf traipse the boundaries between theory and fiction. As Charles Lemert describes Gilman's "fictional" impact in "The Yellow Wallpaper,"

> Herein lies her abiding witness to all women and men who live their lives between doubt and hope, wherein the disciplined practice of social theory begins. Without fiction, there is no imagination; without imagination, no dreams; without dreams, facts hardly matter. Theories are the ways people use their imagination to talk about factual realities that hedge their social dreams. (Lemert 2003, 267)

Where would sociology be without imaginative fiction? "There would be no scientific progress without the imaginative fashionings of the real" (Lemert 2003, 267). Theory, in the Greek origin of the word, is *theoros,* "one who travels in order to see things" or "a spectacle" (Lemert 2003, 277). Social or moral fiction then, like theory, is a kind of spectacle of creative imagination refracting the truths of society.

Because the Ivory Tower of professional sociology and other academic disciplines were largely closed to women at the time of Woolf's authorship, they were sequestered to do their theorizing in literary outlets. One could also make an appeal to a theory of praxis within their writing of fiction. The best way to reach women was not through theory texts—they were mostly read by men. Daniel Bender highlights the popularity of this genre as political tools in his discussion of Gilman's *Herland:* "dime novels were eagerly read by working women and acted as tools to develop a politicized identity as working women, troubled by their condition and dreaming of something richer" (Bender 2010, 67). Like another marginalized sociological writer, DuBois, Gilman, and Woolf found their audience in readers of literary books and magazines. Therefore, finding fiction as its outlet, this type of theorizing "does its work in the always unsettled space between doubt and promise . . . it seeks to describe the possible in order to capture the imagination of others" (Lemert 2003, 267). Further, "far from being stranger than fiction, the strangeness of the factual is that, in many times and places, reality's finest expressions can only be rendered as fiction" (Lemert 2003, 268). Fiction, then, is an appropriate place for a theorist who is marginalized in her society.

Woolf, like her contemporary Gilman, contributed to a sophisticated analysis of gender categories and the idea of modernity as a whole. Focusing on *Orlando,* but also employing intertextual observations from *Mrs. Dalloway* and "A Room of One's Own" (1929), Virginia Woolf offers a groundbreaking examination of women's roles in early modern Britain literary and cultural contexts. In these works, Virginia Woolf demonstrates path-breaking theories of gender and the social construction of identity.

GENDER AND SOCIAL IDENTITY

Within today's mainstream sociological theory, Lorber (1994; 1998) most notably has described the contributions of queer theory to the wider discourse on gender. What Lorber suggests is that the embrace of the concept of queering among mainstream sociology makes possible the observation that "gender roles are merely conventions" and also the rejection of "traditional categories" of masculine-feminine strict dichotomies overlapping onto biological identities. Alongside other "variables," then, the gendered "self" is constructed to belong to a position in society that holds certain responsibilities and role expectations. Additionally, society casts individuals as "actors" in different roles, in performative impersonations, as Judith Butler (1990) has described it. As such, one's identity develops to conform to societal institutions as well as to form an individual sense of inner life: "Identity is based not only on responses to the question 'Who am I?' but also on responses to the question 'Who am I in relation to others?' thus rooting the question in a person's external circumstances" (Alamilla and Howard 2001, 55). In addition to such ascribed traits as race and class, a person's sex is a fundamental characteristic of identity. Its importance is so prominent that a distinction is marked between sex, a person's biological characteristics, and gender, the culturally defined personality traits and patterns of behavior that are associated with a particular sex (Alamilla and Howard 2001, 55). In other words, sex defines whether a person is biologically a man or a woman, whereas (traditionally) gender is the inner sense of whether oneself identifies with the male or the female. That this inner sense of femininity or masculinity is not based on pure biological predetermination can be assumed based on the existence of gender violators such as transsexuals, transvestites, and even those who are born with ambiguous genitalia. While the central attributes of sex and gender do tend to overlap in most people, this phenomenon is based more on societal expectations, rather than on biological imperatives.

In mainstream history of culture within Western civilization, philosophers and scientists were convinced that women were inherently different, and usually inferior, to men in the most basic biological and moral senses. And throughout most Western and Westernized societies touched by globalization, it was and is still largely believed that sex equated with gender. Gender roles were rigidly defined by biological traits, which then *naturally* lined up with societal expectations such as passivity and subservience. In Virginia Woolf's time, for women [according to D.H. Lawrence], "the deepest consciousness is in the loins and the belly. . . . If this is perverted and her flow of energy is upward, to the breast and head, woman may become clever, noble, efficient, brilliant . . . [but] she soon has enough of it, everything goes pop, and she returns to sex, 'which is her business at the present moment'" (Beauvoir 1989, 219). For generations prior to the publication of Virginia Woolf's works, the female sex was devalued and regarded as a lesser/inferior being based on pseudoscientific and religious beliefs. A woman's body gained associations of fragility and wickedness that survived in one form or another to create a societal expectation of the ways in which women acted.

Beset on all sides by "proof" of their weakness and inferiority, a self-fulfilling prophecy emerged as the biological reality of women was engulfed by the cultural construction of what it meant to be female. Women were considered passive and lacking consciousness, because their movements were historically restrained to the point that they were not permitted to do anything worthwhile. In his essay describing the characteristics of individuals and dyads, Georg Simmel argued that prior to modernity, women were the "less individualized sex," meaning that their personalities were generally less developed compared to men (Simmel 1950, 138). By virtue of their dominant role in the workforce and political arena, men were deemed the active agents of society. Likewise, the substandard quality of conventional education for women developed into the perception that females have a secondary intelligence. Simone de Beauvoir eloquently illustrates the dilemma of a girl student in *The Second Sex*: "She will attribute [her weaknesses] not to the mediocrity of her training, but to the unjust curse of her femininity; by resigning herself to this inequality, she enhances it" (1989, 700). Women were forced into the role of a secondary dependent class, with no rights or choices beyond the grudging allowances afforded to them by their fathers or husbands. Nevertheless, some misogynistic scholars denigrated women for acting in the ways in which they were conditioned to behave; one seventeenth-century writer called women "degenerate" from "leading a proud, lazy, and idle life, to the great hindrance of their poor husbands" (Swetnam 2008 [1615], 277). Modern women writers have defended their sex from these criticisms, explaining that people conditioned to believe that they are passive, unintelligent, and unworthy will act in a corresponding way, and reinforce the domains of "separate spheres." "Woman is shut up in a kitchen or in a boudoir, and astonishment is expressed that her horizon is limited. Her wings are clipped, and it is found deplorable that she cannot fly" (Beauvoir 1989, 605). According to women writers, a person's destiny depends not so much on her physical attributes, but on her manifestation of normative cultural expectations and the achievements of her husband. Virginia Woolf's task in *Orlando* was then to undermine these dichotomous categories, and the very time through which those categories had developed—an interruption through disorientation of time.

According to Burns (1994), Woolf plays on a twentieth-century conception derived from the Greek notion of "*alethea*, unveiling"—much like a therapist were to unveil the self-deceptions and faulty perceptions of the psychoanalytic patient. *Orlando* is a roman à clef, about Woolf's sapphic interest in Vita Sackville-West. But it also satirically parallels a Freudian deconstruction of the personhood of her "crush"—the insider knowledge working against masculine constructions of female sexuality (Piggford 1999, 295). In *Orlando* gender roles go through a playful parody/game of "destabilization" and "camp" (Burns 1994; Piggford 1999) both exposing the self, but also the ridiculousness of the two-tiered gendered system.

ORLANDO: THE SOCIAL CONSTRUCTION OF GENDER

As an experiment in deconstructing the doctrine of "separate spheres" but also a semi-biographical novel, Virginia Woolf's *Orlando* presents itself as a pioneer text in the expression of "gendering" and "social constructionist" theories. The importance of culture in the formation of the feminine self is particularly evident in Woolf's *Orlando*, in which the protagonist is born biologically male and becomes biologically female midway through life, and at the same time is characterized by their immortality. Orlando is an intriguing character, because he, and then, she, defies standards of normality by not aging in years and responding to the gender expectations of each time rather unconventionally. Orlando's story emerges at the end of Queen Elizabeth's reign, and she is only middle-aged when the plot of the novel concludes in 1928. In the first half of the narrative, as a man, Orlando displays conventionally (by Woolf's post-Victorian contemporaneous standards) feminine qualities, such as a stress on emotionality, a passion for poetry, tenderness, and an appreciation of nature. His generally docile and melancholic temperament suggests androgyny, but he takes advantage of the independence afforded to a man in Elizabethan until Georgian periods of England.

In Sally Potter's film version of the novel, Orlando is played by the actress Tilda Swinton. Through Orlando's portrayal as a feminine man, Potter is offering a commentary on gender roles at the time of Elizabeth I's reign (a powerful *masculine* woman, played by the famous drag-actor, Quentin Crisp). A key "social influencer" figure of late-Renaissance England is the "poet." The reader of the novel is meant to think of Shakespeare—who is missing from the story—and perhaps Orlando is the court-favored young poet, the avatar of the more famous "Will." Poetry at this time is considered a masculine art form. The character of "the poet" in the story is a very bawdy masculine figure. In the film interpretation, it is only later that poetry, in response to the Enlightenment, and under the reaction within the locus of the Romantics, becomes a "feminine" enterprise, associated with the emotions instead of the "more difficult subjects" of reason-driven philosophy and science. Sally Potter saw Woolf's *Orlando* as a commentary on the "history of literature as the vehicle of consciousness" (Degli-Esposti 1996, 83). Orlando's romantic nature befits him as a man living in the seventeenth and eighteenth centuries. But in the age of science, exploration, and empire—"British masculine-imperialist hubris" (Piggford 1999, 289)—will displace this characteristic into the "feminine."

It is during his stay as an ambassador in Constantinople that Orlando discovers what scholars today have highlighted as the sense of "toxic masculinities" within force, politics, and empire. Then Orlando's metamorphosis from a man to a woman occurs. Orlando who is, therefore, "same soul different sex" retreats into femininity precisely as a response to the corruptions of the force of modern history: the British Empire. Orlando is called to abandon his Ottoman friend for the pursuit of British imperial interests. Experiencing the horrors of war and empire up close, his poetic masculine side is struck voiceless—the old sense of masculinity is no longer relevant. He becomes a woman. At first, alone or in the company of "barbarian" gypsies, Orlando's conduct and appearance remain essentially unchanged:

> Orlando had become a woman—there is no denying it. But in every other respect, Orlando remained precisely as he had been. The change of sex, though it altered their future, did nothing whatever to alter their identity. Their faces remained, as their portraits prove, practically the same . . . her memory then, went back through all the events of her past life without encountering any obstacle. (Woolf 2006, 102–103)

Parallel to the introduction of W.E.B. DuBois's concepts of "the veil" and "second-sight" (1903)—where African Americans are more skilled at seeing the constructions of whiteness and blackness—Orlando's gender awareness begins upon the transformation from man to woman. The novel's prolonged discussion and sociological commentaries about the nature of the female sex's relation to society begins with an awareness of that "otherness" upon Orlando's new identity as female.

Orlando's transition to a female only occurs to her after she is exposed to her own cultural context and notices the differences in society's expectations for women, compared to men. As Okin describes it, "social constructions of gender impinge on Orlando's identity. Having been both man and woman, she begins to see what is 'absurd' about men and women from the other sex's point of view" (1996, 35). She views the world with the sociological imagination and a critical perspective on sex and gender by coming to realize that differences once thought natural or biological are actually rather arbitrary (Okin 1996, 35). She learns that she is dainty from a ship's captain, who offers her shade, delicacies, and companionship. After a sailor almost falls to his death from the shock of seeing her calf, Orlando understands that her sexuality is both dangerous and enticing to men. Little by little, the influence of society drives Orlando to become vainer of her appearance, more dependent on assistance, and more protective of her chastity.

In *Orlando*, Virginia Woolf illustrates that the qualities society attributes to biological sex affect the manifestation of one's gender identity and other aspects of identity—and that we are all in a grand "performance." This insight parallels with a combination of the classical sociological contributions of England's Harriet Martineau and the Chicago school's Jane Addams on standpoint theory (Lengermann and Niebrugge-Brantley 1998, 42–43; 85–86) with that of Symbolic Interactionism's insights on the definition of the situation (Thomas 1931) and the looking-glass self (Cooley 1902). The suspension of accepted gender conventions in these categories, perhaps reified by capitalist categories in the bourgeois production of marriage, creates a disorientation. As George Piggford highlights, "the separation of sex and gender produces a disorientation" creating a "camp effect . . . its deliberate subversion of the dominant sexual discourse . . . through gender performance" (1999, 294). This exposes the way in which the definition of the situation is really fragile; and the extent to which gender, like other aspects of the self is reflecting the social context, both historically and culturally driven.

Woolf also portrays Orlando as a character who breaches the conventional standards of masculinity and femininity in her personality, actions, and worldview. Although Orlando is "bold and active," she does not have the formality, mathematical ability, or "love of power" that are associated with masculinity. Likewise, though she is "excessively tender-hearted" and "prone to tears" like a stereotypical female, she does not possess conscientiousness in her dress or modesty for her accomplishments. Shockingly, Orlando enjoys pastimes habitually only undertaken by men; she raises her own crops, gallops horses, drinks, and gambles in games of chance (*Orlando*, 139–140). By modeling her life in accordance to the tastes of an independent, active man, Orlando retains her individuality and shocks the customary limits of femininity. Even more scandalous, however, is her relaxed understanding of the way in which gender identities link to biological sex. Upon meeting her future husband, Marmaduke Bonthrop Shelmerdine, Orlando and "Shel" recognize their own gender within the other. Woolf relates, "an awful suspicion rushed into both their minds simultaneously. 'You're a woman, Shel!' she cried. 'You're a man, Orlando!' he cried" (184). Orlando's unique experiences and lifestyle open her to the possibility that the female is not limited to women or the male limited to men. Instead, she appears to intuitively understand that the social assumptions of gender are aspects of culture and not of individual personalities. This is an extremely sophisticated theory of gender that does not appear in the sociological literature until much later in the twentieth century. Woolf's contemporary Gilman made no distinction between "sex" and "gender" but, convincingly, as Woolf presented in the love story between the "masculine" female and the "feminine" male, gender (as cultural/psychological comportment) and sex (as biological trait) are distinct.

Woolf's novel presents a suspension of gender, and a theory of general androgyny for all persons. Sasha, Orlando's Russian paramour, is female but skates vigorously like a boy (Woolf 1956, 38). Archduchess Harriet becomes Archduke Harry for more gender confusion (Woolf 1956, 178–179). Orlando's suspension of gender rigidity, in favor of categories of androgyny is not restricted to Orlando themself, but extends to a gamut of attractions and is, thus, an overall gender theory of the "tension between perceived biological sex . . . and self-presentation" which in turn "creates a moment of disorientation and uncertainty" (Piggford 1999, 290). This "disorientation" and cultural dysphoria—akin to Conrad's moral confusion about imperialism—presents us with a sociological critique of the nature of established Victorian gender qualities. Finally, though, in a happy marriage, Orlando, a masculine woman, then must fall in love with Shel, a feminine man.

The key argument for Woolf is not one of deep-seated psychoanalytically driven desires, but it is about the element of disorientation, suspension of given categories, and gender performativity. "The World's a gender stage." Clothes serve as a kind of masque-metaphor—to allude to the use of masques in ancient drama (*personae* as characterization and amplification). *Orlando*'s performative theory is epitomized in the function of clothing in the text of the novel. Conventionally, clothing is one of the most immediately identifiable emblems of a person's public identity, because it outwardly exemplifies the qualities of class and gender. A text entitled "Counsel to the Husband: To the Wife Instruction" clearly demonstrates the historical symbolism of power that clothing had during the English Renaissance: "if the man may not wear woman's apparel, nor the woman man's, how much less may the one usurp the other's dignity . . . or give over his sovereignty to his wife?" (Ste. B. 2007 [1608], 279). Likewise, Virginia Woolf explicitly defines the importance of a person's clothes when she writes, "They change our view of the world and the world's view of us" (Woolf 2006, 138). Dressed for the first time in the proper skirts of a woman, Orlando immediately notices the different treatment she receives from men. In turn, these attentions influence the way she views herself and thus how she will act in the future. After Orlando becomes accustomed to herself as a woman, she begins vacillating between behaviors that would associate her with the feminine and the masculine. At times, she doffs masculine dress to enjoy the freedom of a man's life but then returns to replace her breeches with dresses and petticoats. Tellingly, Woolf describes Orlando's crossdressing as if she is literally changing her sex when she changes her clothes: "She had, it seems, no difficulty in sustaining the different parts, for her sex changed far more frequently than those who have worn only one set of clothing can conceive" (2006, 161). Clothing then is only an outward accentuation of an inward androgyny: "it is only the clothes that keep the male or female likeness, while underneath the sex is the very opposite of what it is above" (2006, 189).

Orlando's choice of clothing is an artifice whereby she does not present her own identity for observation but dresses to represent herself as someone else (Beauvoir 1989, 533). Clothing functions as a metaphor for the way in which culture is an external mask of gender identity. It is a mask that is malleable, thus subverting the social norm that gender is a biological and dichotomous trait.

Sally Potter's film interpretation of *Orlando* consciously displays the protagonist's irregular gender identity and Woolf's symbolic use of clothing. Actress Swinton, who plays Orlando throughout the movie, capably portrays her character first as a feminine man and then as a masculine woman. The overall effect of her performance highlights the androgyny of her features to create "disorientation" and "gender disambiguation" that appears to conceal both the qualities of a man and a woman. The costumes worn by Swinton to portray the male and female Orlando painfully symbolize the relative liberty and expectations associated with each gender. In the opening sequence, Orlando is revealed to be a young man dressed in a rather peculiar period costume that still allows him the freedom to run through a wilderness. This male Orlando is active and independent with a multitude of positions and admirers open to him. He is strongly contrasted with the female Orlando who is powdered, polished, and corseted into immobility, having lost her ability to speak her own opinions as well as the luxury of being able to move about freely. Even at the end of the film, when Swinton is dressed in trousers and steering a motorcycle, she still manages to convey the loneliness of a person who is torn between the feminine and masculine aspects of her character.

MRS. DALLOWAY AND THE SEXUO-ECONOMIC RELATION

The fluidity between masculinity and femininity in *Orlando* are refracted against the rigid roles and notion of separate spheres in the characters within *Mrs. Dalloway* (1925), originally published a few years prior to *Orlando*.

Woolf's feminist pen illuminates the ennui of the housewife, and in the character of Clarissa, the suffocating power of women's age-old reliance on men. For the "separate spheres" thesis, since men are traditionally the breadwinners, the thinkers, and the doers, women are trained to trust in men and accept that the feminine purpose is one of helper, nurse, and comforter. From childhood, women are "taught to accept masculine authority" (Beauvoir 1989, 600). Left alone for the day, Woolf's protagonist Clarissa Dalloway feels disoriented because she is abandoned to her own devices. Without direction from her husband Richard, Clarissa silently wails for his presence: "Richard, Richard! she cried, as a sleeper in the night starts and stretches a hand in the dark for help. . . . He has left me; I am alone forever" (Woolf 1953, 70). The crux of Clarissa's entire life is Richard. Her devotion to him is one born of dependence and trusting, self-giving fidelity. Without Richard, she cannot stand. She is completely dependent upon him. As Jane Ward has described this tragic codependence between men and women, women find fulfillment in emotional self-nullification, and sacrifice of self through emotional labor toward the "significant other." Bringing gender relations forward into today's experience, "even what passes as heterosexual intimacy is often resented by straight women who find themselves doing the emotional heavy lifting for men who have no close friends and won't go to therapy" (Ward 2020, 49). Men in relationships aim "all of these needs at women partners" and men can be "emotional gold diggers" (Rodgers, in Ward 2020, 49). In earlier generations where the "separate spheres" were dominant, this household economy of emotion was more rigid, but by today's standards with double breadwinners, this becomes exhausting for women.

Charlotte Perkin Gilman's systematic sociology describes this unique (in the animal kingdom) characteristic that befalls the human female.

> Humans are the only animal species in which the female depends on the male for food, the only animal species in which the sex-relation is also an economic relation. With us an entire sex lives in a relation of economic dependence upon the other sex, and the economic relation is combined with the sex relation. The economic status of the human female is relative to the sex relation. (Gilman 1898, 5)

Gilman calls this the "sexuo-economic relation." Gilman quotes a poem in the inscription pages of her *Women and Economics* (1898). It might have well been written for Mrs. Clarissa Dalloway: "Ah but he would love her! And she should love but him! He would work and struggle for her, he would shelter and defend her. . . . Weak still he kept her, lest she be strong to flee." (Gilman 1898)

This utter dependence, the result of the fall in Eden, is what traps women and leads to Mrs. Dalloway's peripatetic, nervous nature. Woolf expresses Clarissa's dependence and devotion, "It was her life, and, bending her head over the hall table, she bowed beneath the influence . . . above all to Richard her husband, who was the foundation of it" (1953, 42–43). Woolf's keen insights anticipate Ward's (2020) queer critique of heteronormativity. According to Ward, "The story about the benefits of heterosexuality is also one with wildly differing levels of truthfulness, or explanatory power" (2020, 12). Further, in praise of Virginia Woolf's prescient literary observation, Ward would support the exposition of these gender categories: "when we hold the relationship between misogyny and heterosexuality in full view, we are able to see beyond the male-centric claim that queerness constitutes a tragic and unwilled loss of power, a loss that no one would ever choose (even as it brings sexual pleasure and fosters the 'pride' of the oppressed)" (Ward 2020, 16). Woolf's commentary within *Mrs. Dalloway* describes modes of imprisonment and confinement in rigid doctrines of "separate spheres" in conventional bourgeois marriage, and finds its queer refraction in the experience of *Orlando*. Clarissa Dalloways are in households where they are overshadowed by the authority of their fathers and are married to their husbands before they receive a chance to provide for themselves. Without self-confidence or independence, they must rely on the guardianship of masculine authority figures to support them. But the Shelmerdine-Orlando marriage is a happy, queer, union.

In cultures with dense heteronormative and gendered expectations, marriage becomes an irrepressible societal impulse for women, even though it subjugates them to their husbands by law. For Clarissa Dalloway and others like her, marriage is the only way to survive, because their social upbringing made them incapable of caring for themselves. As an adult, a woman must live as a member of a marital couple; alone and without a husband and family, she is nothing (Beauvoir 1989, 541–542). For Clarissa, the knowledge that she must marry Richard occurred in a kind of premonition: "This [revelation]—that she would marry Dalloway—was blinding—overwhelming at the moment" (Woolf 1953, 92). Such language implies that marriage was not a choice for Clarissa. Instead, it was a destined event, which society and her parents conditioned her to accept throughout her formative years. As Gilman suggests in one example, the composer's wife is defined by her husband's job, being a composer of music, but she is not able to compose (Gilman 1898, 12). However, Clarissa Dalloway's wedding ceremony was not just a religious and familial occasion; marriage was a legal contract that appropriated the bride's rights and conferred them to the husband, according to the popular Blackstone's eighteenth-century articulation: "By marriage, the husband and wife are one person in the law: that is, the very being and legal existence of the woman is suspended during the marriage, or at least is incorporated and consolidated into that of her husband: under whose wing, protection, and *cover* she performs everything" (Dolan 2008, 76).

In other words, upon marriage a woman experienced "civil death," losing any rights as citizen (Weitz 1998, 4). Yet at the same marriage is hyped as "self-realization" through unification with the "self-assured" other. The only freedom or "self" a woman could experience was through being the ornament of her husband's economic achievement. She wore her husband's wealth in jewels or dresses (Gilman 1898, 9). Her rights to property, wages, the custody of her children, and personal safety were waived. In addition, the feminine identity of the woman becomes masked by the masculine identity of the husband after marriage. The woman's new name memorializes the loss of her independent identity as she becomes the property of her spouse. Virginia Woolf obviously recognized the possessive imagery of marital names when she wrote, "She had the oddest sense of being herself invisible; unseen; unknown . . . being Mrs. Dalloway; not even Clarissa anymore" (1953, 14). Practically, marriage often meant the feminine identity suppressing itself in compliance with a husband's opinion. Women see the world through the eyes of their husbands instead of relying upon their own intelligence and critical ability (Woolf 1953, 116).

Cultural expectations for being feminine often created feelings of inadequacy and unworthiness, which women desperately tried to assuage. Clarissa Dalloway pours her energy into planning and hosting parties, an occupation for which she says she has a natural inclination. Furthermore, she muses, the parties make people happy and help Richard further his career as he becomes more personally acquainted with business and political figures. Richard, meanwhile, indulgently tolerates his wife's passion, though he cannot imagine why the parties are so important to her (Woolf 1953, 183). Clarissa's interest in the "trivial" aspects of society—parties, flowers, fashions, and small talk with various rounds of people—is a suitable "feminine" outlet. Yet Clarissa feels ashamed and embarrassed by her accomplishments when her friend Peter visits, believing that her parties are insipid and hollow affairs. Years before, Peter summarized what her life would be like as an adult: "She would marry a Prime Minister and stand at the top of a staircase; the perfect hostess he called her (she had cried over it in her bedroom)" (Woolf 1953, 9–10). Distressed because her interest is not "important" enough from Peter's viewpoint, Clarissa compares herself to the people around her and finds herself wanting. She withdraws from the party: "it was too much of an effort. She was not enjoying it. It was too much like being—just anybody, standing there; anybody could do it. . . . Every time she gave a party she had this feeling of being something not herself" (Woolf 1953, 259). Condemned to meaningless labor and conversation within the bourgeoisie, but still at the gendered margins of society, women like Clarissa Dalloway experienced sensations of failure and guilt, because the work society allowed them to perform did not offer personal satisfaction.

Marianne Weber's contributions to sociological theory are generally overshadowed by her husband's, Max Weber's, stature within the field. But Marianne Weber's insights on gendered patterns of social production within the household economy are not to be overlooked. Weber proposes a "new valuation" of housework and pecuniary independence. "But as is well known . . . this condition is not guaranteed by law, and only recently, in very *narrow* strata of our people been assured by custom" (Weber [1912] in Lengermann and Niebrugge-Brantley 1998, 220). The need for autonomy expressed by Woolf in "A Room of One's Own" is contextualized by contemporaneous feminist authors who describe its very absence. The household economy sets up a power relation, a "master-slave" dialectic which can then lead to the manipulative trickery/tendencies of those held under the "lord and master" (Weber [1912] in Lengermann and Niebrugge-Brantley 1998, 221). Weber makes a link here between cultural toolkits and psychological/personality transformations and the material condition of economic dependency. But for Clarissa Dalloway the manipulation is a dead end; and for women, the ultimate feeling one is left with is failure and guilt.

This failure and guilt are ultimately a product of the status of "Second Sex"—the sense of dependence and feminine ennui. What Clarissa needs are both a sense of independence and meaningful work. Charlotte Perkins Gilman's short story, "The Yellow Wallpaper," refracts this theme. In the story, a woman descends into madness because of inactivity enforced by her doctor and husband. He prescribes a rest cure for depression resulting from a common diagnosis for uppity women of the time, hysteria. The main character in Gilman's "The Yellow Wallpaper" suffers from post-partum-depression-induced paranoia, seeing the material on the wall as designs of peering eyes, monitoring every move. Gilman's main character is driven to insanity because of sheer idleness.

Gilman and Woolf's hidden critique correlates with a Marxian understanding of the human person, namely people suffer from alienation due to lack of meaningful activity (Fromm 2004). Clarissa has no "meaningful work." Work is what defines human happiness. Clarissa is unhappy because she is merely a people-pleaser with no true substance to show for her activity. An insult about the parties being meaningless suggests that even conversation for Clarissa is a meaningless attempt to fill the hole, which is her vacuous self. Her self is defined dependently through her husband. This is because of, in Gilman's terms, the "sexuo-economic relationship" (Gilman 1898). Women were economically dependent upon their husbands and restricted to inane and unimportant domestic duties. Gender, then is mapped onto the power structures rooted in human prehistory, and constituted by an exploitative division of labor: "Gender is a product of the human capacity for conscious, planful, conceptually mediated orientation to each other. Human beings have effectively gendered work, the psyche, the world . . . differentiating our industries, responsibilities and virtues along sex lines" (Gilman 1898, in Lengermann and Niebrugge-Brantley 1998, 119).

For Gilman, like Marx and Hegel before her, "Meaningful work is the essence of human self-realization; restricting or denying the individual access to meaningful work reduces the individual to a condition of nonhumanity" (Ritzer 2004, 298). For Marx, "productive life is the life of the species . . . the whole character of a species . . . is contained in the character of its life activity" (Marx [1844] 1978, 76). Thus, work conditions existential reality. Estranged work, then creates alienation: work is not meaningful activity, but a mere "means to existence" (Marx [1844] 1978, 76–77). Meaningful work is to be found, for Gilman, not in the domestic imprisonment of housekeeping but in, as Virginia Woolf articulates, "a room of one's own," with the autonomy to write and engage in social activism (Ritzer 2004, 298). Like Karl Marx's theory, both Woolf and Gilman "imaginatively theorize" within the frame of historical materialism. They consider the possibility of the roles of history in the development of alienated consciousness. Whereas Woolf and Gilman propose the role of "sex" (our contemporary word would be "gender") play in creating a tiered system, Marx's key theme is the power of "class." Masculinity then creates a pathway for alienation and dominance, differentiation within humans. And glossing on a Marxian theme, both Woolf and Gilman see that this very power of differentiation has taken on a pathological trajectory of history, and this then disconnects us from our unified species-being: "man [sic] is a species-being . . . because he [sic] treats himself [sic] as a universal and therefore a free being" (Marx [1844] 1978, 75).

"THE PROBLEM THAT HAS NO NAME"

Other women attempt to ease their feelings of inadequacy and ennui in *The Hours,* a film that contrasts three women whose only connection is Woolf's novel *Mrs. Dalloway*. The production is based on a book by Michael Cunningham, in which he represents one day in the life of Virginia Woolf, 1950s housewife Laura Brown, and present-day Clarissa Vaughn. Cunningham represents Virginia Woolf as a brilliant writer who suffers from manic depression and is closely monitored by her husband Leonard. Plagued by anomie and ennui in a society that offers very few outlets for women, Woolf pours her frustration at her male-driven world into writing. The movie is bookended by two scenes that agonizingly dramatize Virginia Woolf's final method of escape: suicide. Frustrated with what Michel Foucault has outlined as the stifling and repressive role of Victorian sexual ethics, woman was rendered useless if she did not bear children and serve her husband. As depicted in the film, the depression that Woolf faces shows that late Victorian England did not know what to do with an *independent woman thinker*. That identity would have been a contradiction. The sphere of thinking was reserved for the other sex. Also, facing these contradictions and the "problem that has no name," *pace* Betty Friedan's parsing, Laura Brown's choice may be even more agonizing. Pregnant, discouraged by her inability to complete day-to-day tasks, and overwhelmed by the needs of her husband and son, Brown tries to take her own life. Unable to undertake that final step, Brown waits for her child to be born and then simply abandons the family that is suffocating her. Finally, Clarissa Vaughn mirrors Mrs. Dalloway as she desperately tries to hold her life together by organizing a celebratory party for her AIDS-stricken friend on the day he is to receive a prestigious literary award. After his unexpected death, Clarissa emotionally leans on her partner Sally and her daughter Julia to compensate for the loss of the man she nursed for years. The feminine sense of personal shortcomings is summarized by Simone de Beauvoir's analysis of culture's bifurcated expectations concerning women versus men: "[Men] are willing on the whole to accept woman as a fellow being, an equal; but they still require her to remain the inessential. For her these two destinies are incompatible; she hesitates between one and the other without being exactly adapted to either, and from this comes her lack of equilibrium" (1989, 262). Unsatisfied by their lives, the women of *The Hours* attempt to escape from the gender identities that threaten to suffocate them with emotional demands. Their chief problems are the problem of woman: defining oneself through a relationship with an "other being," a man.

INDEPENDENCE IN "A ROOM OF ONE'S OWN"

Along with hiding from emotional stress, many women also try to repress their intellectual capabilities, as Woolf relates in her essay "A Room of One's Own." Of course, centuries ago, educationally deprived women were barely even aware that they possessed an intellect. As girls, they were denied the opportunity to learn basic logic and grammar, leaving them unprepared for complex studies in theory or the classics (Woolf [1929] 2020, Chapter 3). As time passed, this deprivation furthered the notion that women were incapable of scholarship, and that a woman was somehow "unfeminine" if she enjoyed learning. One male intellectual quoted by Simone de Beauvoir explains, "reason is never useful to them" (Beauvoir 1989, 239). In fact, reason can actually inhibit women from performing proper social duties. An educated or naturally gifted woman is an anomaly, a social misfit who could possibly upset the delicate balance of culture and is therefore considered a dangerous "anarchist" (Beauvoir 1989, 531). Even when women began publishing works of their own, Woolf acknowledges that many women sought to veil themselves by taking male pseudonyms. Currer Bell, George Eliot, and George Sand are all examples of women who hid behind a masculine *nom de plume* to protect their female identities from public suspicion (Woolf 2004 [1929], Chapter 3). For Virginia Woolf, society determines the level of intelligence a female mind is allowed to possess and when her aptitude becomes culturally unacceptable.

Society's anathematizing of strong female intellectuals in previous generations precluded the possibility of genius women of the caliber of Shakespeare or Newton. Virginia Woolf, herself a prolific writer, understood that penning great works of literature takes financial self-sufficiency, uninterrupted time to work, and some sense of tacit societal approval. The sexuo-economic relation stands in the way of this. Women contemporaneous with Virginia Woolf generally did not enjoy access to some or all of these needs, and women living further in the past would have been even further handicapped. She acknowledges that it would have been impossible for a woman in Shakespeare's day to write with such virtuosity, because cultural expectations for women actively repressed flickers of feminine brilliance (Woolf 2004 [1929], Chapter 3). Again, Woolf here applies a theory of base/superstructure in a Marxian tone. The power categories of her generation prevented the ascent of female culture icons. Gilman would suggest that males enforce the tasks of domesticity onto women as a means of preventing them from developing their reflective thinking capacity for other trades. For centuries men knew how to sew, cook, clean, but they were given the intellectual outlets and left women to attend to the less intellectually demanding household duties, thus disadvantaging mental development (Gilman 1898, 8).

Nor do women have hopes for liberatory movements or binding together in intellectual groups. Unlike working class movements, which offer the opportunity for solidarity, the sexuo-economic relation gives rise to individual households, where individuals are linked in dominance pairs that are difficult to break (Ritzer 2004, 300). This is why, in Simone de Beauvoir's observation, women have not had revolutionary movements. They are bound to the internally oppressive unit of the household. This is not to say that Woolf believes that female geniuses did not exist centuries ago, only that the volatile combination of culture and social expectations for women to be docile quashed any hope of a recognized woman genius and squelched the possibility for bringing women collectively together to spark creative ideas in each other, as we find in the eighteenth-century scene of Samuel Johnson conversing with Alexander Pope in *Orlando*. Woolf envisions a gloomy picture of stifled natural talent:

When, however, one reads of a witch being ducked, of a woman possessed by devils, of a wise woman selling herbs, or even of a very remarkable man who had a mother, then I think we are on the track of a lost novelist, a suppressed poet . . . crazed with the torture that her gift had put her to. (Woolf 2004 [1929], Chapter 3)

Where Virginia Woolf focused on the quandary of female literary geniuses, Simone de Beauvoir tackled the issue of women in the sciences. Overwhelmed with the honor of being included in such a "masculine" field, Beauvoir writes that women are "on their best behavior," undermining their ability to create innovative ideas because they mistrust their own originality (1989, 708). Women in the sciences are wary of proffering too risqué or controversial theories, lest they be labeled "irrational." If they conform, they garner legitimacy. In either case, Woolf and Beauvoir essentially embrace the same attitude toward women geniuses. Without the educational, financial, and cultural support which men receive, women may produce competent science and satisfactory literature, but women of true genius will remain anonymous or undiscovered. Woolf suggests this metaphorically by asking what would have been the fate of Shakespeare's sister had she been endowed with the talents of her brother? (Okin 1996, 36).

Finally, in "A Room of One's Own," Virginia Woolf explicitly relates how patriarchal power structures are society's motivation in creating a submissive feminine identity. Until this point, Woolf tiptoed around the subject, allotting most of her attention to the results of gendering but not to its social causes. The subject is first broached when Woolf relates her experience of the prestigious universities in Britain. As a woman, she is tightly limited in her movements, denied the freedom of walking on the manicured lawns of Oxford and the like, where male scholars stride along. Furthermore, her entrance into a library is rebuffed, symbolically illustrating a masculine control over what she is permitted to experience and learn (Woolf 2004 [1929], Chapter 1). Reading scholarly literature regarding her own sex, Virginia Woolf overtly declares that men's social domination of women is a source of power: "when the professor insisted a little too emphatically upon the inferiority of women, he was concerned not with their inferiority, but with his own superiority" (2004, [1929], Chapter 2). Recent commentary concerning cultural power structures confirms that the social construction of gender identities is not based on legitimate scholarship but upon the desire to control limited, desirable sources of authority. "Gender is the basis for macro-level allocation of material resources and opportunities" (Alamilla 2001, 62). With such a gendered power structure in place, men were ensured the best educational, political, and social prospects. Thus, gender is enormously important to male members of a patriarchal society. A man who wishes to become a great ruler, academic, businessman, or politician draws power from the cultural assumption that half of the human race is biologically, intellectually, and morally inferior to him (Woolf 2004 [1929], Chapter 2). "A Room of One's Own" overtly declares Virginia Woolf's belief that the male-dominated society of twentieth-century Britain is a patriarchal power structure constructed through men's cultural domination of women. Woolf's way out, through cultural innovation, is not what feminists would call a complete embrace of the feminine, but rather an acknowledgment of a kind of androgyny: art comes from a very philosophical, erotic view of the dialogue between masculine and feminine. She looks to Coleridge in this observation that "a great mind is androgynous" (Woolf, "A Room of One's Own," quoted in Degli-Esposti 1996, 85).

ORLANDO AND STRUCTURE

Thus, we return to the important function of *Orlando* as a text that suspends structures. *Orlando* suspends two conventional categories important to bourgeois capitalism: time/progress and gender/sex. The fact that Orlando's main character remains in a suspended youth plays an important role, according to Jed Esty: Woolf's ageless characters "cast doubt on the ideology of progress," as commentary on modernist aesthetics linked to colonialism (Esty 2007). Eternal youth is also a master trope of the revolutionary/Enlightenment principles of modernity. "The new!" *Orlando,* Chapter 2 and the conclusion of her time with the ancient society of "gypsies," in Chapter 4, also express a commentary on Orlando's affluence as idle foolishness. Considering colonialism/imperialism, Orlando travels to the "old" world of Asia Minor, the "gypsies," the encounter with an essentialized "Turkish" environment and an androgynization of characters local to Constantinople, all present important scenes bracketing Orlando's both historical and gender transformation. Youthful revolutionary masculinity, progress, colonialism, and its associated power and influence, are rejected by the main character in her transition to the "female sex."

Orlando's character actually suspends the very notion of biological sex categories, as Woolf rejects the binary inheritance of intellectual and social life. In other works, Woolf praises androgyny—not quite the same as "queerness" but as a complete celebration of the suspension of the rigidities of capitalistic notions that exploit one sex at the expense of another. The "great mind" is beyond such a category. In "A Room of One's Own," Woolf writes that it is "fatal for anyone who writes to think of their sex. It is fatal to be a man or woman pure and simple; one must be woman manly or man womanly" (1929, 104). Thus, the writer—or by extension the sociological observer, must always think, analyze, and write with a kind of gender suspension, or gender objectivity. There is a strangeness, and a beautiful liminality in such a role (Simmel 1908; Turner 1969). For Woolf, androgyny is sociological objectivity, while also embracing an artistic imagination. Today one may consider Woolf's theoretical contribution as a rejection of both patriarchal, but also, ironically, the powerful identity politics of deconstructionism—both of these preserve the reification of these identities as prisons and prisms of essentialist perspectives. In this way, we must all be trans- and inter-sexed, or "androgynous" in the project of observing, and writing.

For Plato, and his doppelgänger, Aristophanes, unified and wise beings were seen as androgynous (Degli-Esposti 1996, 86). Offering a sophisticatedly ancient, yet also postmodern, view of creativity, Woolf places herself and calls for all authors to dwell in that liminal position of androgyny. It is perhaps only because of her social context of Victorianism's abiding persistence on defining sex in dichotomies (Okin 1996) that Woolf fell victim to her own depression. Her suicide may have been a martyrdom to the problematic of the "binary" prisons of mental projections and gender-role essentialism (Bell 1972).

CONCLUSION

Through her fiction, Virginia Woolf reflected the sociological imagination of her American contemporary, Charlotte Perkins Gilman. Both authors deconstructed the cultural assumptions of femininity during a period when the social identity of gender, its historical-material cause, and its consequences were barely acknowledged or understood. Woolf's imaginative novel *Orlando* explores the biological and social causes of a person's behavior and implies that (biological) sex is far less important than the cultural expectations of gender. *Orlando* offers a key sociological imaginative technique serving the interests of critical insight over against modern categories. Woolf does this through both "time disorientation" in an eternal character, and "gender disorientation" in the tropes of camp and androgyny. *Orlando* refracts off the texts *Mrs. Dalloway* and "A Room of One's Own," which demonstrate women's reliance on men, the repression of intellect, and their internalized sense of inferiority relating to the legacy of generations upon generations of dependent status in European societies.

Woolf also uses the sociological imagination by highlighting the underlying patriarchal power structures, which offer men resources and opportunities by elevating the masculine while disregarding the feminine. Gilman's articulation of this in the "sexuo-economic relation" was embedded in her literary and theoretical contributions. Long before sociology's acceptance of Queer theory, and also before her sociological peers were attuned to the historical-material and cultural-contextual aspects of gendered relations, Virginia Woolf comprehended one of today's sociology and its most basic principles: that an individual's social identity is strongly affected by outside cultural forces in terms of gender, and that cultural and historical forces may trump biology in their oppressive mechanisms. Woolf's imaginative fiction can be read as sociological commentary that reveals the motivation behind gendering as well its consequences for women throughout the cultural and intellectual history of Britain.

Chapter Seven

The Absurd Christian

The Sociological Imagination of Dostoevsky

Fyodor M. Dostoevsky was born in Moscow in 1821. He had a religious upbringing, and a pedigree of priests on his father's side of the family. His father, an army doctor, was an impoverished "petty tyrant" who was rumored to have been mysteriously murdered by local peasant serfs. Later in life, Dostoevsky was presented in front of a mock firing squad, for punishment with involvement with radical activists of his time. This left a traumatic mark on the man—perhaps triggering later fits of epilepsy—and the writer, as he constantly worked out the tensions between his own view of the noble aims of Western forms of socialist, radical, and liberatory idealism and their "rationalist" erosion of Christian value systems and faith. Inspired by Pushkin's (1829) famous response to modern man in *The Gypsies,* Dostoevsky's didactic literary contribution calls for humility: "Humble thyself, proud man!" (quoted in Nabokov 1981). Dostoevsky's corpus of writing reflects these biographical traumas, in part a product of modernization—playing out in his personality as both a "neurotic" and sentimentalist, according to the eminent and harshly critical literary figure, Vladimir Nabokov (1981, 98–99). Dostoevsky reflects an early form of a sociological imagination—connecting the realms of psychology and ideology—as described by the biographer Joseph Frank (2020). Frank argued that Dostoevsky worked through the tensions of the sociocultural context of nineteenth-century Russia (Miller, in Frank 2020, x–xi). These biographical themes and ideological struggles work their way into plotlines and characterizations in Dostoevsky's last novel, *The Brothers Karamazov*, which is the main focus of this chapter. Dostoevsky is vital to an understanding of the emergence of the problematics of the postmodern, as he anticipated today's extensive, "moral and political instability and latent nihilism" that increases in prevalence as time moves forward (Brodskaya in Frank 2020, xxiii).

THE CONTEXT: DOSTOEVSKY'S SIGNIFICANCE TO SOCIOLOGY

Dostoevsky treats the main theme of the "individual in tension with their society" throughout his novels. Dostoevsky's heroes may be "misfits of Modernity"; Nabokov accuses their creator, and his creations, of highly neurotic temperaments (Nabokov 1981). One can see, however, that a "neurotic symptom" may be an excessive guilt from the over-socialized personality—one that by *modern* standards even embraces morality in an absurd world, rather than rejecting it for a certain form of self-interested egoism. In other words, in Freudian terms, the super-ego is no longer relevant, so why trouble oneself with this guilt? Building on this observation, the introspective element within the characterizations of Dostoevsky's protagonists reflects the spirit of the time: "it is . . . precisely he . . . who bears within himself the heart of the whole . . . while others in the epoch . . . have been torn away from it" (Dostoevsky, quoted in Bird 2012, 200). Dostoevsky's "neurotic voice" within his own historical period comes across to the reader in the somewhat reflexive questions of the self's role within society. This is a voice that anticipates later literary moments that will reject all morality, and embrace the absurd, as Goldmann observes about the modernist period within the arts and literature, "where the human being has lost all essential reality either as an individual or a community" (1975, 138). This is also an important conundrum for the dawn of social psychology, as it is found in the sociological theories of Charles Horton Cooley (American, b. 1864), and of French thinker Emile Durkheim (b. 1858). Norbert Wiley has explored the introspective element within the social self, via the literary theorist Mikhail Bakhtin's description of "voices" (Wiley 2016). Bakhtin, writing on the dialogical character of Dostoevsky's poetics, reflects an important bridge between sociological theory and the study of literature. The sociologically significant psychoanalyst Sigmund Freud is also an important link between social science and Dostoevsky—Freud saw *Brothers Karamazov* as the finest novel ever written (Cassedy 2005, 16). Dostoevsky as a "psychological" and "philosophical" writer is an acknowledged line of research. What this chapter seeks to do is view Dostoevsky with the lens of sociology of religion, and the power of the "bridge" of religion as a cultural system that ties the individual to the larger society. Dostoevsky's sense of "religion" is not exactly Orthodox, but nevertheless, it gives the reader a projected formula for a specific sociological problem. This is a blueprint for religious practice within secularization. In this way Dostoevsky's work is a companion to the concept of "lived" religion as Robert Orsi (2002) and other sociologists have described it. Lived religion is not so much high-level conceptual nor focused on "correct" theology of belief. Rather through the expedient, imagination-driven method of fiction, Dostoevsky offers images of the actual "practice" of the sanctification (or demonization) of everyday life. Religion is both a toolkit for building a better future, and driven by a longing for a sense of what was lost, from the past. Dostoevsky's "creations" and lived religion are infused more by a religious "imagination" rather than formal doctrine or dogma. This makes possible an "atmospheric" level of faith-in-narrative. Fiction thus presents itself in an important methodological kinship to the framework of "lived religion" within sociology of religion. This is because of its power of narrative over the dogmatic; "belief in practice" is a great deal more than following "imperatives" or great commandments (Williams 2011, ix).

MODERNIZATION AND SECULARIZATION

According to a generalized sociological narrative of history—one that Dostoevsky articulated in his characterizations and the moral dilemmas in which he places his some of his characters—the ties that bind an individual to society transform (or even evaporate) over the course of "modernization." Modernization is an historical concept important to both Dostoevsky and the origins of sociological theory. The question of how to conceive of a "new" response to the problems of rapid industrialization and secularization dominated the trajectory of Saint Simon's, Durkheim's, Marx's and Weber's sociological thought in the mid-nineteenth to early twentieth century. Socialism emerges as a solution for these thinkers—with different methodological emphases and nuances. It has resurged in our discussions today. An important consideration, that we are revisiting today in "late Capitalism" or "late Empire" is that of Durkheim's key concept of solidarity-as-trust. Trust is an essential element in society and the vital "glue" of socialism. It is an "emergent reality"—meaning, one cannot point to it, but its absence can be painfully palpable. The absence of trust is also an important theme in the more contemporary observations of Ulrich Beck and Anthony Giddens on risk-society and surveillance.

Dostoevsky's contribution to the sociological imagination is a response, but not a simplistically reactionary one, to the problematic of modernity's crisis of trust and the dissolution of the "old solidarities" that hold social ties together. Through "tradition" Christian ethics give shape to responsibility and obligations. Tying this into the contemporary sphere, there are a few brief mentions of going to "America" as a metaphor for modernity in *The Brothers*

Karamazov. It is an escape into "freedom," individualism, license, and the will, or, "vanity" (Part IV, Book XI. Chapter IV, "A Hymn and a Secret"). In this way, Dostoevsky presents the journey to America as the immigrant's hopes to free themselves from the fetters of the "old ties." One observation on the works of Dostoyevsky is that they are a continued meditation on the tensions between "old and new"—reflected both philosophically and sociologically in his statement on "truth and Christ" where Dostoevsky famously chose "Christ before truth." Many pietists have championed this saying by Dostoevsky as a negation of the new. However, looking more deeply into the (sometimes) complex categorizations and vagaries of Dostoevsky's faith, these are affirmations and emboldened statements that Dostoevsky proclaimed about the murkiness of faith within a fallen world.

"CHRIST BEFORE TRUTH"

In Rowan Williams's interpretation, Dostoevsky's famous biographical affirmation of the choice of "Christ before the truth" reflects the reality that it is the *divine* in us—not the human—that draws us to be responsible for one another in ways that are supra-human. This is our freedom from the realm of necessity and the viciousness of selfishness and ego. If we want to obey the divine spirit of connection and solidarity, we must disobey the selfishness in ourselves. As Fr. Zosima reminds the reader, when humans acknowledge their human weakness, then we are available to the Other's face concretely displayed in our neighbor. A new "iconography" is necessary for the individual, one in the image of Christ in the time of lost icons, the death of God, the emergence of Western ideals. Redemptive grace needs to be enacted within the warmth of practice rather than the coldness of dogma. Like Durkheim's sense of solidarity, humans complete one another through a reliance on their respective talents (like the sense of organic solidarity) but with the overlay of spiritual love (not unlike the "old" ties of obligation via mechanical solidarity).

Dostoevsky's socialist critics, like Leontyev, argued that this did not create a successful formula for "utopia" but it seems that they missed the very point—Dostoevsky's critique of materialism is foundational to the human level of existence in "conceptuality" or "consciousness." "Culture" and human consciousness come into being in the very moment humans recognize the possibility of limitation and death—according to Cassedy, Dostoevsky's anthropology is that humans are the *animal metaphysicum* (2005, 174). The need for an affirmation of immortality follows from here. But for Dostoevsky, "heaven" was not so much a place, but an attempt at making a meaningful narrative of life. "Immortality" is less about the "reward" of martyring oneself through the so-called "lacerations" (as a chapter is titled in *Brothers Karamazov*) but about the coherent whole of one's social and personal history. This immortality bids us to do the good—it forms one element of social glue which acts as a proviso for *true* love of humanity (Williams 2011, 80–81). What distinguishes Dostoevsky's conception of "immortality" from a more Orthodox rendering is its universalism—all are welcome. As Fr. Zosima expressed: "All is Truth." In attempting to reconcile the brothers, Zosima expresses this unity through the phrase, "on behalf of all, for all," which is taken from the Orthodox liturgy. Some later authors, like Jean-Paul Sartre and Julia Kristeva, saw Dostoevsky as expressing a proto-theory of existentialist human freedom, especially when considering the philosophical asides on "choice and necessity" in *Crime and Punishment* (Bird 2012, 117). But that deserves more attention elsewhere.

The question of order and the roots of mechanical solidarity, or obligation, is fundamental to Dostoevsky's characters' navigation of responsibility and action. For Dostoevsky, interconnection is the fundamental human reality—we are all one. The ego, amplified in Western ideologies, tells us, falsely, that we are separate, or even free from each other. The Kantian formula of autonomy elides with a Napoleonic "superman" and this is definitely what Dostoevsky wishes to critique, especially evidenced in the epitomized "before" redemption characterization of Raskolnikov in *Crime and Punishment* (Nielsen 2013). In the words of biographer Robert Bird, "Dostoevsky's faith is not an escape from the harsh forces of necessity, but a contrarian challenge against them" (Bird 2012, 54). This is both the power, but also presents the potential for the trappings, of Dostoevsky's embrace of an "old world" sense in *the pillars of tradition*. Family, patriotism and religion are synergistic "conservative" forces that are threatened by the uncertainty of modernity—the anomie that Durkheim discusses. Dostoevsky's characters face the empty realism of modern life, its anomic abandon and loneliness (nihilism) and some ponder, and some even commit suicide. This is a "horror" where everything is permitted, but humans are left with a choice. Modernity brings with it the absurdity of choosing the good. Ivan's devil is the patron saint of the "modern existentialist"—one can anticipate the likes of Camus in the future (Williams 2011, 72–73). Why do the good? What's the point, in morally vacant contexts like pandemic, war, societal breakdown? Freedom seems to be found in licentiousness in this context and anything but self-preservation seems absurd. If God, as a universal, is indeed "dead," what sustains the Christian to make a choice for the good?

A conjured, magical sense of embodied Durkheimian "collective effervescence" or, for Dostoevsky, "grace of the Christ"—especially noted in his famous speech on the legacy of Pushkin (1881) and its projection of a call for cultural conversion—lacks a sensitivity to the trajectory of Russian history. In the twentieth century, socialism takes over, the iron necessity of material history. Dostoevsky "ignored the fact that masses of people are not ruled by ideas alone, but by a variety of social currents largely outside of their individual control" (Nielsen 2013, 113). But this does not make the religious and cultural arguments of Dostoevsky categorically "wrong"—even if he was "on the wrong side of history." The Christ was also on the wrong side of history in *The Grand Inquisitor.* Perhaps a truly sacramental imagination, rather than a noumenal image of the Christ, would have unified the elements of "bread" as a message of delivery both in the physical and spiritual realms. This is the failure of the "writer's" spiritually projected utopia, but a cultural source of inspiration and sensitive understanding of the roots of projected utopias. As Daniel Vokey on the philosopher Alasdair MacIntyre has expressed, "there are no standards for rational judgments that are not internal to socially and historically conditioned traditions" (2001, 49). Thus, Dostoevsky's Christianity is cultural and atmospheric; it creates a reality through which the characters' choices, lived experience, and inner "dialogues" express a struggle with making sense of life through a Christian meanings, symbols, and tropes. *Brothers Karamazov* is a dramatized fictional biography of these entanglements and conscience.

DRAMAS OF DISINTEGRATION

Dostoevsky's stories are imbued with his own biography—as "dramas of disintegration" and the fragmentations of modern life's social-psychological realities (Bird 2012, 30–31). How can the divide be healed—the (reluctantly ancient) inner life weighted by tradition, with the chaos and uncertainty of freedom and progress? How, in the words of Robert Bellah's discussion of these terms in Durkheim, can the conundrum between *Gemeinschaft* (tradition/community) and *Gesellschaft* (modernity/progress/society) be resolved (see also Tönnies ([1887] 1961))? Christ then answers—but hopefully it is a Christ that embraces the true reality of the absurdity of the human condition. Dostoevsky's *Brothers Karamazov* is a dramaturgy and contains a series of purposely theatrical and sophisticatedly "Plato-like dialogues" between the "voices" of the desires of the Napoleonic individual and the call of the collective conscience. Durkheim and Dostoevsky converge as social psychological writers, in their exploration of the tension between the individual and society. As Donald Nielsen states, they were both "fascinated by the role of religion in the social order, and the balance between the competing demands of the individual and society" (Nielsen 2013, 96). Dostoevsky saw the problematics of the experience of "modernization/Westernization" following his broken, disappointed (and punished) experimentations with Western utopianism. Like Joseph Conrad, writing a few decades later, one level of Dostoevsky's contribution to sociology is that the individual is in a dangerous sea of anomie—awash with the chaos of self-interested sharks (the individual's fellow humans). For both authors, the question was not socialism or capitalism but the two novelists came down on different sides in responding to the weight of institutions and tradition. Conrad resolved this into a sense of how the individual must preserve himself from institutions. Dostoevsky, on the other hand, embraced a "lived" religion and culturally infused Christianity where the individual subsumed himself in the poetic imagination of the aesthetic but also transformative function of the icon; *theosis*. This divinization of the human transforms the spiritual to a lived, worldly, cultural possibility (Rosenshield 1994, 495). Perhaps there was an unintended generational/cohort effect here as Joseph Conrad's father, Apollo (b. 1820)—of Dostoevsky's (b. 1821) generation—had a favorite saying: *ubi crux, ibi poesia*—where there's a cross there is poetry. A crucifixion is albeit a more Roman Catholic motif as quoted by Conrad's Polish father. But lent to the Orthodox worldview, suffering is the crux and symbol of transformation for Dostoevsky's embrace of the poetic imagination. This comes through self-revealing in both the characters Ivan, and Dmitry.

Dostoevsky uses the brothers' character development—their actions, their psychological dispositions—to play out the drama of the human family and make a commentary on its potential dissolution, but also the power of Christian forgiveness and reconciliation. The "world" of a family drama that Dostoevsky conjures is not so much like the hues of the canvas of a Christian worldview on an icon painting, but more like incense that floats in the air during the divine liturgy. A radical immanence of the spirit of the divine-as-incarnate is the theological trope of this Christian writer—and the image of Christ as God-man (Rosenshield 1994; Nielsen 2013, 100) inspires the reader to be divine, even despite our human failings. This is the glue-as-forgiveness, as grace, that holds society together; the mostly absurd kiss of Christ to the Grand Inquisitor. As W.I. Thomas (1931, 69) suggests in *The Unadjusted Girl*, "A dying reprobate [assumed to be, anecdotally, Rabelais] petitions for forgiveness: *Dieu me pardonnera; C'est son métier.*" And the community wishes to grant such grace; as long as the sinner repents. For Dostoevsky, repentance is lost to modern ways of political-economic-social life: both capitalist, and socialist, as these are methods of rationalist-calculative vacuums of morality.

Modern life—including capitalism and socialism, both sides of the "catastrophe" in the observations of the phenomenological and Christian philosopher, Michel Henry—present the problems of nihilism and egoism. Nietzsche read Dostoevsky, but he only comes to express a societal shift that had been taking place as a result of modern western values. Nietzsche's will-to-power is ironically the impetus behind both systems of capitalist and socialist governance and economy. As Dostoevsky observes, how can one build a paradise on a *tabula rasa*? (letter in 1866, Nielsen, 2013, 99). Socialism (and Dostoevsky lumped socialism, nihilism, and materialism into one ideological matrix) is inspired by an impulse to destroy. Like Chronos, the advance of time presents how in the socialist impulse, "the revolution eats its children." And in modernity's other alternative, the capitalist orientation toward time is expressed in Benjamin Franklin's quip, "Time is Money" (Weber 2001).

One interpretation of the *Grand Inquisitor* suggests that it is Christianity "made manifest in speech"; thus, the parable of Christianity since the 'death of god' and its resurrection in socialism, is "the parable of the rise and betrayal of socialism" (Orr 1977, 72). The Inquisitor's final words reflect this: "For if anyone has deserved our fire, it is you. Tomorrow I shall burn you. *Dixi!*" (quoted in Orr 1977, 72). The element of "speech" and the *said* of these radical philosophies reflect an "alienation" within the "talk" about praxis versus the "pure charisma" of the silent service of Christ—which is the "empty" sense of suffering as emptying/*kenosis*. The prophet can only be silent when they see what the workings of history and human failing does to their prophecy (Orr 1977, 71). The alternative to "empty speech" is living the message of Christlike sacrifice-into-the divine.

This emptying, embodied rather than spoken, sense of divinization/*theosis* suggests the novelist's alternative in cultural Christianity that "permeated everyday life" from the most mundane activities to new forms of human association in the imitation of Christ (Nielsen 2013, 101). For Dostoevsky this required a collective embrace of a unified moral order. But what about today's context and what Durkheim noticed in the increasing differentiation of the "division of labor" as a metaphor for diversification of the collective conscience? Is Christianity absurd in modern contexts, given this diversity of cultural systems, values, and beliefs?

REANIMATION OF THE CHRIST

Anyone can observe, namely on the part of voices which testify to the "vanished whole" or a lost "center," in American society today: there is a crisis of trust. We stand at the threshold of a pervasive "heart of darkness"—with gun and knife violence, terrorism (from sources home-grown and abroad), potential war with nuclear capabilities, and political divisiveness. All of these heighten the awareness of an absence of trust. Yet interestingly enough, in this context a bio-pic on a Presbyterian minister media figure from the 1970s to 1990s, Mr. Fred Rogers, was produced and screened domestically and internationally over the holiday season of 2019. What is this odd coupling? The paradoxical pairing of discourse on neighborly love and mass violence may not be causally linked, but their simultaneity poses an interesting problematic in modern life that Dostoevsky (though a very different personage in vocation/avocation compared to Mr. Rogers) asks the same question: would you be, or won't you be, my neighbor—are we all our brothers' keeper?

Speaking within a vocation (not existing at the time!) of a sociological religionist, Dostoevsky calls for the "religious reanimation of society" (Nielsen 2013, 103). *Crime and Punishment* character Raskolnikov reflects the end-point of the trajectory of modern thinking and Western ideals—the oppressive isolation of the Napoleonic complex (Bird 2012, 101–103). Dostoevsky experiments with the literary method of incarnational and redemptive love in the face, and embrace, of Sonya in *Crime and Punishment*. This literary trope finds its way into *Brothers Karamazov*. This is not so much a tragic realism, but the struggle with the human condition as the contradiction or synthesis between embodiment and redemptive possibility. This paradox *haunts* the author's life. Again, the possibility of redemption floats in the air, immanent like the incense and smoke of the divine liturgy. Modernity works against this sacramental presence. As Donald Nielsen argues, both Durkheim and Dostoevsky were concerned with modernization's "excesses of egoism, nihilistic derangement of experience, and collective madness, including suicide. Both held out hope, in differing ways, for a religious renaissance" (Nielsen 2013, 96). Modernization inspires a reactionary response. But both Durkheim and Dostoevsky were calling for more of a religious renaissance. For Durkheim this is "civil religion"—perhaps in a Jewish-Catholic cultural mode of an expression of religion (see Geertz 2000). In Dostoevsky—his "Christ before truth" is not intended to be reactionary rejection of modernity, but a call for a cultural level of divinization—through the medium of incarnation. This is a distinctively Orthodox *mysticism*, but not necessarily the Western perspective, which one might see the in the institutional and power-ridden aspect of "Religion." Dostoevsky's characters parallel the historic development, engagement, and ultimately tension with "European" modes of the Enlightenment and its projected utopias. As in *Faust* (1976), the demonic force speaks French. The demonic force also pulls away from the "incarnational" to the conceptual in speech and dogma—this is one of the lessons of *The Grand Inquisitor* (Williams 2011, 82–83).

THE PROBLEMS WITH SOCIALISM

In Dostoevsky's rendering, through the mode of literary expression, "Russian experience had been molded and largely perverted by Western scientism, materialism, socialism, egoism, and a variety of movements claiming to liberate Russians from the inherited fetters of Czarism, Russian Orthodoxy, and their related social institutions" (Nielsen 2013, 98). For Dostoevsky, unlike Durkheim, socialism was not the answer. At its foundation, as exampled most famously by Nicolai Chernyshevsky's utopian novel *What is to be Done?* socialism is ultimately a misguided rationalist endeavor, with an underlying motivation from utilitarianism. Lost is the important glue of mechanical solidarity and Christ-like connection with sacrifice, obligation, responsibility, or a realistic attention to one's neighbor. As Rowan Williams has argued (2011), Dostoevsky's call for a uniquely Christian solidarity (and a religious mode of socialism is possible within the writings of Durkheim) is the sometimes difficult and awkward embraces of neighborly obligation and responsibility, rather than instrumentalized connections of self-interest and convenience. Both Durkheim and Dostoevsky see the animation of social life through spiritual coherence and (for Dostoevsky) consensus: a global transformation of human solidarity and interconnection via "free theocracy," where Dostoevsky found inspiration in Vladimir S. Solovyov (Williams 2011, 84). Perhaps a contemporary continental philosopher of religion might call this "church beyond Church." Across the globe, Melville's *Moby Dick* (written a few decades earlier) experimented with this idea, albeit through Queequeg as he was worshipping at the "First Congregation of the whole worshipping world . . . human kind."

The project of socialism, in Dostoevsky's perspective, was based on rationalism and materialism (Frank 2020). Dostoevsky was responding to a famous call by Vissarion Belinski, who saw religion as the conventional "opium" anesthetizing the hopes for revolution, awakening, and a rational coming to terms with reality (Nabokov 1981). Religion, then, prevents a coming-to in sober senses, as presented in Marx's famous terms from "Contribution to the Critique of Hegel's Philosophy of Right" (1844), and the Manifesto of the Communist Party (1848 [1888]) (Marx in Marx and Engels 1978, 54; 476). Belinski's famous quote in 1847's "Letter to Gogol": "It is not preaching or prayers that Russia needs . . . but an awakening among her common folk of a sense of human dignity . . . lost amid the mire and manure . . . conforming not with the teaching of the Church, but of common sense and justice" (Quoted in Nabokov 1981, 97). The appeal of Enlightenment hopes/projections of the common sense/reason driven society was important to a youthful Dostoevsky—but what is resolved within the conclusion to both the *Grand Inquisitor* narrative and the very conclusion of *Brothers Karamazov* is the answer of the absurdity of faith: Christ, and Alyosha, give the kiss of all-forgiving love. The desire for rational manifestations—even within a theological scope—is the human, but the divine takes the leap into the unknown, transcending all categories of rationality, into the absurdity of faith (Frank 2020, 173).

In the writings of Gillian Rose, the British social thinker describes modernity via the problematic of a "broken middle." This is shown by the sense of rupturing of life within modern philosophy, but is also rooted sociologically in what Eugene Halton describes in *Bereft of Reason:* as the rationalist, nominalist, and self-interested foundation of modernity. This problematic is not solved by a materialist socialism, even with its noble and highest aims. The gap between the "is-and-the-ought"—between the individual (*particulier*) conscience and the collective conscience—is the very dilemma that Durkheim explores in the "Dualism of Human Nature." Even in Dostoevsky himself this fissure was not healed in a biographical—or perhaps psychiatric—assessment of his life in tension with the characterizations in his novels. This "split" characteristic of the distance between words, hopes, and aims, and one's actual character traits and actions is more common among the modern psyche—this is the psychological condition of the broken middle. Another way of articulating this is that it reflects the social-psychological consequences of the incompleteness of the transition between *Gemeinschaft to Gesellschaft* (Tönnies [1887] 1961). These tensions play out in the character "portraits"—somewhat like icons—within Dostoevsky's fiction.

A NEW (AND ANCIENT) ICONOGRAPHY

As modern novels emerged, in what Lukács referred to as the "Post-Dostoevskian" literary moment, characterization became a replacement for iconography, in the death of icons (through secularization) but also through the reproduction of images, and the historical emergence of the photograph in the late nineteenth century (Bird 2012, 160–161). Walter Benjamin has reflected on the power of distance and "aura" versus modernity's "immediacy" of the image, social life, politics, and so on. According to Bird (2012) Dostoevsky's characters' faces are more like voices—obscured/distanced icons speaking. They are, in a sense, the inspirational "portraits" of the personages they reflect. In this way, Dostoevsky's method as modern icon painter in the form of words can reflect both human-and-divine properties. Fr. Zosima is himself an icon of a deeply serious, but practicable solidarity-as-love that must serve as a glue for society. Christ-like love unifies humans into one single moral entity (Nielsen 2013, 106). But it is not a naïve, rather ephemeral utilitarianism guiding motivations, as in secular forms of solidarity and "love of mankind." As Dostoevsky reflects on neighborly love within *Brothers Karamazov*, the voice of the pastoral Fr. Zosima's relays a story of a doctor:

"I love humanity," he said, "but I wonder at myself. The more I love humanity in general, the less I love man in particular. In my dreams," he said, "I have often come to making enthusiastic schemes for the service of humanity, and perhaps I might actually have faced crucifixion if it had been suddenly necessary; and yet I am incapable of living in the same room with any one for two days together, as I know by experience. As soon as any one is near me, his personality disturbs my self-complacency and restricts my freedom. In twenty-four hours I begin to hate the best of men: one because he's too long over his dinner; another because he has a cold and keeps on blowing his nose. I become hostile to people the moment they come close to me. But it has always happened that the more I detest men individually the more ardent becomes my love for humanity." ("A Lady of Little Faith")

Fr. Zosima reflects on the difficult journey of *real embodied and messy Christian* love—which is different than today's myopic secularized "celebration" of otherness: "Love in dreams is greedy for immediate action, rapidly performed and in the sight of all. Men will even give their lives if only the ordeal does not last long but is soon over, with all looking on and applauding as though on the stage" ("A Lady of Little Faith"). Today's sense of a thin "celebration" of one's neighbor seems to require the spark of innocent attraction, fascination, entertainment. Real charity requires us to go further, in the voice of Zosima:

"Active love is labor and fortitude, and for some people too, perhaps, a complete science. But I predict that just when you see with horror that in spite of all your efforts you are getting farther from your goal instead of nearer to it—at that very moment I predict that you will reach it and behold clearly the miraculous power of the Lord who has been all the time loving and mysteriously guiding you.

"Strive to love your neighbor actively and indefatigably. In as far as you advance in love you will grow surer of the reality of God and of the immortality of your soul. If you attain to perfect self-forgetfulness in the love of your neighbor, then you will believe without doubt, and no doubt can possibly enter your soul. This has been tried. This is certain." ("A Lady of Little Faith")

Active love is the hard work of "striving" to love . . . in the face of great annoyance, weariness, and fatigue—at the level of the suffering crucifixion and sacrifice—always pointing toward the good, hoping for the good, directing toward the good in a meaningful narrative whole, and sharing responsibility with others. These are the redemptive qualities for Christian love in Dostoevsky's vision—painful, challenging love and co-responsibility.

So, what does this mean for a sociology of trust and building community? Can we engage Dostoevsky in contemporary social life without some of the problematic baggage of Christian nostalgia via Fascism, nationalism, and so forth? The building blocks of civil society are trust, solidarity, bonds/ relationships. In the assumption of a common whole, these should pervade institutions, such as economics, culture, religion. The commonality of civil society is mortar holding those blocks together. For Dostoevsky the possibility of loving one's neighbor is diminished by modernity's force of freedom and license. This presents us with the "two voices" in Dostoevsky—the tension between 1) tradition and 2) progress/freedom. "*C'est du nouveau, n'est-ce pas*" is presented rather flippantly, and diabolically (The Devil. Ivan's Nightmare). Marx's famous quotation of the humanist perspective from Terence, "Nothing human is alien to me," is the diabolic projection into the license of the Napoleonic/ Nietzschean entrance of the will to power. The entitlement to crime, then, to allude to *Crime and Punishment*, is the selfishness and ultimate discourse of freedom/progress in the voice of the über-mensch. Dostoevsky's own sense of the Hobbesian ego-as-modern-man may have been inspired by the writings of the proto-Nietzschean, Max Stirner (Cassedy 2005, 39). The reader cannot ignore the egoism within the character Raskolnikov—even the contemporary adaptation of the television movie version of *Crime and Punishment* (2002, directed by Menachem Golan) shows the picture of Nietzsche hanging on Raskolnikov's apartment wall. The battle between egoism and communal good is a constant sociological theme in Dostoevsky. And this also relates to the questions of agency and freedom.

Throughout the philosophical dialogues within *Brothers Karamazov*, there is an ongoing battle between the philosophies of social context conditioning, necessity, and the call to responsibility and obligation. Durkheim sensed this very "tug of war" in his reflections on the "dualism of human nature" (1973)—the beastly ignorance of material philosophies (both within capitalism and an ill-conceived socialism) and the commandment to be attentive to one's responsibility is the struggle within the modern context.

CAN HUMANS BE GOOD WITHOUT GOD?

This is a frequent question, articulated by the atheists and immoral throughout the course of *Brothers Karamazov*. Interestingly enough, those who doubt or struggle with faith-as-morality come to entertain this question—and they are the interesting characters who show substance of character in the novel. What religious ethics from a Christian perspective point to is the very collapse of the need/impulse to be good with this very individual autonomy and "vacuum of responsibility" that goes along with modern (Western European) erosion of what Eduard Shils has called a "central value system." An abiding question throughout and drawn from *Brothers Karamazov* is how can "man be good without God"? A humility about the limits of secular-as-acquisitive-love is an important part of recognizing our need for a spiritual orientation. Our embodied and barriered nature that separates us from each other (modernity's "original sin" is individualism) is something the principle of common humanity of more secular ideologies forgets and may prevent us from being "good neighbors." The *divine* in us—not the human—draws us to be responsible for one another in ways that are supra-human. If we want to obey the divine spirit of connection and solidarity we must disobey the selfishness in ourselves: that individual "truth" of egoism. As Fr. Zosima reminds us, when we acknowledge our human weakness, then we are available to the Other's face concretely displayed in our neighbor.

Faced with the problem of suffering, especially the senseless suffering of innocents in our "fallen" world, Dostoevsky argues for, via Alyosha, the important choice to love in a child-like fashion. This action of love in good deeds in a dreary world leads to salvation not only in a projected "life after death," but also "here on earth as well. As Zosima implies, the world could be a paradise if only we wanted it to be so" (Nielsen 2013, 110). This is only if humans recognize their mutual responsibility through grace. However, the story is not as simple as this.

Dostoevsky (the person) had the reflective, and perhaps honest, moment of clarity, to jot down in his final notebooks, "We are all nihilists . . . we are all Fyodor Pavloviches" (Bird 2012, 8). Perhaps the modern age comes to people of faith in the form of anticlimactic apocalyptic of bureaucratic and instrumental rationalities and their accompanying absurdities—something akin to the perverse introspections and images in Nicolai Gogol's *The Overcoat*. "Something is very wrong and all men are mild lunatics engaged in pursuits that seem to them very important while an absurdly logical force keeps them at their futile jobs" (Nabokov 1981, 57). "Infinite cubicles" of life today may be an endless dark tunnel of bureaucracy, litigious culture, minutiae within contracts, and other absurdities. The sociological thinker Max Weber, who in the dawn of the new century ([1905] 2001) sensed the trajectory of modern social life into "specialists without spirit and sensualists without heart," was aware of these "disenchanting" dynamics.

What sociologists, journalists, and other commentators could call out today is a latent phenomenon of submissive, authoritarian, and anomic disconnect and conflict in capitalist culture—the manifest phenomenon of this is outright violence in our streets, houses of worship, shopping malls, and schools. Dostoevsky's message—relevant for today—conveys an understanding of the dualism in human nature. Durkheim reminded his reader, via Pascal, that humans are neither angel nor beast. Humans have a vast potential for good, or malice. As Robert Bird reflects upon in a biography of the Russian author, "None of [Dostoevsky's] protagonists—is ever granted a final illumination of his 'true' face. Even Zosima stinks in the grave . . . [his] characters exist towards their images, but only as exempla of spirit-made-flesh and flesh-made-spirit" (Bird 2012, 15). Fr. Zosima's miraculous divinity is that he is profoundly human. His corpse stinks—contrary to the expectation for the saintly, within the Orthodox tradition.

IVAN/ZOSIMA

The lessons drawn from *Brothers Karamazov* and Dostoevsky's own life suggest that Christianity should never make its practitioners comfortable—this is where it escapes the Fascist trap. For Dostoevsky, Christians should be especially hesitant when faith comes packaged in haughty confidence in a naïve sense of superiority. Like the confessee with Fr. Zosima, the moment we know we are so incapable of love is the moment we become truly loving. Oddly, the words of Fr. Zosima are spoken by protagonist Ivan (a "nonbeliever" who publishes theological writings) later in the book, in the chapter just before the famous *Grand Inquisitor* section of the novel.

> Ivan reflects with Alyosha: "I must make you one confession . . . I could never understand how one can love one's neighbors. It's just one's neighbors, to my mind, that one can't love, though one might love those at a distance. I once read somewhere of John the Merciful, a saint, that when a hungry, frozen beggar came to him, he took him into his bed, held him in his arms, and began breathing into his mouth, which was putrid and loathsome from some awful disease. I am convinced that he did that from 'self-laceration,' from the self-laceration of falsity, for the sake of the charity imposed by duty, as a penance laid on him. For anyone to love a man, he must be hidden, for as soon as he shows his face, love is gone." ("Rebellion")
> "Father Zosima has talked of that more than once," observed Alyosha; "he, too, said that the face of a man often hinders many people not practiced in love, from loving him. But yet there's a great deal of love in mankind, and almost Christ-like love. I know that myself, Ivan." ("Rebellion")

Why place this dialogue in a later chapter? This is the reflexive/self-critical voice of nonbelieving Ivan—who is ironically the author of many theological treatises. Cassedy (2005) notices the dramatized parallels between Ivan/Zosima throughout *Brothers Karamazov*. This doppelganger might suggest a "new Christian church" of world-embracing—"bathing the earth in tears of joy." Dwelling in and loving the earth, embracing reality (Cassedy 2005, 156)—that's what Ivan's "voice" constantly challenges Alyosha to do. Perhaps Ivan is the "adult faith" protagonist of *Brothers Karamazov*, in contrast with the child-like faith of Alyosha. But where Ivan seems physically—and by extension morally—sick at times, Zosima presents the possibility of a graceful "order" to existence. But it doesn't point to an abstraction or projection of heaven, but rather earth: loving all on earth.

CONCLUSION: A HOLY, ABSURD, SYNTHESIS

Dostoevsky presents us with a self-critical approach to the Romanticist preservation of a thin Christian ethic in the absurdities of modernity. According to biographer Robert Bird, this Romanticism "is an unsustainable consolation" (Bird 2012, 17). Does the author call us to a deeper charity, an engaged extension of an earthly understanding and compassion that is not instrumentalized into the (thin) exchange for an abstraction of otherworldly salvation? In Rosenshield's (1994) analysis, this reflects a lower-level or more primitive form of piety. Numerous theological commentaries on *Brothers Karamazov* have suggested a mystical bricolage, even pan-theistic character to the teachings of Zosima. They are infused by (and somewhat retorting) the thinking of Schleiermacher, Kant, Victor Hugo and Jean-Jacques Rousseau, just as much as Eastern Patristics (Cassedy 2005). In Fr. Zosima's final homily, before his death, he states, "he who has faith, has faith in God's people." For Zosima's mystical orthodoxy, faith moves out from the individual's self-consumption, but not in a naïve way. Atheism is internally self-enclosed, self-obsessed. But true faith must absorb other forms of thought, and encounter doubt, before it moves to active love. Active love counters atheists with that engaging mysterious element of Christian love (in Zosima's parsing), and active love is able to see that the "house has many rooms." Gracefully, active love affirms that even those who attack Christianity still may come to practice its ideals. Whereas other (secular) logics choose hell precisely because those persons, bathed in pride and arrogance, reject both the need and the possibility of forgiveness: "they will burn in the fire of their own wrath." But this message of Zosima is not expressing condemnation, but one of interconnection, co-responsibility, and the divine grace that covers all human relationships. Even Nabokov observes this "weight" of responsibility within his reading of *Brothers Karamazov*. Through the lens of the reader, in a mystery novel trope, each of the brothers seem somehow culpable of, and reflect guilt for, the murder of Fyodor Karamazov—even the saintly Alyosha (Nabokov 1981, 133).

In a syncretistic fashion, the theology of Zosima actually absorbs a favorite quotation of the cosmopolitan atheist. The Latin poet Terence's famous line is incorporated and made holy, thus shifting it away from its "diabolical" association: "Nothing human is alien to me"—"Satan *sum et nihil humanum a me alienum puto*" ("The Devil: Ivan's nightmare"). This was also the one of the famed atheist Karl Marx's favorite quotations (Marx 1865). In one reading, this ontology-embracing principle—spoken through or "framed" with a diabolic voice within the text of *The Brothers Karamazov*—is potentially absorbed and coopted through Christological icon of Zosima. In his "last sermon" to Alyosha, the Zosima states "all is truth"—an embrace of all creation gives us access to the possibility of becoming divine. This message comes to the "innocent" Alyosha at the height of his mystical experience. This might suggest there is a grand "amnesty" umbrella—forgiveness but not acceptance of the new radical philosophies of Dostoevsky's day (Frank 2020, 181). Rosenshield makes the connection between mystery and a grounded ethics—but what place does this have today, or even in Dostoevsky's context of the Nietzschean problem of the advancing "death of God"? From an Orthodox view "Grace is the presence of God within us which demands constant effort, but these efforts, however, in no way determine grace, upon our liberty as if it were external or foreign or foreign to it" (Vladimir Lossky, quoted in Rosenshield 1994, 499). This expresses the mysterious connection between grace and human freedom. The "absurdity" of Christianity in a modern context follows not from the fact that God is dead and we should be left to do whatever the ego chooses—but it is rather that the mystery of "God's death"—Jesus in the tomb—calls us to be responsible to one another. Hans Holbein's painting "The Body of Christ Dead in the Tomb" was influential to Dostoevsky, who visited Basel in 1868 (Bird 2012, 124). If the Western mode of consciousness had "killed God," then Dostoevsky's work is an embrace of the mystery of faith after the "death of God" in modern life and a vision of the mystical unity of "cosmic consciousness." In this new form, perhaps "absurd," expression of Christian life requires a *choice* of an ethic of responsibility. This "Christ before truth" reflects the *choice* the self should make in responsibility to others before and beyond the trappings of ego and power, recognizing infinite solidarity with, and connection and responsibilities to, others: in Zosima's terms, "All is Truth" ("The Russian Monk").

Dostoevsky's kiss from Christ to the Inquisitor, and Alyosha to Ivan, expresses this graceful and open theology of Zosima. Dostoevsky embraces his comrades in a leap of faith—prepared to forgive them, but not accept them, because a "lack of faith" could revert to tyranny (Frank 2020, 181). The absurd Christian is able to acknowledge that the world does not make rational sense, but still have faith without embracing nihilism or hedonism. The universe can never "make sense" in rational terms, but this does not let us "off the hook"—the absurd Christian, and all, must choose Christ, freely and with moral autonomy, while acknowledging the irrationality of human desires, drives, and actions. This is the final lesson of the all too human narrative of the family drama of *Brothers Karamazov*.

Chapter Eight

Conclusion

Stories in the Dawn of Capitalism— Crisis and Narrative in Boccaccio's Decameron

INTRODUCTION: CRISIS AND *COMMUNITAS*

The legacy of Karl Marx's writings reminds us that ultimately capitalism brings humanity to point of crisis. Whether it is in the psychological contradiction between the need for cooperation and a culture of competition, or the rapid changes in production technology, or economic collapses, a point arrives where: "all that is solid melts into air, all that is holy is profaned, and man is at last compelled to face with sober senses his real conditions of life, and his relations with his kind" (Marx and Engels [1848] 1976, 476). The discipline of sociology arose out of a need for a critique of these paradoxes of modern industrialism. The founders give us powerful "moments of clarity," especially through the insights of Marx, Weber, Durkheim, DuBois, Simmel, and others. However, what this volume has addressed was a discussion of how the founders' literary contemporaries, Hawthorne, Melville, Conrad, Gilman, Woolf, and Dostoevsky, created narratives as responses to these "breakages/crises" in modern capitalism, and for Dostoevsky, socialism as well.

In today's period of history, after the various disruptions of the Trump presidency, emergence of neo-Fascist elements, the COVID crisis, humanists of all sorts are called to reassess the power of narrative. Both academic and, better yet, the "civilian" humanist who actualizes through pragmatic applications of humanism within everyday life, should look back on these "great tales" with a new appreciation for literature as it describes the origins of this crisis, and, through the power of narrative, help us with applied ethical reasoning to function and cope within this crisis, or transform the situation altogether.

As academic institutions at all levels—from universities to middle schools—defund humanities and the arts in favor of S.T.E.M. programs, Max Weber (2001) might observe the way in which modern capitalism creates bureaucratic and technical functionaries—specialists without spirit and sensualists without heart. What better niche can destructive authoritarian psychologies, cultures, and leaders thrive than in an absence of ethical and humanistic education. As the theologically trained sociologist Jacques Ellul was known for observing in the 1960s, education in the humanistic tradition provides an essential guard against the influence of propaganda and fascism (Alves 2014).

The COVID crisis was not only a sociopolitical and public health wake-up call. It also presents an opportunity to renew interest in the humanities and social sciences wherein students are called to weigh particular moral inquiries and situations into a "deeper" sense of ethics and personhood. It suggests a time for reflection. In *The Ritual Process,* Victor Turner (1969) outlines the modes of ritual time, especially that of the "betwixt and between" experience of liminality. Turner's concept of liminality—or literally something between two realms, within a threshold/doorway (*limen*)—presents a suspension of social structures and hierarchy, and is a departure from "the normal." In this context, ritual, as a form of narrating powerful mythic stories, becomes a way of expressing intense emotions due to uncertainty and chaos, bracketing the experience of individuation and individualism, relaxing the forces of competition and ego in favor of togetherness and *"communitas."* This moment in ritual fosters a sense of connection, unity and solidarity via communion, community, commonality, and commonweal.

In the early stages of COVID there was a profound surge of "good will" discourse—commercials, public officials, and so on, urged kindness, patience, neighborly connection, and altruism. What stories became important in these times? The "great epics" and ballads of baby boomers, gen-Xers, millennials were popular on the radio and television, downloaded: *Lord of the Rings, Harry Potter, Indiana Jones, Marvel Heroes, DC Comics, Star Wars.* "We must come together" and *"*The evil must be defeated" took on a cultural overtone in these popular genres, and even in the voices of politicians. But eventually this sense of solidarity evaporated with the murder of George Floyd, and it may have also been exposed as "hype" by other experiences of violence, unemployment, and frustrations in the lower realms of the precariat economy. Where did the solidarity go? Was it ever there in the first place? This brings us to the cultural (mass) production question—did all these "good will" media serve as a kind of toxic salve, or opiate, during the time of COVID, masking the true inequalities and injustices, only to come out later, and to some extent be reified, in the Black Lives Matter protests and iconography?

DECAMERON: EARLY CAPITALISM AND CULTURE

A larger historical question presents itself: what is the function of art in capitalist society's times of crisis? Starting with the very dawn of capitalism—Giovanni Boccaccio's fourteenth-century Florence and his *Decameron*—these are a few concluding thoughts on the role of moral reflexivity and a sociological imagination within the context of fictional narrative. This moment where art captures the imagination presents rich potential for psychosocial insights. This is especially important in the meaning-making process following collective traumas and crises. Artistic expression can be on the one hand a vehicle for interpreting and processing cultural trauma. But on the other hand, art can also be a suspension of/numbing out or holding that very meaning-making and reflexive process at bay. It may serve as an anesthetic power, whereby it preserves the overall status quo. This opens up the possibility for a meditation on the role and social function of the imaginative in the suspension of time in the liminal. But as demonstrated by Boccaccio, this very suspended storytelling is also an opportunity for wider sociocultural critique.

Boccaccio's *Decameron* is a (lengthy) set of stories—and raucous escapades—narrated by voices of the nobility, told over ten days. The text anticipates class-differentials in the experience of plague in its first pages. What the *function* of this text reflects is how the earliest forms of "capitalist" class division, as evidenced in fourteenth-century Florence, give way to a materially based psychology and culture of self-indulgence of those not in the realm of dire necessity. The self-absorption of the elites in the story reflect how empathy (or the lack thereof by ignoring the suffering around oneself), has class dimensions. As Boccaccio stages the storytelling, the elite, while self-pampering, indulge in stories of brutality, sexual escapades, and exploitation. Boccaccio's muted/minimized voice brackets these bawdy tales, and is one of a Christianity-infused criticism. The (early) Renaissance humanist employs satire as a method of critical consciousness. Boccaccio's "voice" asks, "what is the place of compassion in these times?" "Where has responsibility for one's neighbor and the important practice of Christian *caritas* gone?" The leveling power of plague exposes the very social construction of reality—because plague is a natural tragedy: "overcoming all obstacles, disregarding all frontiers . . . all life is turned to death" (Falvo 1999, 145). Overall, the key message of *caritas* evaporating in the outside world in Boccaccio's Florence, is akin to how rapid changes in consumption opportunities and patterns created a culture of narcissism in late-modern capitalism, corresponding with the rapid collective personality transformations of the 1970s to 1980s (Lasch 1979).

Plague or pandemic has a leveling power—all become vulnerable, rich and poor. In the time of Boccaccio, plague presented itself as a process of "undifferentiation" and altered social structures and institutions (Falvo 1999, 144). Although one could note that today in late capitalism, those on the racial and economic margins of society have been disproportionately devastated by COVID, as numerous current studies have shown. The bubonic plague was less discriminatory. At Boccaccio's time there was a reflection on a connection between "disease" and "disorder" because of this (René Girard, cited in Falvo 1999, 148). Paralleled in the twentieth century, Albert Camus's novel uses plague as a metaphor for the social disruption of war. David Steel writes, that in addition, "the plague played havoc with the established social order of fourteenth-century Florence, bringing in its wake economic disruption, political anarchy and a progressive deterioration of manners." Paralleling with Camus, illness experienced as an individual, "forces the relaxation of social and moral attitudes so disease on a vast social scale liberates cynicism and lawlessness" (Steel 1981, 90). Steel also notes a powerful shift in a "genealogy of modernity" within Boccaccio—this presents the dawn of modern causality wherein "the historical circumstance of the plague as direct cause, or one of them, of the shift in moral outlook to which *The Decameron* itself testifies and of which it is the greatest contemporary literary monument. There is a sense in which the age of modern fiction was ushered in by a virus" (Steel 1981, 90).

Referring back to Victor Turner's thesis, the suspension of structure, or the Bakhtinian potential for "carnival" of plague opens up the question about the meaning of order—and also creates a place for what Mazzotta has defined as the importance of "play." History-causality-destiny are an interesting matrix of concerns that plague brings about—not necessarily a Heideggerian "being unto death," but rather the plague is a "switchman" of history that makes possible some of the logics that Calvinist theology, especially predestination—a critical connection to the notion of "elect" in capitalism. "Where human mortality is concerned, notions of chance, destiny and predestination are uncomfortably sharpened in times of plague" (Steel 1981, 91).

A rerouted religious response to plague, in some sense, then, ushered forth the kernels of both modernity and religious reaction. As Kathryn Mogk connects religious and artistic meaning-making in times of social distress:

> Religion's entanglement with pandemic is just as old as its ties to art. Historically, pandemics have fueled religious movements in the societies they disrupt. . . . While the aftermath [of the Black Death] included artistic masterpieces—most famously, Boccaccio's *Decameron*—religious responses were far more profound. The possibility of sudden death, seared into collective memory by pandemic, made religion everyone's business. (Mogk 2020)

Mostly for ill, religiosity in response to COVID's existential uncertainty has led to a surge of new COVID clusters. As Mogk notes again on the context of fourteenth-century Europe: "The decades that followed saw new forms of lay devotion, vernacular translations of the Bible, and enthusiasm for a "mixed life" that brought monastic practices into the household and workshop. Some of the best aspects of the Protestant Reformation—its determination to bring the gospel to every ploughboy, its insistence that each person go to God with no mediator but Christ—were extensions of this movement" (Mogk 2020). We can see for Boccaccio's time, there is a link between individualization of faith, questioning of religious authorities (especially their hypocrisy) and the somewhat "nondiscriminatory" visit of the angel of death—upon the righteous or unrighteous. This "tyranny of chance" (Mazzotta 1986, 19) and the arbitrariness of the experience of death problematizes a religious worldview as somehow "irrelevant." Thus, with the notion that religion and obedience to God results in no specific positive outcome, again, presents a turn toward the dawn of the "modern." The *Decameron* is essentially a leisurely "wasting of time" for the key storytellers—contrary to the new emerging capitalistic ethic of efficiency. Similar to the scenes of Ingmar Bergman's famous *The Seventh Seal* (1958), the participants play chess—they themselves may be pawns in the "Game of Death, or its shadow, the agon of Time" (Mazzotta 1986, 46). Additionally, within the inscribing action of the manuscript itself, Clarke (2018) links this use of "catchwords" within the pages to the marginalia markings; support a case for the text as an exercise in a fanciful liminality. This method speaks to the process of the scribe—likely clergy—and suggests a moral message, expressing the importance of the experience of timelessness. Within Turners' definition of timeless liminality—the storytelling exhibits both "forward and backward motion." The personified figure of Death is ever lurking, as in Bergman's famous robed movie character. The "threat of loss is constant" both as transition and potentiality within the liminal moment (Clarke 2018, 36) of the pre-bound form of the text—it is a call to attention to the manuscript inscriber's moral reflexivity, rather than the reader. The force of death, here, disregards the hierarchical structures of scribe/knight/peasant. Death has a democratic force.

ESCAPISM AND STORYTELLING

What is the place of fictional storytelling within this context where life is constantly precarious, and Death looms over all? Escapism plays a role in storytelling fantasies amidst realities of death. According to Mazzotta: "for him the visionary power of the imagination, its play and pleasure, constantly takes its flight from the real and it constantly stumbles against the unyielding, necessary laws of the business of living" (1986, 10). Art has both a "discrepancy and kinship" to reality/life. Art can reflect life. Art also helps the audience/viewer/reader escape the drudgery of life. Art can also shape existence and transform such drudgery into a more hopeful existence. Art and life are symbiotic, just as much as the dialectic between utopia/history, and hope for a better reality must also pay heed to an honest reckoning with life's limitations. For Boccaccio the response is not tragic or forlorn, but playful: "it is a mode drawn under the sovereignty of play, which is both a stance and a style of effacement of the boundaries between the real and the make-believe, the serious and the unserious, the useful and the useless . . . the worst illusion of all is to believe we have no illusions" (Mazzotta 1986, 11). Play, then, embraces the "real" even while it is a suspension of it. This is in contrast to more modern notions of the "mass culture" system and branding as a kind of distraction that "dulls" and dissociates people in marketing culture, distancing us from our possibility for other forms of imagination toward liberation (Wright and Hutchison 1997).

For Boccaccio the act of storytelling engages more of a participatory and critical element through the mechanism of allegory. In allegory the author disguises their own imagined normative vision (Jameson 2019, 12). But even while this is suspended directly, Boccaccio uses lewd stories as exposure of the "sickness" of society—as an extended metaphor and measured allegory. This suspension is at the very heart of "the literary art" where the hopes of the artist are "obfuscated by the questions of universalism, the human condition"—in Boccaccio's descriptions of sex vs. death—and the "eternal story" (Jameson 2019, 12). Thus, "ideology is at the heart" of the inscribing of narrative forms; it constitutes the "intersection between the biological individual and the collective" expressed in "language itself" (Jameson 2019, 12). Ideas, in Jameson's description, are not simply words, but syntax connected with meaning. Thus, the project of the narrative allegory connects the individual to the larger moral/meaning questions. Anticipation of the "End" also adds to the liminal element of the experience of time. There is in *Decameron,* "a generative link between a cause and its effects, the law of causality is suspended—temporal continuity is broken up by the loom of death" (Mazzotta 1986, 22). The stories then become a "diversion" or "distraction"—culture is then druglike, a "sweet poison." Ritual then, reflecting Turner's (1969) concepts is a suspension of structure/reality, rather than a reification of those categories of "the system."

The medieval and ancient sense of culture's power to distract through creating "effervescence" had some parallels to today's understanding of culture's anaesthetizing properties. This observation was not in any way a "new finding" via the Marxian perspectives so common in Marx's early works, as they are brought into the interpreters of twentieth- to twenty-first-century Critical

Theory. Boccaccio in "Genealogy of the Gods" interprets the Christian philosopher Boethius's observations in *Consolation of Philosophy*, addressing a description of the "bad muses who nurse the sick with sweet poison (*dulce venerium*)" (Mazzotta 1986). Boccaccio distinguishes these from the good muses, trusted by the poets to cure those sick of mind. It is the "poet-haters," he passionately argues, who bawl at the "modest muses" as if they were "women in the flesh" and accuse them of being "disreputable, obscene, witches, harlots" (Mazzotta 1986). Poetry-as-feminine seduces the reader-as-masculine, and the "witchcraft" here is an extended metaphor for the power of *bad* culture to distract.

The debate here between "Truth" and "Poetry" is a medieval (or early Renaissance) rehearsal of the classic question of exiling the emotional from the reason-based governance in Plato's *Republic*. Yet, the mediating character here is Boethius's *Lady* Philosophy. And the difference between the Platonist sense of banishing poetry is not what the medieval orientation embraced. In the Middle Ages, "poetry was made to please and to teach, or more precisely to please in order to teach" (Green, in Boethius 1962, xxi). Fiction-as-fantasy, inherited from a kind of early sense of "dreamwork" here serves as a framework for moral allegory. Boethius's reflections come in the prison of the "soul-in-the-body"—or reason to the vicissitudes of Fortune (Green, in Boethius 1962)—but the key to escape is the very Lady of Philosophy. Through the mediation of *caritas*, and courtly love, poetry and philosophy can unite the soul to the body—but certainly philosophy is not the (sole) solution, or proper response, to the problem of plague, because it does not constitute a "rational" or "logical" series of observations about causality and the punishment of the just/unjust seems arbitrary. All are vulnerable to death from the plague. Boethius may have dismissed such "bad" poetry as a "strumpet muse" but *Lady* Philosophy herself, Boccaccio concludes, cites "many a fragment of verse and poetic fable to soothe and console Boethius" (Mazzotta 1986). So here we have a very curious (to modern notions, but perhaps not medieval ones) fusion between the philosophical and the poetic.

Nietzsche might observe there is a play here between the Apollonian and Dionysiac (1993). Fractured in the ancient world and modernity, one must remember that these forces are fused in the Medieval imagination, and their extremes resolved within a notion of Christian love. Additionally, there are "good" and "bad" forms of poetry. For the ancients, Apollo, the god of (helpful rather than destructive/Dionysiac) poetry is also representative of the art of medicine. This is developed within Boccaccio (and also before) through the metaphoric bond between reason and medicine. Ovid gives precepts (avoid theater and love-literature, never drink wine in moderation, either abstain or overdo it, do not eat onions) which, taken together, "are a transparent burlesque of the rhetoric of pedagogical treatises and in themselves are useless to control the unbounded play" (Mazzotta 1986). This marks the ongoing symbiosis between literature and philosophy, and literally makes a joke of the "consolation"—perhaps functioning with some sort of anesthetic properties—of philosophy.

To further problematize the way a modern reader might interpret the modes of the Apollonian and Dionysiac, in the *Decameron,* the accounts of lascivious activity go alongside descriptions of great religiosity and ritual scrupulosity. One interpretation of this may be that this is the game of utopia, which is to be understood as the imaginative project to reverse and parody the corruption of the city the storytellers have left behind. In fourteenth-century Florence, the body politic was crumbling, and there was emerging a new proto-bourgeoisie. Again, in the cloak of allegory, "law is the medicine of the body politic," and the body politic and society itself—as the Christian Church was seen as the very "body of Christ"—were "crumbling in the midst of corruption and bodily decay" (Falvo 1999, 144).

Whereas in today's COVID crisis, we see the pandemic unmasking the harsh health care access inequalities and government instability of our society, in Boccaccio's interpretation during his time, the plague itself was a naturalized metaphor for the sickness of society and democratizing power of death. Alongside emerging capitalism, Boccaccio's satire presents the first glimmering of a capitalist context that drives a critical sociology. This critique is presented through the power of naturalized metaphors at the dawn of Western capitalism—a skillful means at presenting a critique of his social context. The "plague" was seen not as a divine punishment, but within a (new) sociological vision of the "sickness" of society. Boccaccio's genius is to present this through the means of the naturalism of allegory and metaphor. Like a good Renaissance version of Durkheim (1973), observing breakdown of norms in a system that is changing, Boccaccio's "subtext" presents an early idea about capitalist-driven *anomie.*

There is another (albeit earlier historical context) social theory parallel with Marx's concept of alienation, and Boccaccio's commentary suggests that the foundation of moral life is being swept away in his context, leaving a sense of a dehumanized humanity. As Mazzotta highlights: "if the most elementary works of mercy, such as the burial of the dead and the caring for the sick, are neglected; if community can only be defined by the communication of the infection; if the exercise of reason, eclipsed in man, seems the attribute only of animals who roam freely through the fields and, unguided" (1986, 41). These observations perhaps are an earlier historicized expression, with culturally Christian moral overtones, about the logic of "capital" driving selfishness deprived of human decency. Boccaccio refers to humans losing conscience: animals "roaming unguided," in what the ancient world dubbed mere animalistic plane of "slavish necessity" (Greek: *ananke*). This disconnects humans from our required sense of freedom, but also sociability via "species being"; the observation is akin to Marx's 1844 Manuscripts on dehumanization into "animal" functions, self-interested behavior and alienation/atomization (Fromm 2004).

ART IS MOCKED BY ART: THE POWER OF UTOPIA

In addition to social selves' need to perform and receive *caritas*/charity, for Boccaccio's time, what makes humans human is also their capacity for "reason." For Boccaccio reason was understood as restraint (*ragione*) rather than abstract rationality of Descartes, or the Enlightenment's inheritance. The danger-zone is halfway between the reality of restraint and the imagined utopia. The Edenic-like garden setting of the story telling reflects a broken utopia. The world in plague expresses the lingering effects of Adam's fall from the Garden of Eden. Boccaccio's text presents an irony: as these (privileged) youngsters move into the idyllic space, halfway between reality and an imagined world, this "storytelling" within the *Decameron* is fantasy because the "Edenic" metaphors create a utopia as a *false* projection of safety. It is the allure and illusive nature of ontological security—but the reality is mortality and precariousness, a hint that the safe bounds of the garden are just as illusory for them as they were for Adam (Mazzotta 1986, 42).

The underlying subtext here is that theorizing, and projected utopias, are borne of leisure: a famous saying of the time was, art is mocked by art (*l'arte e dall'arte schernita*) (Mazzotta 1986, 44). In another rendering, "art can delude itself." This is a reminder that art can both deny and provoke the powerfully destructive emotions which lie just beneath the surface. Yet the artistic imagination allows the liminal moment of entertainment and distraction, an anesthetic power.

The stories reflect the perversion of humanity, and that very form of alienation which comes from too much wealth and idleness (against an old Aristotelian "mean"). Privilege is to be read as "idleness," here: Boccaccio "proffered this my travail to idle women and not to others" (from the Epilogue). Different themes in the stories express how "desire turns into aggression, philosophy into madness, learning a weapon of power, promises of either scholar or strumpet into deceptions" (Mazzotta 1986, 44). They are both a reflection of societal sickness, as the sickness exists in the "atmosphere"—this liminal space explores both sides of natural sickness (psycho-social and its metaphor within the body's symptoms).

COVID: CULTURE IN 2020

These reflections now move toward Phase Two of COVID-America, Summer 2020—the Great Awakening of the Black Lives Matter movement after the murder of George Floyd. Our "hype" about solidarity was exposed. The sickness of the *inequality* of the body of society was manifest; it could not be ignored. Mainstream media began to embrace the reality about how *fractured* American society really is. As a response, imagined utopias (both futuristic and nostalgic) became popular—the present "does not exist in epics" (Moretti 1996, 88). This, via Ernst Bloch's (1977) observations on the non-synchronous' role in dialectics, reflects a symptom of the delusions of capitalistic cultures, but also a constructive response to both collective and individual trauma, sometimes the response to rapid historical change and changes in a situation. New images for a hopeful future are vital in times of crisis, just as powerful as fascistic images of nostalgia about the past prevent the dialectic process from unfolding. All in all, cultural forms, imagined utopias (past or future) all play through like a couch potato's movie-binge on Netflix. But another possibility—can they be transformative? One more modern example is the method of Dostoevsky's introspective "dialogues" and his own suffering of "epileptic fits" as an "amplification" of self-consciousness (Bird 2012, 129). The trauma of Dostoevsky's "mock firing squad" served as an existential "limit experience" in the sense of Maurice Blanchot's and George Bataille's philosophies—an opening to a sense of timelessness—alluding to an anthropological sense of liminality. This leaves the student of Dostoevsky to an observation that one can only know oneself in "instants of apocalypse" (Bird 2012). Therefore, to transfer from the individual suspension of time to that of the collective, a society comes to know itself within its time of crisis, even if the powers of the media-info-tainment industry-center seek to create a level of hype. It is an awakening within consciousness that episodes of dramatic events, which gives birth to better visions of society. It is in this very opening that repeats the very essence of the birthing of the sociological imagination, from what Stephen Buechler (2011) has defined in "critical sociology"—a hope-driven lens for a better future. But at least for Boccaccio, according to Mazzotta, these utopic imaginings may all be a fantasy.

An important lesson from Boccaccio's realism reflects that utopia and play may just be projected illusions and, according to Mazzotta, "the worst illusion of all is to believe we have no illusions" (1986, 11). Art reflects life, while it is also seeking a better one, but it is a reminder that engaging in discussions of utopia has a touch of frivolity and privilege. Lukács's first edition of *The Theory of the Novel* presents a link between Boccaccio and the mood of withdrawal from the world during the disasters of World War I. The collective psychosis of COVID and its accompanying political upheavals reflects the need for a liminal space where people step back from the world and "tell stories"—attempting to understand themselves and others, through narration and reflection (Lukács 1971, 11–12). For Lukács, these conversations presented the opportunity to reflect on what he termed a "post-Dostoevskian" world—a world that eclipses "total art" and pure, untainted heroes, a world of psychological complexity and ambiguity.

Boccaccio, writing at the dawn of capitalism, might appreciate how our stories of today are illuminating of and illuminated by late capitalism. The earliest version of those cultural shifts, seeds planted in the unconscious of the capitalist psyches of the 1300s, have grown into a thicket of social problems, creating selfishness and inequality. According to Paula Findlen, Boccaccio's "*Decameron* described in hilarious, yet bitingly pointed detail how humans repeatedly deceived and failed to understand or care enough for each other, and how readily they traded their ideals for more immediate pleasures and tangible rewards. Human arrogance and greed, knowledge and deceit, lust and love, laughter and passion fill the pages of his collection" (Findlen 2020). Self-indulgence, arrogance, lust, greed, all are the "sins" of capitalism—perhaps Marxians today would see these observations rooted in categories that are far too Christian, but certainly they corroborate with some of the aspects that contribute to Durkheim's categories of modern anomie and Marxians' definitions of alienation. Further, as an early experiment in a critical social perspective within capitalism,

> Boccaccio's clear-sighted vision of the world as it is, and not as it ought to be, was his ultimate gift to a generation that endured a truly dreadful disease. With his pen Boccaccio subtly reminded his fellow Florentines—and many generations of readers everywhere who have delighted in his stories—that plague arrived in his city not because the constellations had aligned badly, not because it was God's will, but as the inevitable consequence of a restless and consuming society ever on the move (Findlen 2020).

To see disease and plague as not an abstract divine force, but one with social causes is a profound revolution in artistic, scientific, philosophical consciousness, and Boccaccio's commentary within the "stories" presents evidence of the kernels of modern thinking.

The homiletic response within *The Decameron,* is that the human is not satisfied or fulfilled through knowledge or the pursuits of philosophy. But rather, met with the problem of time and the quandaries of existence, suffering and death, we are called to love. This is not unlike Dostoevsky's conclusion in *Brothers Karamazov.* According to Mazzotta, Boccaccio accounts for love as "a disease and a child of time (as the mythic account of Venus' origin from Chronos' emasculation shows), and is bound, that is, to a temporal scheme of memory and imagination" (1986, 45). As with Umberto Eco's modern novel (*The Name of the Rose,* 1983*)* in a reference to the heritage of the classic, "The Romance of the Rose," (ca. 1270) death's sovereignty over the world of generation and corruption, can only be combated by the embodied, the humorous, the charged power of sexual reproduction . . . yet as Eco's narrative would have it, the philosophical force and establishment of institutions of Religion seek to obliterate this element within the authoritative tradition of theology, the poetic imagination bridled by restraint of body and emotions.

CONCLUSION: COVID AND DARK CARNIVAL

In *The Decameron*'s epilogue humanity's finitude with respect to the experiences of love/time is contrasted with that realm of the divine as essentially a-temporal/eternal. A suspension of time—in the liminal—teaches the principle of erotic enjoyment, or at least the discussions of such a pastime. This is also through the characterological technique of play, feigning and framed narratives, though within the restraint mechanisms of reason. Within the framework of ritual theory as it is influenced by Durkheim's observations, the function of this "liminal" space is to create solidarity and collective effervescence. But like champagne's effervescence wears off, so the liminal space must come to a conclusion. Structure returns. For as the conclusion to this posits, "Who knoweth not that wine, though, according to Cinciglione and Scolajo and many others, an excellent thing for people in health, is hurtful unto whoso hath the fever?" (Epilogue). Sweet wine can be poisonous, just as culture can distract those with such "fevers." Plague inevitably problematizes community: requiring private instead of public ritual practice (Falvo 1999, 147). This points to an inevitable decline in the potency of sacrament: ritual performance does not seem to be linked to sacramental efficacy (Falvo 1999, 147). This leads to all sorts of ethical hypocrisies and the problem of empty ritual/ritualism; these criticisms of "hollow" religion are also explored within the individual stories of the text. But this experience, in Boccaccio's description, may also serve as a gateway to a new, more "emergent" kind of ritual *communitas* (Falvo 1999, 150), based more on a new vision of self-constructed society where the storytellers escape to the countryside.

Though embedded in "Christian" culture and themes, Boccaccio leaves us, in the Epilogue, with a warning about the abuse of religion, bad interpretations, and hypocrisies that arise to "solve" social problems in times of crisis—that salve which also kills: "What books, what words, what letters are holier, worthier, more venerable than those of the Divine Scriptures? Yet many there be, who, interpreting them perversely, have brought themselves and others to perdition." This is perhaps a warning, and a projection for today. This anticipates the carnival-driven apocalyptic political and religious *Elmer Gantries* of our days, accompanied by the prosperity gospel. This peculiar Christianity expresses our American context's particular blending of modern capitalism and religion. They are the creators of a dark carnival (Langman and Ryan 2009; Lundskow 2012; Thorpe 2019), rather than true *communitas*/social solidarity. They enhance and capitalize upon the time of social upheaval. They are the ones who create the flood and then save the day in their self-proclaimed ability to part the waters.

References

Achebe, Chinua. (1977) 2006. "An Image of Africa: Racism in *Heart of Darkness.*" In *Heart of Darkness,* Norton Critical Edition 4th edition, edited by Paul Armstrong, 336–349. New York and London: WW. Norton.
Adepitan, Titi. 2003. Review of Achille Mbembe's *On the Postcolony. Canadian Literature* Issue 178 (Autumn): 155–156.
Adorno, Theodor, Walter Benjamin, Ernst Bloch, Bertolt Brecht, and Georg Lukács. 2007. *Aesthetics and Politics.* With an Afterword by Fredric Jameson. London and New York: Verso.
Ahmad, Eqbal. 2018. "Terrorism: Theirs and Ours." In *Approaches to Peace: A Reader in Peace Studies, Fourth Edition,* edited by David P. Barash, 145–150. New York: Oxford University Press.
Alamilla, R.M. and J.A. Howard. 2001. "Gender and Identity." In *Gender Mosaics: Social Perspectives,* edited by Dana Vannoy, 54–63. New York: Roxbury.
Alfaro, Mariá Jesús Martinez. 1996. "Intertextuality: Origins and Development of the Concept." *Atlantis* 18 (1/2): 268–285.
Almond, Gabriel, R. Scott Appleby, and Emmanuel Sivan. 2003. *Strong Religion: The Rise of Fundamentalisms around the World.* Chicago and London: University of Chicago Press.
Alves, Artur Matos. 2014. "Jacques Ellul's 'Anti-Democratic Economy': Persuading Citizens and Consumers in the Information Society." *Cognition Communication Cooperation* 12 (1): 169–201.
Arendt, Hannah. 2000. *The Portable Hannah Arendt.* Edited by Peter Baehr. New York: Penguin Classics.
Badiner, Allan Hunt. 1990. *Dharma Gaia: A Harvest of Essays in Buddhism and Ecology.* Berkeley, CA: Parallax Press.
Baxandall, S. and S. Morawski (editors). 1973. *Marx and Engels on Literature and Art.* Candor, New York: Telos Press.
Beauvoir, Simone de. 1989. *The Second Sex.* Trans. H. M. Parshley. New York: Vintage Books.

Begam, Richard and Michael Valdez Moses. 2007. *Modernism and Colonialism: British and Irish Literature, 1899–1939.* Durham, NC and London: Duke University Press.

Bell, Quentin. 1972. *Virginia Woolf: A Biography.* Orlando, FL: Harcourt.

Bellah, Robert. 1992. *The Broken Covenant.* Chicago: University of Chicago Press.

Bellah, Robert, Richard Madsen, William Sullivan, Ann Swidler, and Steven Tipton. 1985. *Habits of the Heart: Individualism and Commitment in American Life.* Berkeley: University of California Press.

Bender, D. 2010. "In Women's Empires: Gynaeocracy, Savagery, and the Evolution of Industry." *American Studies* 51 (4): 61–84.

Bensick, Carol Marie. 1985. *La Nouvelle Beatrice: Renaissance and Romance in "Rappaccini's Daughter."* New Brunswick, NJ: Rutgers University Press.

Bird, Robert. 2012. *Critical Lives: Fyodor Dostoevsky.* London: Reaktion Books.

Blanchot, Maurice. 1993. *The Infinite Conversation.* Translation and foreword by Susan Hanson. *Theory and History of Literature,* Vol. 82. Minneapolis: University of Minnesota Press.

Bloch, Ernst. 1977. "Nonsynchronism and the Obligation to Its Dialectics," Trans. Mark Ritter. *New German Critique* 11 (Spring): 22–38.

Boccaccio, Giovanni. (1886) 2007. *The Decameron.* Translated by John Payne. New York: Walter J. Black. Project Gutenberg, accessed August 2020: http://www.gutenberg.org/files/23700/23700-h/23700-h.htm

Boethius, Anicius Manlius Severinus. (523) 1962. *The Consolation of Philosophy,* translated with an introduction by Richard Green. Indianapolis: Bobbs-Merrill Publishing.

Brooks, David. 2000. *Bobos in Paradise: The New Upper Class and How they Got Here.* New York: Simon & Schuster.

Brooks, David. 2020. "What the Voters are Trying to Tell Us." *New York Times,* November 5, 2020. https://www.nytimes.com/2020/11/05/opinion/trump-biden-voters.html

Bruenig, Elizabeth. 2019. "Jesus, Mary, and Mary." *New York Review of Books.* November 21: 25–27.

Buechler, Stephen. 2011. *Critical Sociology.* Boulder, CO: Paradigm Publishers.

Burns, Christy. 1994. "Re-dressing Feminist Identities: Tensions between Essential and Constructed Selves in Virginia Woolf's *Orlando.*" *Twentieth Century Literature* 40 (3): 342–364.

Burrow, Colin. 2020. "The Last Whale." *London Review of Books,* 42:11. June 4, 2020, last accessed July 20, 2021. https://www.lrb.co.uk/the-paper/v42/n11/colin-burrow/the-last-whale

Butler, Judith. 1990. *Gender Trouble: Feminism and the Subversion of Identity.* New York: Routledge.

Calhoun, Craig, Joseph Gerteis, James Moody, Steven Pfaff and Indermohan Virk. 2012. *Classical Sociological Theory* 3rd edition. New York: Wiley.

Camus, Albert. 1988. *The Stranger.* Translated by Matthew Ward. New York: Vintage.

Caplan-Bricker, Nora. 2018 "Leaving Herland." *The Point Magazine,* 16: April 23, 2018. https://thepointmag.com/politics/leaving-herland/.

Caputo, John. 2013. *The Insistence of God.* Bloomington: Indiana University Press.
Caputo, John. 1997. *The Prayers and Tears of Jacques Derrida: Religion without Religion.* Bloomington: Indiana University Press.
Caputo, John and Gianni Vattimo (editors). 2007. *After the Death of God.* New York: Columbia University Press.
Carroll, W.C. 1999. "Discourses of the Feminine." In *Macbeth: Texts and Contexts,* edited by W. Shakespeare and W.C. Carroll. Boston: Bedford/St. Martin's: 344–352.
Cassedy, Steven. 2005. *Dostoevsky's Religion.* Stanford, CA: Stanford University Press.
Chesler, Phyllis. 2003. *Woman's Inhumanity Toward Woman.* New York: Penguin.
Christensen, Andrew G. 2017. "Charlotte Perkins Gilman's Herland and the Tradition of the Scientific Utopia." *Utopian Studies* 28 (2): 286–304.
Clarke, Kenneth. 2018. "Text and (Inter)Face: The Catchwords in Boccaccio's Autograph of the *Decameron.*" In *Reconsidering Boccaccio: Medieval Contexts and Global Intertexts,* edited by Olivia Holmes and Dana E. Stewart, 27–47. Toronto: University of Toronto.
Conrad, Joseph. 1983. *The Collected Letters of Joseph Conrad,* Volume 1. 1861–1897. Edited by Frederick Karl and Laurence Davies. Cambridge: Cambridge University Press.
Conrad, Joseph. (1899) 2006. *Heart of Darkness.* Norton Critical Edition 4th edition, edited by Paul Armstrong. New York and London: W.W. Norton.
Conrad, Joseph. (1906) 2011. *The Mirror of the Sea.* Floating Press.
Conrad, Joseph (1907) 2013. *The Secret Agent: A Simple Tale.* Haddonfield, NJ: J.P. Piper.
Cooley, Charles Horton. 1902. *Human Nature and the Social Order.* New York: Scribner's: 179–185.
Coppola, Francis Ford, director. 1979. *Apocalypse Now.* Omni Zoetrope.
Dahms, Harry. 2019. "Ignoring Goethe's Faust: A Critical-theoretical Perspective on American Ideology. *Fast Capitalism* 16 (2): 9–30.
Daldry, Michael, director. 2002. *The Hours.* USA: Paramount.
Dameron, J. Lasley. 1994. "Faust, the Wandering Jew, and the Swallowed Serpent: Hawthorne's Familiar Literary Analogues." *Nathaniel Hawthorne Review* 20 (1): 10–17.
Degli-Esposti, Cristina. 1996. Sally Potter's "Orlando" and the Neo-Baroque Scopic Regime. *Cinema Journal,* 36 (1) 75–93.
DiFranco, Ani. 1998. "Pulse." *Little Plastic Castle.* Righteous Babe Records.
DiGangi, M. and William Shakespeare. 2008. "Gender, Sexuality, and the Family." In *The Winter's Tale: Texts and Contexts,* 174–175. Boston: Bedford/St. Martin's.
Dolan, Francis E. 2008. *Marriage and Violence: the Early Modern Legacy.* Philadelphia: University of Pennsylvania Press.
Dostoevsky, Fyodor. 2009. *The Brothers Karamazov.* Translated by Constance Garnett. New York: The Lowell Press. Project Gutenberg, last accessed July 18, 2021. https://www.gutenberg.org/ebooks/28054.

Dow, George Francis. 1988. *Every Day Life in the Massachusetts Bay Colony.* Mineola, NY: Dover Editions.

DuBois, W.E.B. (1903) 1989. *The Souls of Black Folk.* New York: Bantam Books.

Dumont, Lucile. 2018. "From Sociology to Literary Theory." *Symbolic Goods* 3. Translated by Jean-Yves Bart. L'Ecole Pratique des Hautes Etudes. Presses Universitaires de Vincennes.

Durkheim, Emile. 1973. *On Morality and Society: Selected Essays.* Edited with an introduction by Robert Bellah. Chicago: University of Chicago Press.

Durkheim, Emile. (1912) 1995. *Elementary Forms of Religious Life.* Translated by Karen Fields. New York: Free Press.

Eagleton, M. 2005. "Nice work? Representations of the intellectual woman worker." *Women's History Review* 14 (2): 203–221.

Eco, Umberto. (1983) 1994. *The Name of the Rose,* translated by William Weaver. Harvest Books.

Eichner, Hans. (1971) 1976. "The Eternal Feminine: An Aspect of Goethe's Ethics." In *Faust* Norton Critical Edition, translated by Walter Arndt and edited by Cyrus Hamlin, 615–624. New York and London: W.W. Norton.

Eliot, T.S. 1925. "The Hollow Men."

Eliot, T.S. [1943] 2014. *Four Quartets.* Orlando, FL: Harvest Books, Harcourt.

Ellul, Jacques. 1964. *The Technological Society,* translated by John Wilkinson. New York: Vintage.

Erdinast-Vulcan, Daphna. (1991) 2006. "The Failure of Metaphysics." In *Heart of Darkness.* Norton Critical Edition 4th edition, edited by Paul Armstrong, 415–421. New York and London: W.W. Norton.

Esty, Jed. 2007. "Virginia Woolf's Colony and the Adolescence of Modern Fiction." In *Modernism and Colonialism: British and Irish Literature, 1899–1939,* edited by Richard Begam and Michael Valdez Moses, 70–90. Durham, NC and London: Duke University Press.

Falvo, Joseph. 1999. "Ritual and Ceremony in Boccaccio's *Decameron.*" *MLN*, 114 (1): 143–156.

Findlen, Paula. 2020. "What Would Boccaccio say about Covid?" *Boston Review,* April 24, 2020, accessed August 2020. http://bostonreview.net/arts-society/paula-findlen-what-would-boccaccio-say-about-covid-19

Forster, E.M. 1921. *Howards End.* New York: Vintage.

Foucault, Michel. 1980. *The History of Sexuality: Volume I.* New York: Vintage Books.

Frank, Joseph. 2020. *Lectures on Dostoevsky.* Edited by Marina Brodskaya and Marguerite Frank, With a Foreword by Robin Feuer Miller. Princeton and Oxford: Princeton University Press.

Franssen, Thomas and Giselinde Kuipers. 2015. "Sociology of Literature and Publishing in the Early 21st Century: Away from the Centre." *Cultural Sociology* 9 (3): 291–295.

Freedman, William. 2014. *Joseph Conrad and the Anxiety of Knowledge.* Columbia, SC: University of South Carolina Press.

Friedan, Betty. 1997. *The Feminine Mystique.* New York: W.W. Norton.

Freud, Sigmund. (1930) 2005. *Civilization and its Discontents.* New York: W.W. Norton.
Fromm, Erich. 1955. *The Sane Society.* Greenwich, CT: Fawcett Publishers.
Fromm, Erich. [1968] 2021. "Political Radicalism in the United States and its Critique." Reprinted in *Fromm Forum* 25: *Political Dimensions of Psychoanalysis,* 115–126.
Fromm, Erich. 1990. *Man for Himself: An Inquiry into the Psychology of Ethics.* New York: Holt Publications.
Fromm, Erich. [1961] 2004. *Marx's Concept of Man.* New York: Continuum.
Foucault, Michel. [1977] 1980. *Power/Knowledge: Selected Interviews and Other Writings 1972–1977.* Edited by Colin Gordon. Translated by Colin Gordon, Leo Marshal, John Mepham, and Kate Soper. New York: Pantheon Books.
Gawkowska, Aneta. 2012. "Woman, Self-Giving and Receiving: New Feminism, Theology of the Body and Society." *Polonia Sacra* 16 (34): 173–186.
Geertz, Clifford. 2000. *The Interpretation of Cultures.* New York: Basic Books.
Genovesi, S. J. Vincent. 1987. *In Pursuit of Love: Catholic Morality and Human Sexuality.* Collegeville, MN: Liturgical Press.
Gergen, Kenneth. 1991. *The Saturated Self.* New York: Basic Books.
Gessen, Masha. 2017. "When Does a Watershed become a Sex Panic." *The New Yorker,* November 2017, last accessed January 2020. https://www.newyorker.com/news/our-columnists/when-does-a-watershed-become-a-sex-panic
Giddens, Anthony. 1992. *The Transformation of Intimacy: Sexuality, Love & Eroticism in Modern Societies.* Stanford, CA: Stanford University Press.
Giffin, Michael. (1999) 2013. "Joseph Conrad on Colonialism: From Evolution to Evil in Heart of Darkness." Adapted from "Psychology Takes the Linguistic Turn: The Early Twentieth Century." *Introduction to Religion in the English Novel.* Lampeter, Wales: Edwin Mellen Press. Kindle Edition.
Gilman, Charlotte Perkins. (1916) 1998. *Herland.* Dover Thrift Editions.
Godwin, Sandra E. and Barbara J. Risman. 2001. "Twentieth Century Changes in Economic Work and Family." In *Gender Mosaics: Social Perspectives,* edited by Dana Vannoy, 134–144. New York: Oxford University Press.
Goethe, Johan Wolfgang von. 1976. *Faust: Norton Critical Edition.* Translated by Walter Arndt and edited by Cyrus Hamlin. New York: W.W. Norton.
Goldman, Jane. 2013. "Virginia Woolf and the Aesthetics of Modernism." In *The History of British Women's Writing, Vol. 8: 1920–1945,* edited by M. Joannou, 57–77. London: Palgrave MacMillan.
Goldmann, Lucien. 1975. *Towards a Sociology of the Novel.* London: Tavistock.
Gramsci, Antonio. 1971. "The Intellectuals." *Selections from the Prison Notebooks.* Translated and edited by Quentin Hoare and G.N. Smith, reprinted, last access in May 2021: https://www.marxists.org/archive/gramsci/prison_notebooks/problems/intellectuals.htm
Greeley, Andrew. 2000. *The Catholic Imagination.* Berkeley: University of California Press.
Grey, Robin (editor). 2004. *Melville & Milton: An Edition and Analysis of Melville's Annotation on Milton.* Pittsburgh: Duquesne University Press.

Halton, Eugene. 1995. *Bereft of Reason: On the Decline of Social Thought and Prospects for its Renewal.* Chicago: University of Chicago Press.

Halton, Eugene. 1986. *Meaning and Modernity.* Chicago: University of Chicago Press.

Hamblin, James. 2018. "This is Not a Sex Panic." *The Atlantic Monthly,* January 2018, last accessed in January 2020. https://www.theatlantic.com/entertainment/archive/2018/01/this-is-not-a-sex-panic/550547/

Hawthorne, Nathaniel. (1878) 2008. *The Scarlet Letter.* Project Gutenberg, accessed in July 2021. https://www.gutenberg.org/files/25344/25344-h/25344-h.htm.

Hawthorne, Nathaniel. 1957. "Young Goodman Brown." In *Great American Short Stories.* Edited by Wallace and Mary Stegner, 53–68. New York: Dell Publishing.

Hochschild, Adam. 1998. *King Leopold's Ghost: A Story of Greed, Terror and Heroism in Colonial Africa.* Boston & New York: Houghton-Mifflin.

Hochschild, Arlie. 2018. "Male Trouble." *The New York Review of Books.* October 11.

Isackson, Peter. 2020. "Steven Pinker and the Debate over Cancel Culture." *Fair Observer,* July 22, 2020, last accessed in March 2021. https://www.fairobserver.com/region/north_america/peter-isackson-steven-pinker-george-orwell-cancel-culture-news-78461/

James, C.L.R. (1953) 2001. *Mariners, Renegades & Castaways: The Story of Herman Melville and the World We Live In.* With an Introduction by Donald E. Pease. Hanover, NH: Dartmouth College Press.

James, Henry. 1879. "Hawthorne." Last accessed in March 2021. http://xroads.virginia.edu/~DRBR/james_1.html

Jameson, Fredric. 2019. *Allegory and Ideology.* London and New York: Verso. Kindle.

Jameson, Fredric. 2013. *The Antinomies of Realism.* New York and London: Verso. Kindle.

Jasanoff, Maya. 2017. *The Dawn Watch: Joseph Conrad in a Global World.* New York: Penguin Books.

John Paul II. 1997. *Theology of the Body: Human Love in the Divine Plan.* Jamaica Plain, MA: Pauline Books.

Johnson-Bogart, Kim. 1992. "The Utopian Imagination of Charlotte Perkins Gilman: Reconstruction of Meaning in 'Herland.'" *Pacific Coast Philology* 27 (1–2): 85–92.

Keillor, Garrison. 1993. *The Book of Guys.* New York: Viking.

Kilbourne, Jean, director. 2010. *Killing Us Softly IV.* Northampton, MA: Media Education Foundation.

Kipnis, Laura. 2017. *Unwanted Advances: Sexual Paranoia Comes to Campus.* New York: HarperCollins.

Klein, Naomi. 2008. *The Shock Doctrine: the Rise of Disaster Capitalism.* London: Picador.

Langman, Lauren. 2020. "The Dialectic of Populism and Cosmopolitanism." In *Cosmopolitanism in Hard Times,* edited by Vincenzo Cicchelli and Sylvie Mesure, 339–354. Leiden: Brill.

Langman, Lauren and Maureen Ryan. 2009. "Capitalism and the Carnival Character: The Escape from Reality." *Critical Sociology* 35:4.

Lasch, Christopher. 1979. *The Culture of Narcissism: Life in an Age of Diminishing Expectations*. New York: W.W. Norton.
Lawrence, David Henry. 1922. *Women in Love*. New York: Modern Library.
Lemert, Charles. 2003. "Charlotte Perkins Gilman." In *The Blackwell Companion to Major Classical Social Theorists*, edited by George Ritzer, 267–289. Malden, MA: Blackwell.
Lengermann, Patricia and Jill Niebrugge-Brantley. 1998. *The Women Founders: Sociology and Social Theory 1830–1930*. New York: McGraw-Hill.
Lepenies, Wolf. 1988. *Between Literature and Science: the Rise of Sociology*. Translated by R.J. Hollingdale. Cambridge, UK: Cambridge University Press.
Levinas, Emmanuel. 1998. *Otherwise than Being or Beyond Essence*. Translated by Alphonso Lingis. Pittsburgh: Duquesne University Press.
Liquette, Felisa Lopez. 1991. "Melville, an Existential Humanist," *Revista de Estudios Norteamericanos* 1: 49–57.
Loonam, John. 2019. "Review of, *Ahab's Rolling Sea: A Natural History of Moby-Dick*, by Richard King." *Washington Independent Review of Books*, November 1, 2019, last accessed July 19, 2021. http://www.washingtonindependentreviewofbooks.com/index.php/bookreview/ahabs-rolling-sea-a-natural-history-of-moby-dick
Lorber, Judith. 1998. "Believing is Seeing: Biology as Ideology." In *The Politics of Women's Bodies: Sexuality, Appearance, and Behavior*, edited by Rose Weitz, 12–21. New York: Oxford University Press.
Lorber, Judith. 1994. *Paradoxes of Gender*. New Haven, CT: Yale University Press.
Lukács, Gyorgy. 1971. *Theory of the Novel. A Historical-Philosophic Essay on the Forms in Great Epic Literature*. Translated by Anna Bostock. Cambridge, MA: Massachusetts Institute of Technology Press.
Lundskow, George. 2012. "Authoritarianism and Carnivalization in the 2008 Presidential Election and the Return of Right-Wing Populism." In *Alienation and the Carnivalization of Society*, edited by Jerome Braun and Lauren Langman, 119–132. New York: Routledge.
Martin, Robert K. 1986. *Hero, Captain, and Stranger: Male Friendship, Social Critique and Literary Form in the Sea Novels of Herman Melville*. Chapel Hill and London: University of North Carolina Press.
Marx, Karl. 1865. "Confession." April 1 1865. Transcribed by Andy Blunden. Last accessed July 20, 2021. https://www.marxists.org/archive/marx/works/1865/04/01.htm
Marx, Karl & Friedrich Engels. 1978. *The Marx-Engels Reader*. Edited by Robert Tucker. New York: W.W. Norton.
Marzagora, Sara. 2016. "The Humanism of Reconstruction: African Intellectuals, decolonial Critical Theory and the Opposition to the 'Posts' (Postmodernism, Poststructuralism, Postcolonialism." *Journal of African Cultural Studies* 28 (2): 161–178.
Mazzotta, Giuseppe. 1986. *The World at Play in Boccaccio's Decameron*. Princeton University Press.
Mbembe, Achille. 2003. "Necropolitics." Translated by Libby Meintjes. *Public Culture* 15 (1): 11–40.

MacMillen, Sarah L. 2020. "From Herland to #MeToo: Utopia or Dystopia?" *Soundings* 103 (2): 243–263.

MacMillen, Sarah L. 2020. "Neighborly Love in 2020." *Genealogies of Modernity,* May 4, 2020, accessed July 2020. https://genealogiesofmodernity.org/journal/2020/4/30/neighborly-love-in-2020

McLaughlin, Dan. 2018. "The Scarlet Letter is Back: It Never Really Went Away." *National Review,* May 23, 2018, last accessed July 20, 2021. https://www.national-review.com/corner/the-scarlet-letter-is-back-it-never-really-went-away/

McKinley, Kathryn. 2020. "How the Rich Reacted to the Bubonic Plague has Eerie Similarities to Today's Pandemic." *Nation of Change,* April 17, 2020, accessed August 2020. https://www.nationofchange.org/2020/04/17/how-the-rich-reacted-to-the-bubonic-plague-has-eerie-similarities-to-todays-pandemic/

Melville, Herman. 1967. *Moby-Dick.* Harrison Hayford and Hershel Parker, eds. New York and London: W.W. Norton.

Miller, Perry. 1957. *The American Transcendentalists: Their Prose and Poetry.* Garden City, NY: Anchor Books/Doubleday.

Mitcham, John C. 2016. *Race and Imperial Defence in the British World.* Cambridge: Cambridge University Press.

Mogk, Kathryn. 2020. "Art and Religion in a time of Plague." *Genealogies of Modernity,* May 18, 2020, accessed July 2020. https://genealogiesofmodernity.org/blog/2020/5/18/kathryn-blog-post

Montgomery, Marion. 1984. *Why Hawthorne was Melancholy Volume III.* La Salle, IL: Sherwood Sugden and Company.

Moore, Alex. 1989. *Concord Authors: Biographical Notes.* Concord, MA: Anaxagoras Publications.

Moretti, Franco. 1999. *Atlas of the European Novel 1800-1900.* London: Verso.

Moretti, Franco. 1996. *Modern Epic: The World System from Goethe to Garcia Márquez.* Translated by Quintin Hoare. London and New York: Verso.

Morris, Aldon. 2017. "W.E.B. Du Bois at the center: from science, civil rights movement, to Black Lives Matter." *British Journal of Sociology* 68 (1): 3–16.

Moses, Michael Valdez. 2007. "Disorientalism: Conrad and the Imperialist Origins of Modern Aesthetics." In *Modernism and Colonialism: British and Irish Literature, 1899-1939,* edited by Richard Begam and Michael Valdez Moses, 43–69. Durham, NC: Duke University Press.

Mumford, Lewis. (1929) 1967. "Moby Dick as Poetic Epic." In *Moby Dick*, edited by Hayford and Parker, 631–633. New York and London: W.W. Norton.

Nabokov, Vladimir. 1981. *Lectures on Russian Literature.* Edited with an introduction by Fredson Bowers. New York: Harcourt Brace Jovanovich.

Najder, Zdzislaw. 1976. "Conrad and Rousseau: Concepts of Man and Society." In *Joseph Conrad: A Commemoration,* edited by Norman Sherry, 77–90. New York: Palgrave MacMillan.

Nava, Alejandro. 2017. "The Souls of Black Folk: Ralph Ellison's Tragicomic Portrait." In *Search of Soul: Hip-Hop, Literature, and Religion*, 143–168. Berkeley, CA: University of California Press.

Nielsen, Donald. 2013. "Dostoevsky in the Mirror of Durkheim." In *Durkheim, Durkheimians and the Arts,* edited by Alexander Riley, W.S.F. Pickering and William Watts Miller, 95–118. Oxford, New York: Berghahn Books. https://www.jstor.org/stable/j.ctt9qcrxf.9

Nietzsche, Friedrich. 1993. *The Birth of Tragedy.* Edited with an introduction by Michael Tanner. Translated by Shaun Whiteside. London: Penguin Books.

Niland, Richard. 2005. "Conrad's Language of Retrospection: Youth, Poland, and the Philosophy of History." *The Polish Review* 50 (2): 155–186.

Nisbet, Robert. 2017. *Sociology as an Art Form.* New York: Routledge. Kindle Edition.

Noble, Trevor. 1976. "Sociology and Literature." *British Journal of Sociology* 27 (2): 211–224.

Noll, Birgit. 2010. *Herman Melville and the German* Roman. Dissertation in Comparative Literature. St. Louis, MO: Washington University.

Okin, Susan Moller. 1996. "Sexual Orientation, Gender, and Families: Dichotomizing Differences." *Hypatia* 11 (1): 30–48.

Olson, Charles. (1947) 1967. "Ahab and His Fool." In *Moby-Dick*: Norton Critical Edition, edited by Hershel Parker, 648–651. New York: W.W. Norton.

Olson, Jeane N. 1993. "E.M. Forster's Prophetic Vision of the Modern Family in Howards End." *Texas Studies in Literature and Language* 35 (3): 347–362.

Orr, John. 1977. *Tragic Realism and Modern Society: Studies in the Sociology of the Modern Novel.* London and Basingstoke: MacMillan.

Orsi, Robert. 2002. *The Madonna of 115th Street: Faith and Community in Italian Harlem: 1880-1950.* Yale University Press.

Otto, Rudolph. 1958. *The Idea of the Holy: An Inquiry into the Non-Rational Factor in the Idea of the Divine.* Translated by John Harvey. New York: Oxford University Press.

Phillips, Caryl. 2003. "Out of Africa." *The Guardian,* February 22, 2003, accessed March 2019. https://www.theguardian.com/books/2003/feb/22/classics.chinuaachebe

Piggford, George. 1999. "Who's that Girl? Annie Lennox, Woolf's *Orlando,* and Female Camp Androgyny." In *Camp: Queer Aesthetics and the Performing Subject, A Reader,* edited by Fabio Cleto, 283–299. Edinburgh, UK: Edinburgh University Press.

Pilger, John and Alan Lowery, directors. 2010. *The War You Don't See.* Dartmouth Films.

Porter, J.S. 2020. "Comfort in the Time of Covid." *The* Hamilton Spectator, March 23, 2020, accessed July 2020. https://www.thespec.com/opinion/contributors/2020/03/23/comfort-in-the-time-of-covid-19-some-thoughts-on-music-that-brighten-dark-days.html

Potter, Norris Whitfield Jr. 1943. *The Critical Theory and Literary Practice of Joseph Conrad.* Boston University Theses and Dissertations. Department of English.

Potter, Sally, director. 1994. *Orlando.* Sony Pictures Classics.

Quirk, Tom. 2007. *Mark Twain and Human Nature.* Columbia, Missouri and London: University of Missouri Press.

Ritzer, G. 2004. "Early Women Sociologists and Classical Social Theory, 1830–1930." In *Classical Sociological Theory*, 217–303. New York: McGraw Hill.

Rogers, Mary F. 1991. *Novels, Novelists and Readers: Toward a Phenomenological Sociology of Literature*. State University of New York Press.

Rose, Gillian. 1992. *The Broken Middle: Out of Our Ancient Society*. Oxford: Wiley Blackwell.

Rose, Gillian. 1996. *Mourning Becomes the Law: Philosophy and Representation*. Cambridge: Cambridge University Press.

Rosenshield, Gary. 1994. "Mystery and Commandment in 'The Brothers Karamazov: Leo Baeck and Fedor Dostoevsky." *Journal of the American Academy of Religion* 62 (2): 483–508.

Said, Edward. 1993. *Culture and Imperialism*. New York: Alfred Knopf.

Sapolsky, Robert. 1997. "Testosterone Rules." *Discover Magazine,* March 1997, accessed January 2020. http://discovermagazine.com/1997/mar/testosteronerule1077

Sapolsky, Robert. 2019. "This is Your Brain on Nationalism: The Biology of Us and Them." *Foreign Affairs,* March/April 2019. Accessed January 2020. https://www.foreignaffairs.com/articles/2019-02-12/your-brain-nationalism?utm_medium=newsletters&utm_source=special_send&utm_campaign=summer_reads_2019_newsletters&utm_content=20190901&utm_term=newsletter-summer-popup-2019

Servitje, Lorenzo. 2016. "'Triumphant Health' Joseph Conrad and Tropical Medicine." *Literature and Medicine* 34 (1): 132–157.

Sewall, Richard. (1950) 1967. "Moby-Dick as Tragedy." In *Moby-Dick* Norton Critical Edition, edited by in Hershel Parker, 692–702. New York: W.W. Norton.

Sherrill, Rowland A. 1979. *The Prophetic Melville: Experience, Transcendence and Tragedy*. Athens, GA: University of Georgia Press.

Shriver, Lionel. 2019. Cruel and Unusual Punishment. *Harper's Magazine,* February 2019, accessed January 2020. https://harpers.org/archive/2019/02/cruel-and-unusual-punishment-2/

Simmel, Georg. (1903) 1950. "The Metropolis and Mental Life." In *The Sociology of Georg Simmel,* translated and edited by Kurt Wolff, 409–424. New York: Free Press.

Simmel, Georg. (1908) 2012. "The Stranger." In *Classical Sociological Theory: A Reader,* edited by Craig Calhoun, et al., 361–365. New York: Wiley.

Simmel, Georg. 1950. "The Isolated Individual and the Dyad." In *The Sociology of Georg Simmel,* edited by Kurt Wolff, 118–144. New York: Free Press.

Smith, Zadie. 2019. "Fascinated to Presume: in Praise of Fiction." *New York Review of Books,* October 24, 2019

Steel, David. 1981. "Plague Writing: From Boccaccio to Camus." *Journal of European Studies* 11 (42): 88–110.

Steele, Anne. 2020. "Classic Rock gives comfort to music fans during Covid lockdown." Business section. *Wall Street Journal,* April 25, 2020, accessed July 2020. https://www.wsj.com/articles/the-soundtrack-of-the-coronavirus-pandemic-oldies-11587819602

Steiner, George. 1989. *Real Presences*. London: Faber and Faber.
Ste. B. (1608) 2007. "Counsel to the Husband: to the Wife Instruction." In *Othello: Texts and Contexts*, edited by W. Shakespeare and K.F. Hall, 278–280. Boston: Bedford/St. Martin's.
Sten, Christopher. 1996. *The Weaver God, He Weaves: Melville and the Poetics of the Novel*. Kent, OH and London, UK: Kent State University Press.
Stern, Milton. 1991. *Contexts for Hawthorne: The Marble Faun and the Politics of Openness and Closure in American Literature*. Urbana and Chicago, IL: University of Illinois Press.
Stetson {Gilman}, Charlotte Perkins. 1898. *Women and Economics: a Study of the Economic Relation Between Men and Women as a Factor in Social Revolution*. Boston: Small Maynard and Company.
Stetson, {Gilman} Charlotte Perkins. (1899) 1999. The Yellow Wallpaper. Project Gutenberg, accessed July 17, 2021. https://www.gutenberg.org/files/1952/1952-h/1952-h.htm
Swetnam, J. (1615) 2008. The Arraignment of Lewd, Idle, Froward, and Unconstant Women. *The Winter's Tale: Texts and Contexts*, edited by W. Shakespeare and M. DiGangi, 275–282. Boston: Bedford/St. Martin's.
Tamaki, Jillian. 2020. "Why Michael Eric Dyson Would Demote Heart of Darkness from the Canon." *New York Times*, June 4, 2020, accessed March 2019. https://www.nytimes.com/2020/06/04/books/review/michael-eric-dyson-by-the-book-interview.html?action=click&module=Well&pgtype=Homepage&section=Book%20Review
Tawney, R.H. (1926) 1998. *Religion and the Rise of Capitalism*. With an introduction by Adam B. Seligman. New Brunswick, NJ: Transaction Publishers.
Thomas, William I. 1931. *The Unadjusted Girl: With Cases and Standpoint for Behavioral Analysis*. Boston: Little and Brown Company.
Thorpe, Charles. 2019 "The Carnival King of Capital." *Fast Capitalism* 17 (1): 87–108.
Thorpe, Charles. 2016. *Necroculture*. New York: Palgrave MacMillan.
Tocqueville, Alexis de. [1839] "'Tyranny of the Majority' from *Democracy in America*." In *Classical Sociological Theory: A Reader*, edited by Craig Calhoun, et al., 361–365. New York: Wiley.
Tönnies, Ferdinand. [1887] 1961. "*Gemeinschaft and Gesellschaft.*" In *Theories of Society*, edited by Talcott Parsons. Glencoe, IL: Free Press.
Turner, Victor. 1969. *The Ritual Process*. Ithaca, NY: Cornell University Press.
Vokey, Daniel. 2001. *Moral Discourse in a Pluralistic World*. Notre Dame, IN: University of Notre Dame Press.
Wallerstein, Immanuel. 2004. *World-Systems Analysis: An Introduction*. Durham, NC: Duke University Press.
Ward, Jane. 2020. *The Tragedy of Heterosexuality*. New York: NYU Press. iBooks edition.
Watt, Ian. 1976. "Impressionism and Symbolism in *Heart of Darkness.*" In *Joseph Conrad: A Commemoration*, edited by Norman Sherry, 37–53. New York: Palgrave MacMillan.

Weber, Max. 1968. *On Charisma and Institution Building*. Edited with an introduction by Shmuel N. Eisenstadt. Chicago, IL: University of Chicago Press.

Weber, Max. 2001. *The Protestant Ethic and the Spirit of Capitalism*. Translated by Talcott Parsons. With an introduction by Anthony Giddens. New York and London: Routledge Classics.

Weitz, Rose. 1998. *The Politics of Women's Bodies: Sexuality, Appearance, and Behavior*. New York: Oxford University Press.

West, Harry. 1974. "Hawthorne's Magic Circle: The Artist as Magician." *Criticism* 16 (4): 311–325.

Westbrook, Laurel and Kristen Schilt. 2013. "Doing Gender, Determining Gender." *Gender & Society* 28 (1): 32–57.

Wiley, Norbert. 2016. "Bakhtin's Voices and Cooley's Looking Glass Self." In *Inner Speech and the Dialogical Self*, 134–149. Philadelphia, PA: Temple University Press.

Williams, Raymond. 1977. *Marxism and Literature*. Oxford, UK: Oxford University Press.

Williams, Rowan. 2011. *Dostoevsky: Language, Faith and Fiction*. Waco, TX: Baylor University Press.

Woolf, V. (1929) 2020. "A Room of One's Own." Project Gutenberg, last accessed July 20, 2021. http://gutenberg.net.au/ebooks02/0200791.txt

Woolf, V. (1925) 1953. *Mrs. Dalloway*. New York: Harcourt, Brace & World.

Woolf, V. (1928) 2006. *Orlando: A Biography*. M. DiBattista, ed. Orlando, FL: Harcourt.

Woolf, V. 1956. *Orlando: A Biography*. Orlando, FL: Harvest Book, Harcourt, Inc.

Wright II, Earl. 2020. *Jim Crow Sociology: The Black and Southern Roots of Sociology*. Cincinnati, OH: University of Cincinnati Press.

Wright, Talmadge and Ray Hutchison. 1997. "Socio-spatial Reproduction, Marketing Culture, and the Built Environment." *Research in Urban Sociology* 4: 187–214.

Zapf, Hubert. 2012. "The Rewriting of the Faust Myth in 'Young Goodman Brown.'" *Nathaniel Hawthorne Review* 38: 1, 19–40.

Zimmer, Heinrich. 1975. *The King and the Corpse: Tales of the Soul's Conquest of Evil*. Edited by Joseph Campbell. Princeton, NJ: Princeton University Press.

Index

Achebe, Chinua, 18, 62–66, 71
Adorno, Theodor, 2, 15, 31, 68, 82
archetypes, 7, 9, 15, 20, 24, 28, 31, 35, 57, 69, 86–87, 97
authoritarianism, 15, 26–27, 56–57, 69, 73, 136, 142

de Beauvoir, Simone, 94, 105, 110, 111, 112, 116–18
Bellah, Robert, 26, 56, 57
Black Lives Matter, 15, 65, 142, 150
Boccaccio, Giovanni 3, 7, 21–22, 141–53
Brooks, David, 2, 38

Calvinism/Puritanism, 16–17, 23–40, 44, 47, 59, 88, 144
Cassedy, Steven, 124, 126, 135, 137, 138
Catholicism, 17, 20, 23, 25, 33, 47, 72, 95, 97–98, 129, 131
colonialism, 1, 6, 18, 61–70, 77, 82, 85, 101, 119
Conrad, Joseph, 3, 4, 13, 14, 18–19, 43, 54, 57, 61–82, 86, 101, 102, 109, 129, 141
Cooley, Charles Horton, 39, 72, 108, 124

Dahms, Harry, 31
Dostoevsky, Fyodor, 3, 7, 14, 15, 20–21, 73, 123–39, 141, 150
DuBois, W.E.B., 1, 56, 64, 66, 102, 107
Durkheim, Émile, 1, 8, 13, 21, 35, 53, 57, 59, 72, 73, 124–36, 141, 148

Ellul, Jacques, 12, 34, 67, 142
Emerson, Ralph Waldo, 25, 27–28, 30, 32, 45
Engels, Friedrich, 8, 48, 64–65, 132, 141
environmentalism, 44, 45, 57–58

Frank, Joseph, 123–24, 132–33, 139
Friedan, Betty, 116
Fromm, Erich, 5, 39, 42, 46, 57, 66–67, 72, 94, 114, 149

Giddens, Anthony, 92–94, 97, 125
Giffin, Michael, 18–19, 70–71, 74
Gilman, Charlotte Perkins (Stetson), 3, 6, 14, 20, 83–99, 102, 103, 109, 111–15, 117, 120, 141
Goldmann, Lucien, 2, 4, 5–6, 11
gynocracy, 85–86, 95

Halton, Eugene, 43, 44, 55–57, 59, 133

Hawthorne, Nathaniel, 3, 14, 17, 23–39, 42–44, 50, 53, 55, 141

imperialism, 2, 6, 7, 14, 18–19, 44, 56, 59, 61–82, 91, 101, 109, 119
instrumental rationality, 33–34, 67, 132, 136

James, C.L.R., 1, 18, 21, 41, 47, 48, 50, 55, 56, 57
Jameson, Fredric, 11–12, 19, 33, 45, 50, 82, 146
Jasanoff, Maya, 54, 66, 74–75, 77, 80–82

Lepenies, Wolf, 8–9, 45, 82
Lukács, Gyorgy, 1–6, 11, 13–15, 21, 67–68, 70, 75, 82, 133, 150–51

MacIntyre, Alasdair, 74, 128
Marx, Karl, 1, 2, 4–5, 7–8, 32, 42, 46–48, 57, 58, 64–65, 70, 72, 73, 81, 85, 115, 125, 132, 135, 138, 141, 146, 148, 149
Mbembe, Achille, 62, 67, 69
Melville, Herman, 3, 4, 14, 17–18, 21, 24, 25, 28, 29, 31, 41–59, 132, 141
MeToo movement, 83–99
Moretti, Franco, 10, 15, 33, 35, 41, 49, 57–58, 62, 74, 77–79, 150
Moses, Michael Valdez, 18, 61, 77

Nabokov, Vladimir, 123, 124, 132, 136, 138
Nisbet, Robert, 1, 11

Orr, John, 61, 68, 81, 130
orthodoxy (religion), 124, 127, 129, 131–32, 137–39

racism, 18, 59, 62, 63–70
religion, 7, 17–18, 20–22, 23, 43, 50, 53–54, 132, 135, 123–40, 143–53

Said, Edward, 14, 18, 61, 62, 65, 67–68, 69, 70, 77–79, 80
Simmel, Georg, 1–2, 47, 82, 105, 120, 141
Smith, Zadie, 9–11
Steiner, George, 16

Tawney, Richard Henry (R.H.), 17, 27, 29, 30, 32, 34
Thomas, W.I., 35, 108, 129
Thoreau, Henry David, 28, 32
Thorpe, Charles Robert, 9, 66–67, 74, 153
Tönnies, Ferdinand, 1, 25, 128, 133

utopia, 20, 81, 83–96, 126, 128, 146–52

Wagner, Richard 13, 57, 78
Weber, Marianne, 114
Weber, Max, 1, 8, 9, 17, 21, 27, 29, 32, 34, 38, 45, 47, 57, 114, 125, 130, 136, 141, 142
Williams, Raymond, 3–5, 12, 70–71, 72
Williams, Rowan, 125–27, 132
Woolf, Virginia, 3, 5, 6, 14, 19, 20, 99, 101–121, 141

About the Author

Sarah Louise MacMillen (Ph.D. in Sociology at the University of Notre Dame, Indiana) is an associate professor of sociology and the director of the Peace, Justice, and Conflict Resolution Minor Program at Duquesne University in Pittsburgh, Pennsylvania. Primarily using qualitative methods and the tools of sociological theory, she has published and taught on topics related to religion, social philosophy, gender/sexuality, and peace studies. She also has a strong commitment to bridging discussions with the arts and humanities—both in research and the classroom. Her hobbies include singing in a choir, swimming, playing tennis, jogging, and hiking.

www.ingramcontent.com/pod-product-compliance
Lightning Source LLC
Chambersburg PA
CBHW020123010526
44115CB00008B/951